BLOODY RIDGE
AND BEYOND

BLOODY RIDGE
AND BEYOND

A World War II Marine's
Memoir of Edson's Raiders
in the Pacific

MARLIN "WHITEY" GROFT
and LARRY ALEXANDER

BERKLEY CALIBER, NEW YORK

THE BERKLEY PUBLISHING GROUP
Published by the Penguin Group
Penguin Group (USA) LLC
375 Hudson Street, New York, New York 10014

USA • Canada • UK • Ireland • Australia • New Zealand • India • South Africa • China

penguin.com

A Penguin Random House Company

This book is an original publication of The Berkley Publishing Group.

BLOODY RIDGE AND BEYOND

ISBN: 978-0-425-27300-5

An application to register this book for cataloging has been submitted to the Library of Congress.

First edition: October 2014

PRINTED IN THE UNITED STATES OF AMERICA

10 9 8 7 6 5 4 3 2 1

Interior text design by Tiffany Estreicher

This book is dedicated to the memory of Ken Bowers,
who gave his life in the cause of freedom;
to my buddy Bill Waltrip, who still calls me "son"; and
to the brave men of Edson's Raiders, the toughest Marines to
ever wear the Globe and Anchor

CONTENTS

PREFACE

On the warm, sunny Sunday morning of August 6, 1989, I and a number of my colleagues of the 1st Raider Battalion, the famed Edson's Raiders, stood on the grounds of the Marine base at Quantico, Virginia, not to train for war as we had done forty-seven years prior, but to remember our departed brethren and our Raider legacy. We had returned to where it all began for the Raiders in order to dedicate a memorial as part of the Quantico National Cemetery.

I am more than a little proud of the fact that the idea for the memorial had been first floated by me six years earlier during the funeral of Ben Howland, who had been something of a legend in the Raiders. A tenured professor of landscape architecture at the University of Virginia after the war, Ben had become both a teacher and mentor to my son Eric, who was studying at the university's School of Architecture.

At the reception following Ben's death, several Raiders commented that Ben had not been buried at Arlington, but rather was interred at the Quantico cemetery, which, we noted, incorporated some of the very ground we had trained on in 1942. Would it not be appropriate, I mused, if a memorial to the Raiders would be erected on the site?

Coincidentally that summer, Eric had an internship as a student landscape architect with the Veterans' Administration's National Cemetery Service. The Quantico National Cemetery had just recently been opened and was being viewed as a "replacement" cemetery for Arlington. In his capacity as a landscape architect, Eric embraced the idea of the memorial, which we envisioned as being placed alongside a memorial path through the woods.

The idea took wing and over the following year, a memorial committee was formed. Eric donated his time to work on concepts and ideas that were presented at the annual Raider Reunion in February 1984. Since our reunions were held at Quantico, we walked the memorial trail. Getting the needed approvals proved somewhat frustrating, with government bureaucracy being notoriously slow. Plus we had to raise funds, although after all this time, I no longer recall how much we needed. Finally, it all came together.

Eric's plan called for the creation of a small parklike setting shaded by towering oak trees and partially enclosed by a low stone wall. A path weaves through a series of low granite boulders emerging from the ground, each representing one of the islands where we Raiders fought and bled, principally Guadalcanal, Tulagi, Makin, New Georgia, and Bougainville. The design included a bench that overlooked the cemetery and our former training grounds. The ground-cover vegetation assumes the role of the Pacific Ocean, lapping around the granite "islands." A large boulder near the bench holds a bronze tablet that briefly outlines the Raiders' history and our stand on Bloody Ridge.

A number of invited guests attended the dedication, including the sons of our late commander, Austin and Robert Edson. Dedicatory remarks were made by General Alfred M. Gray, the Marine Corps Commandant, and the memorial marker itself was unveiled by the widows of Lew Walt and Ben Howland.

As Taps was blown to conclude the ceremony, I paused to reflect on the pride each of us Raiders felt that day; pride in our commander, in our unit, and in ourselves.

The Raiders were formed on February 16, 1942, and existed until February 1, 1944, fifteen days shy of two years. More than eight thousand men served in what eventually became four Raider battalions. Of that number, 892 never returned home.

Yet over that short period of time, we carved a legend for ourselves on far-flung battlefields like Hill 281 on Tulagi, Tasimboko, the God-awful Bloody Ridge, and along the Matanikau River on Guadalcanal, and in the jungles around Enogai and Bairoko on New Georgia.

I was a member of the 1st Raider Battalion, serving under Colonel Merritt A. Edson. By being a member of that magnificent organization, I was among the very first Americans to take the war to our enemies as we landed on Tulagi, an hour before the Guadalcanal fight began. As part of Edson's reconnaissance patrol, I scouted the barren hilltop that would become known as Bloody Ridge, and stood with him atop that blood-soaked ridge as thousands of Japanese tried to sweep us aside in two desperate nights of hand-to-hand fighting. I was with the Raiders in the fierce fighting amid the stinking jungles on New Georgia, and remained a member of the unit until its disbanding.

Counting myself among those who served in this valiant battalion of the finest men in the United States Marine Corps is perhaps the proudest achievement of my life.

These are my remembrances, which I hope will serve as a legacy to the brave Marines who fought beside me and shared my hardships, preserved for my grandsons and for future generations of my fellow Raiders.

Semper Fi,
Marlin "Whitey" Groft
Lancaster, Pennsylvania
May 2014

INTRODUCTION

In my twenty-plus years of being a journalist, I have had the distinct honor of interviewing combat veterans from every American war of the twentieth century, from World War I through Iraq. In each instance, I have found their valor, courage, and willingness to put themselves in harm's way for their nation to be inspiring. In a few cases, most particularly Major Richard D. Winters and Sergeant Forrest Guth, both with the famed "Band of Brothers," they became friends.

The same can be said for Marlin F. "Whitey" Groft.

I met Marlin in 2009 when I was looking for a veteran on whom to write a newspaper story to run on Veterans Day. I knew Whitey had been a Marine during the war, and that he had served on Guadalcanal. I did not know until I began the interview that he had been a member of one of the Marine Corps's most famous World War II fighting organizations, Edson's Raiders.

As a historian who specializes in the Second World War, I certainly knew who Merritt Austin Edson and what were sometimes referred to as his "do-or-die men" were and what they had done. I had studied the Battle of Guadalcanal intensely and also read many of the fine accounts written about the Raiders, including *Edson's Raiders* by the eminent military historian Joseph H. Alexander, who is, so far as I know, no relation. So as Whitey spoke about Bloody Ridge during our interview, I could follow the action in my head.

Of all the Pacific battles, to me the Guadalcanal campaign is the quintessential struggle. Not just because lessons the American commanders learned during this first land offensive were put to use in later invasions, but because it was the only land battle after America went over to the offensive that America came seriously close to losing. It was hastily planned, poorly executed, abysmally supplied and supported, and at one point, the Marine ground commander, Major General Alexander Vandegrift, was authorized by his superiors to surrender his forces if necessary. And of all the many individual battles on Guadalcanal, the Raiders' valiant two-day stand against an overwhelming number of Japanese soldiers on what is called both Edson's Ridge and Bloody Ridge was the most important fight of the entire campaign. Had the Japanese taken the ridge, they'd have plunged straight through the Marine defensive perimeter, taken Henderson airfield, split the American forces in half, and, quite likely, forced the surviving Marines into the jungle to fight as a disorganized guerilla force, or to simply starve to death, because there would be no American Dunkirk from a U.S. Navy still reeling after Pearl Harbor.

Edson's recognizing the strategic value of the ridge and knowing the consequences of its loss, plus his dogged defense against odds of three or even four to one, and the ability and courage of his men to stand and smash wave after wave of enemy attackers, combined to make Bloody Ridge one of the most crucial battles in American military history.

Yet, ironically, the Marines Corps high command never wanted the Raiders. Indeed, the Raiders were the bastard child foisted off on the Marines by Colonel James Roosevelt through his father, the President of the United States. Young Roosevelt was a devotee of Lieutenant Colonel Evans Carlson, who studied the tactics of the Red Chinese forces fighting the Japanese in China. An eccentric man who had a habit of rubbing people the wrong way, a trait that lost him popularity with his superiors, Carlson devised a raider concept to strike at the enemy behind his lines, where he least expected it. Edson, too, was working on a similar concept, and the two men would become bitter rivals.

What President Franklin D. Roosevelt liked most about the raider idea, and why he ordered it initiated, was that America's military had suffered a string of humiliating defeats starting with Pearl Harbor, and the morale of the troops, not to mention the folks on the home front, needed some type of victory. The smashing American victory at the Battle of Midway had been a start, but more—much more—was needed. The idea behind the Raiders was to launch sizeable attacks behind enemy lines, taking the war to the enemy and letting him know that America was down but not out. This, Roosevelt believed, was imperative. The Marine high command, however, did not feel the need for some type of elite fighting force, considering as they did that all Marines were elite. To them, the Raiders were redundant and resulted in nothing more than a serious drain from the regular ranks of some of the Corps's best fighting men.

Whitey Groft was there. He lived what I had simply read about. He was personally interviewed by Edson for the Raiders (and was initially turned down), and he had several personal stories about his own interactions with the famed commander.

As we spoke that day in 2009, he showed me a fifty-seven-page memoir he had entitled "Under the Southern Cross and Beyond," which covered his time with the Raiders, as well as his eventual reassignment to the 29th and, later, the 22nd Marines on Okinawa, and in China, guarding a vital airfield against Communist Chinese forces after the war ended.

After the newspaper story ran on November 11, I kept in touch with Marlin. He had mentioned to me that he'd always wanted to convert his short memoir into a book, and in 2012 we began to convert that wish into reality. Using his memoir as a starting point, plus adding many hours of interviews with Marlin, as well as phone calls to his friend and machine gun squad leader, Bill Waltrip, and to former Raider Robert Youngdeer, as well as consulting various historical sources to flesh out the action on Tulagi, Guadalcanal, and New Georgia, Marlin and I have combined to create an intimate look at one of American's most dynamic fighting units, by a man who was a part of it from start to finish.

I wish to thank my editors at Berkley for their help in allowing us to tell this story. A big thank-you goes to Holly Bowers Toth for information and photos of her uncle, Kenneth E. Bowers, Whitey's best friend who died on Tulagi. Thanks also to Bob Gilbert of the Kenneth E. Bowers VFW post in Nazareth, Pennsylvania, for putting me in touch with the Bowers family.

My heartfelt thanks also goes to my wife, Barbara, who sacrificed our family time while I worked on this project.

Lastly, my personal thank-you to Marlin Groft and all the other Raiders for doing their part to halt the Japanese aggression in the Pacific, and to all the men and women who served in World War II, in whatever capacity they were called on to provide, for doing their part in preserving freedom across the globe.

Larry Alexander
December 2013

BLOODY RIDGE
AND BEYOND

CHAPTER ONE

FROM "SKINHEAD" TO RAIDER

The midday sun shone down brightly on the city of Lebanon, Pennsylvania, its beams sparkling off the windshields, chrome bumpers, and grillwork of the cars that cruised along Cumberland Street. A number of the city's 27,206 inhabitants, some bundled in winter coats despite the warming rays bathing the city, leisurely strolled the sidewalks on this quiet Sunday. Church was out, but from somewhere across town came the low, mournful *bong-bong* of a steeple bell.

It was December 7, 1941, and I and a few of my buddies were sitting on the steps outside the front doors of the William Penn Restaurant and Bar, which had been opened thirteen years earlier by its Greek owner, Constantinos "Gus" Levendis. I had been born in this city, the second youngest child of fourteen—seven boys and seven girls—born to John and Emma (Barshinger) Groft, who had spaced us out over so broad a gap in time that many of my older siblings had married and left home before I started school. One brother, Ernie, died of an illness when he was seven years old.

I had graduated from Lebanon High School in 1939, and since the country was still in the grips of the Great Depression and jobs were at a premium, I entered the Civilian Conservation Corps, one of President

Franklin Roosevelt's federally run public works programs. The CCC bounced me around to different locations, mostly in Pennsylvania, although my last post was in Washington, D.C. There I lived and worked at Rock Creek Park, operating a dragline excavator to help dredge the waterway. Following my one year of service, I returned home.

My parents no longer lived in Lebanon but had moved to Lancaster County sometime after Dad's crippling. My father had been an ironworker for the Lebanon division of Bethlehem Steel, and when I was about three years old, he had been horribly burned by molten steel, thus ending his working career. There was no workers' compensation in those days, and he received some pitiful payout of $400 or so, if my memory serves me. Survival from that point on became a total family affair, with all of my brothers and sisters of working age and ability getting jobs and chipping in.

For myself, I had just been hired as a silk-screen printer in a textile mill, so as I sat on the steps of the hotel that Sunday, I was feeling good about my future prospects. That was when a man came out of the restaurant and asked if we had heard the news on the radio.

"What news?" I asked, squinting up at him in the bright sunlight.

"The Japs just bombed Pearl Harbor," he replied breathlessly. "It's war."

War, I thought. That was one wrinkle in my future plans that I had not considered. Naturally, I was aware of the fighting in Europe and how Adolf Hitler was kicking just about everybody's ass over there, and I knew the Japs were fighting in China. But I had not planned on anyone, least of all the Japanese, having the balls to attack us.

My first thought now was to answer the call of my country. As a boy, I had grown up with my father's stories of his time in the Spanish-American War. He had joined the cavalry, and although the war ended before he had gotten any farther than some drab Texas Army base, he loved to tell stories about Teddy Roosevelt and the Rough Riders. Those tales danced across my imagination, and now as a new war opened, I was determined to follow in my father's boot prints. I'd join the U.S. Army and volunteer for the cavalry. I tried to encourage my friends to sign up with me, but after a week of waiting for them to follow my lead, I grew impatient and ended up being the only one ready to jump on the enlistment bandwagon. Since my parents were living in Lancaster, I traveled there the next day and informed them of my plans. Having done that, I mounted the concrete steps leading into the General Charles P. Stahr Armory on North Queen Street to sign the papers. Inside, I strode confidently into the Army recruiter's office. A sergeant in a green uniform, sitting behind a desk, looked up as I entered. I told him I wanted to be a cavalryman, and a thin smile creased his otherwise emotionless face.

"Cavalry is becoming obsolete, son, a remnant of a bygone era," he told me. "We only have one active unit, and there is no way in hell you are going to be assigned to it."

He explained how the Army was moving toward mechanized warfare, abandoning horses for tanks and half-tracks.

"The Krauts proved that point in Poland," he told me. "Their tanks made hamburger out of the Polish cavalry."

The vision of going into battle inside a sort of steel chariot held no appeal for me.

Crestfallen, I turned away. As I wondered what I wanted to do next, I glanced into another office. There I spotted a man standing just inside, in a snazzy blue uniform, with red piping accenting the pants and jacket, a white leather belt around his waist, and a white peaked hat on the desk. Fixated on the uniform, I entered the office and asked him what branch of the service he represented.

"I'm a United States Marine," he replied matter-of-factly.

In truth, I didn't know much about the Marines, having never met one, but neither did I dwell on it too long. The uniform had won me over and I found myself signing the papers.

Since I had a few days to kill before I departed for what the recruiter called boot camp, I spent the time readying myself and bidding farewell to my parents and friends. Next thing I knew, I was standing on the railroad platform at Lancaster, suitcase in hand and all alone, my parents being unable to travel. All around me were young men. A few were chatting, but most looked as lonely and bewildered as me. The eastbound train chugged into the depot, and I stepped into the Pull-man car that would carry me to Philadelphia.

I was now truly on my own. Settling back in the seat, I listened to the wheels clank along the track as the train rolled east. We made periodic stops along the way, during which more young men, some with buddies, some alone, and all just as nervous as me, stepped on board. By the time we arrived in Philly, our contingent of men had grown quite large.

We were met at the cavernous 30th Street Station by several Marine NCOs, who cast disparaging looks at this crop of recruits they'd been ordered to shepherd. Their bellowing orders of "form up here" and "fall in," laced with a few hearty "god damnit"s, echoed off the Classical Greek–style architecture until they finally got us outside and on board waiting buses for a trip to the Philadelphia Navy Yard. Arriving at the base, we were herded into a large, nondescript redbrick building and told to strip down to our birthday suits for physical examinations.

I was about to embark on a most exciting ten years as a United States Marine.

During World War II (and this is still the case even to this day), men living west of the Mississippi River who enlisted or were drafted into the Marines were sent to San Diego for training. For men like me, living east of the Mississippi, our new home would be Parris Island, South Carolina, five miles south of Beaufort, the second oldest city in the state.

A Marine training base since November 1, 1915, Parris Island grew in leaps and bounds. Between 1941 and 1945, about 204,000 men would pass through its gates.

Following my physical examination and numerous inoculations that stung as if the medical orderlies were using square needles, I and the rest of the recruits boarded another train that was already teeming with men from New York City and points north. As this train rumbled south, we made stops in the cities of Dover, Baltimore, Washington, Richmond, and seemingly at every small town rail whistle stop, mailbox, and fence post in between, and every time more young men crammed on board.

At around dusk, the train slowed to a halt in Yemassee, South Carolina, a tiny rail town near Parris Island. Stepping down from the Pullman, I looked around and realized there were more guys on the train than there were residents of this rinky-dink hamlet. A short walk from the station I noticed a number of large wooden shacks.

A sergeant began bellowing, "Line up! Come on, gentlemen! Get in line. You waitin' for an invitation? Move your asses!"

We did as ordered, although hardly with the parade ground precision that would become second nature to us over the next several weeks.

Once we were in line, the sergeant snarled, "Nicely done."

We were certain he didn't mean it.

"This is home for the night," the sergeant growled, jerking a thumb toward the row of shacks. "The trucks will be here in the morning to take you to the training center."

With that, we were divided into groups of twenty-five or thirty men, and each group was assigned to a shack that, we now discovered, had been converted from a chicken coop. There I spent a sleepless night, both from apprehension about the future and from the nighttime cold that the uninsulated plank walls did little to block.

As promised, a column of drab green two-and-a-half-ton trucks arrived with the sun the following morning. Hoisting ourselves on board and settling on the benches that lined both sides of the truck bed, we felt more than a little anxious as the drivers turned over their engines. Then we were off, the deuce-and-a-halves rattling down the unpaved roadway toward that mysterious place known as Parris Island, where they made boys into men. The trucks, which we secretly believed had been given to the Marines by the Army after the shock absorbers were first removed, jolted and jarred us for close to an hour. Then, with a squeal of brakes, our convoy passed through the training center's main gates and halted on a dirt street, lined by more wooden shacks.

"Everybody out," the call came. "Out! Move!"

Leaping down from the truck beds, we were herded a short distance down the road and into a large, drab brick building. As we milled about in a confused mass, Marine NCOs moved through and divided us randomly into platoon-sized groups of twenty-five to thirty men, much like the night before. In batches, we were next taken to a smaller adjacent building, where we were ordered to strip off all our clothes. Then our flock of naked men—this was obviously no place for the modest—were given "chemical baths" by running a gauntlet of medical orderlies who, with sadistic glee, we suspected, hosed us down as we moved passed them. We were then ushered into a room where our hair was shaved to the skin. The next room contained men from the quartermaster corps, who handed us our day uniform, called dungarees; underwear, or skivvies; boots, known as boondockers; a pith helmet like I'd seen actors wearing in jungle movies; plus blankets, toilet gear, and a duffel bag to keep it all in. We quickly dressed and shoved everything else into our bags. We then ran out a rear door, our freshly shaved heads making us feel like plucked chickens.

A corporal formed my group into a line, paired us up, and led us to a broad field of tents perfectly erected in straight lines, with the rows separated by wide, immaculately kept company streets.

"This will be your home," he said. "You men are now platoon 101 of the 2nd Recruit Battalion. Remember that. I'm not one for repeatin' things."

He then began assigning two men to each tent.

"Groft! Bowers! In here," he barked, indicating a tent, then moved on to the next.

I and the young man the corporal referred to as Bowers entered our new quarters, and looked around. The tent had two canvas cots, one to each side, with a coal oil space heater squatting at the rear, to stave off the nighttime chill. How good that would've felt last night. A naked lightbulb hung from a cord attached to the tent's ridgepole. I claimed a cot and sat down. Bowers plopped down on his. We grinned foolishly at each other.

"Not bad," Bowers said. "More comfy than I expected."

We introduced ourselves to each other and shook hands.

My tent mate was a good-looking kid named Kenneth Bowers. Four months short of his twenty-first birthday, Bowers told me he was born in Stockertown, Pennsylvania, but that he and his family were now living in Nazareth, Pennsylvania. Like me, he came from a large family, with nine sisters and three brothers, although two sisters and a brother had died early. Then Bowers proudly showed me a photograph of his parents, Fred and Lillie.

Since Nazareth was less than seventy-five miles from Lebanon, we felt as if we had been neighbors, and we took an instant liking to each other.

It was the start of a wonderful, but tragically short, friendship.

B right and early the next morning we were rousted from our bunks by shouts, curses, and blowing whistles. Scrambling into our dungarees, we formed up on the street in front of our tents. There we found ourselves face-to-face with the two men who, for the next ten weeks, would be for us the most influential and, at times, the most terrifying individuals on Earth: our drill instructors.

They were Sergeants Ward and Rebel, both former China Marines, a distinction they earned for having served with the 4th Marine Regiment in Shanghai, protecting American interests and citizens as the Sino-Japanese War threatened to engulf everything and everyone. These men were hard-ass Leathernecks, veterans, and we were awed by them as they stood ramrod stiff, their uniforms neatly pressed and their campaign-style hats, bearing the globe and anchor device, planted firmly on their heads as if screwed into place. Beneath the circular brim of the hats, their faces were impassive, their jaws set, their eyes glaring menacingly at us as we stood at rigid attention. It was into their capable but unsympathetic hands that the Marine Corps had placed our fate.

"Do you believe this?" Ward asked his assistant DI as he surveyed us.

"Pitiful," Rebel replied, shaking his head pathetically. "I've scraped better stuff off the bottom of my shoes."

Ward turned a hard eye on us.

"My name is Sergeant Ward," he announced in a loud, raspy voice.

"This is Sergeant Rebel. If you need to address us, that is how you do it. You don't call us 'sir,' and God help the man who calls either of us 'Sarge.'" He waved a clipboard. "Your names are on this here list, but this list don't mean shit to us. You have no names. You have no past. You have no life outside the gates of this camp. That life you had out there is over. Forget it. And forget that special girl. Some 4-F is probably already in her pants. All you need to worry about right now is us." He indicated the two of them. "You are skinheads. That's it. Skinheads. The lowest form of animal life God put on this planet. You are not men, and you sure as hell ain't Marines. As skinheads, you are now property of the United States Marine Corps, lock, stock, and asshole. And the Marine Corps gave you to us."

Ward then laid out the day's training program, including close-order drill, calisthenics, and physical training. We were ordered to double-time everywhere and salute any Marine we met who was not a fellow boot.

Thus began what was to be our ten-week initiation into the Marine Corps. Every morning started with bunk inspection. Each cot had to be made to regulation, the blanket tight as a drumhead, otherwise Rebel and Ward hurled the bed—mattress, cot, and all—out into the company street, and the unlucky boot had to start all over again. Needless to say, every day, fewer and fewer beds got tossed out, as we learned the Marine way to square our bunks.

The training was tough, and Ward and Rebel rode our asses relentlessly. Both men were perfect examples of what being a Marine is all about, and as I look back over those early days I know I was truly blessed. Years later, when I, too, would become a drill instructor, these men were at the forefront of my mind as I dealt with my boots.

Despite the ruggedness of the training regimen, I enjoyed my time in boot camp due in no small part to Sergeants Ward and Rebel, who guided us through those hectic weeks. But our stay at Parris Island was cut short because of the increasing numbers of new recruits who kept constantly coming through the gate. As a result, after just five weeks or so, we found our platoon on its way to Quantico to complete our last phase of training, which was the firing range.

Quantico was more important than Washington, D.C., so far as the Marine Corps was concerned. It was *the* Marine camp, and we were delighted to be there, although we were, technically, still boots, even if Ward and Rebel had stopped calling us skinheads.

At Quantico we were issued a piece of regulation equipment we all grew to cherish, the 1903 bolt-action Springfield rifle. Weighing in at 8.67 pounds and measuring 43.9 inches in length, this excellent weapon was manufactured by either the Remington Arms Company or the Smith-Corona Typewriter Company.

"Take care of her and treat her well, and she'll do the same for you every time," Sergeant Ward told us. "Even a broad can't promise that."

The weapon was fed by a five-round stripper clip, which consisted of five .30-caliber rounds placed in a grooved, stamped-metal strip. With the weapon's bolt open, one end of the clip was placed in a receiver at the rear of the breech, and using a thumb, the shooter pushed the rounds down into the breech and off the clip, which was then removed either by hand or by closing the bolt, which automatically ejected it. By the breech, on the left, was also a magazine cut-off switch. When the switch was open, the weapon took a full clip. Close the switch, and the Springfield became a single-shot, bolt-action rifle.

After being issued our weapons and memorizing the serial number, we learned the various parts of the rifle, right down to the smallest screw. We were also drilled over and over on how to field strip, clean, and reassemble the piece.

And heaven help the man who dropped his rifle or referred to it as a "gun" in front of his DI.

Then we were off to the rifle range to sight in these beauties. I loved the range and did quite well, qualifying as a sharpshooter. However, the weapon I found that I liked best was the .45-caliber, 1911 model Colt automatic. Being enlisted men, we were not issued .45s, but being Marines, we learned to shoot them, along with every other weapon in the Marine arsenal, including the Browning Automatic Rifle. I was awarded the expert badge for my handling of the Colt .45 and drew high praise from my instructor.

Boot camp was drawing to a close, and soon we would do what we really came to do; that is, join the ranks and become one of those storied men known as U.S. Marines.

As the day of our graduation finally arrived, word came down that a special Marine unit called the Raiders, similar to British commandoes, was recruiting volunteers. We'd never heard of these Raiders, but we had heard talk about their commander, Lieutenant Colonel Merritt Edson, who was said to be a hard-fighting leader. Bowers and I studied the notice on the camp bulletin board, and we turned to each other as if we could read each other's mind.

"Let's volunteer," Bowers said with a gleam in his eye. "We joined the Marines to fight, right?"

Bowers was correct. This is what we had signed up for in the first place, a chance to fight the Japanese. Now that opportunity was calling out to us. We submitted our names without further delay.

A few days later, Bowers and I, along with several other men, were ordered to report to A Barracks. As I recall this time seventy years later, I can again feel the excitement as I sat in that outer room inside A Barracks, awaiting my turn to see the great man. This was a colonel, for Christ's sake, the highest-ranking officer I had ever met, let alone spoken to, and a man destined to become a legend in the Marine Corps. I cannot describe how I fought to control my nerves as my turn drew ever nearer.

"Oh God, give me the strength to stand firm through that door!" I thought to myself.

Merritt Austin "Red Mike" Edson was Vermont-born and attended the University of Vermont for two years before enlisting in the National Guard in 1916. Following a brief stint on the Mexican border, he returned to the university later in 1916, but a year after that, he quit again, to join the Marines. He was commissioned as a second lieutenant and served with the 11th Marines in France during the First World War, but saw no action.

In the 1920s he applied for flight training and earned his gold wings in

1922. Assigned to the Marine Air Station in Guam, he remained in the Mariana Islands until 1925. Assigned then to Kelly Field in Texas, Edson studied advanced aviation tactics, followed by the Company Officers' Course at Quantico, Virginia. There he graduated with the highest grades ever attained up to that time. For some reason—physical, we heard—he gave up flying in 1927 and soon was assigned to the Philadelphia Naval Yard as an ordnance officer. That was quickly followed by an assignment to the cruiser USS *Denver*, where Edson found himself en route to Central America and action against Sandino bandits in Nicaragua. Between 1928 and 1929, Edson, now in command of 160 hand-picked, specially trained Marines, fought twelve sharp engagements against the bandits and earned his first Navy Cross plus a Silver Star and the Nicaraguan Medal of Merit.

In 1936 Edson enrolled in the Senior Officers' Course at the Marine Corps School at Quantico, and a year later he was off to Shanghai as operations officer with the 4th Marines. In July of 1937, war broke out between the Japanese and the Chinese, giving Edson a unique opportunity to study the Japanese military under combat conditions. It provided our future commander with some valuable insights.

By June 1941, Edson was back at Quantico and in command of the 1st Battalion, 5th Marines, which, the following January, would be redesignated the 1st Special Battalion, the prelude to the 1st Marine Raider Battalion.

The idea of an elite raider force grew in the minds of two men, Edson and Lieutenant Colonel Evans Carlson, who had also served in China and studied guerilla tactics, mostly with Communist forces led by Mao Tse-tung. This close association with Mao would later prove something of a political and professional liability to the tall, gangly New Yorker. Carlson's number two man was Captain James Roosevelt, son of our president. Hoping to sell the Marines on the concept, Roosevelt wrote to Marine commandant General Thomas Holcomb on a topic he called the "Development Within the Marine Corps of a Unit for Purposes Similar to the British Commandoes and the Chinese Guerillas." But Holcomb wasn't buying. The feeling was that the

Marines, already considered an elite fighting force, did not need another elite force within their ranks. However, Holcomb did not take into account Roosevelt's clout, as the son appealed to his father, who put pressure on the men below him, specifically Admiral Chester Nimitz, overall naval commander in the Pacific. Nimitz soon relented and ordered the formation of a command-style fighting force. Holcomb grudgingly complied, but decreed that the force be known as raiders, rather than the too-British-sounding term "commandoes," or the Shock Battalion, as was suggested by Marine General Holland Smith.

On February 16, 1942, the 29 officers and 667 men of Edson's 1st Special Battalion became the 1st Marine Raider Battalion, and training began. Within days, though, Edson was ordered to detach 7 officers and 190 men to "seed" a 2nd Marine Raider Battalion that would be commanded by Carlson. Bitterly, Edson transferred his entire A Company under Captain Wilbur Meyer to Carlson in San Diego, and was thoroughly outraged when the eccentric Carlson reinterviewed all of the men Edson had hand-picked, and refused to accept many of Edson's so-called "easterners," preferring to train men in his own fashion. This deliberate snub evolved into a festering wound between, not just the two commanders, but also the men in their two battalions, and would lead to bad feelings and more than one knockdown brawl.

———

The loss of an entire company was as severe blow to Edson, and created a void he quickly needed to fill, which is how Ken Bowers and I found ourselves sitting in a waiting room inside A Barracks. We had both seen Edson before. One day, during our two-week rifle qualification period, he showed up on the firing line. Lifting a Springfield to his shoulder at the five-hundred-yard mark, he pumped five rounds into the bull's-eye as fast as he could work the bolt. We were suitably impressed.

Bowers and I fidgeted nervously as we awaited our turn to go inside and meet the great man. Would he like us? Would he accept us? And what the hell were we getting ourselves into? All of these questions, and more, sifted through our brains as we watched men walk in, and men walk out, of the inner door.

Then our turn came. I was in front of Ken, so I was ushered inside first.

The room was barren except for a desk, behind which Edson sat in a wooden, straight-backed chair. I strode crisply across the room to within three feet of the desk, stopped, and saluted.

"Private Marlin Groft," I announced, and rattled off my serial number.

Edson returned the salute then glanced at papers on his desk. As he studied the documents, I nervously watched the top of his head, with a fire-red crop of close-clipped hair.

"At ease," he said without looking up.

Then he turned his gaze toward me, his steely blue eyes boring into mine. I could not hold his stare. I could feel my legs getting weaker, and it occurred to me that this must be what it was like to stand before St. Peter. Later, of course, I would discover that Edson was, in fact, one rung higher.

"From what I am reading here, you seem like a good man," Edson said. "You come from Pennsylvania Dutch country. That's good, hearty German stock. I like that. I know a lot of good men from Pennsylvania."

I was starting to feel encouraged.

"Your training records look good, except for swimming," Edson said.

"It's not my strong point," I conceded. "I'm no Johnny Weissmuller, sir, but I passed the boot camp course."

"You did," Edson said. "Just. But I need more than that. We are going to be a commando-style unit, and the men may be required to swim to shore while also lugging gear and equipment. For that, I'm looking for strong swimmers. I'm sorry, son. I don't think I can accept you. The fact that you are not a good swimmer could result in your death, as well as the death of others. But I thank you for volunteering."

The whole time he spoke, his eyes never left mine, and I could feel those blue bolts burning through my head as he rendered his decision. Crushed, I saluted. Edson returned the salute, and I turned and left. On my way out, I could not even look at Bowers as he passed me on his way into the office. This was the first real disappointment I had ever felt over something that I had cared about in my life, and as I returned to my barracks I was convinced I would end up walking guard duty in some navy yard and never get to see a Japanese, much less fight one.

My mood was not enhanced when a beaming Ken Bowers returned to the barracks and announced that Edson had selected him. When I told him I had been rejected, he was as bitterly disappointed as I was. It had never occurred to either of us that we'd be separated.

"I'm sorry, Marlin," he told me.

"It's OK," I told my friend. "I'm happy for you."

"Maybe I'll ask to be dropped from his unit," Bowers said. "I'd hate for us to get separated."

I chided him. "Don't be an idiot. It's what you want, so do it, and best of luck to you. We'll stay in touch."

I'm not sure I believed that last, as the rejection weighed on my mind, especially when Bowers got his orders to transfer to C Barracks, where the men selected for the Raiders were being billeted.

My depression lasted three days. Then, out of the blue, new orders arrived for me. As I read them, I was stunned. I was to report to C Barracks for duty with the Raiders. I felt it had to be a mistake, but I wasn't about to question it. So I hastily shoved my belongings into my barracks bag, hoisted it up on my shoulder, and hurried toward C Barracks, one of three large buildings on Bartlett Avenue. Entering, the first person I spotted was Bowers, and we embraced in a joyful reunion.

"Thank God," Bowers said. "I'm so glad you're here. How'd it happen?"

"I have no idea," I told him in hushed tones. "And for Christ's sake, don't ever bring it up."

I never knew by what means I came to be accepted as a Raider, and believe you me, I never asked. Still, for the next several weeks, as we underwent Raider training, I kept waiting for the mistake to be discovered, possibly by Edson himself. I envisioned him spotting me in the ranks, then the hammer dropping, booting me out of the unit to which I desperately wanted to belong.

But for now I was here. The adventure of my life was about to begin.

CHAPTER TWO

TRAINING AND DEPLOYMENT

Officially a member of the 1st Raider Battalion, at least for now, I and my closest buddy, Ken Bowers, found ourselves being assigned to the 2nd platoon of D Company.

Dog Company was under the command of Captain Justice "Jumpin' Joe" Chambers, who was recruited by Edson on March 23. An exceptionally fine officer, as were all the leaders Edson hand-picked, Chambers's claim to fame was that his mother was a relative of Valentine Hatfield, head of the Hatfield family, whose bloody, twenty-eight-year-long family feud with the McCoy family in West Virginia and Kentucky took no fewer than twenty lives.

Actually, Chambers was not our first CO. The first, Captain Henry Cain, died suddenly of a heart attack in March 1942, while on a march. Captain Ira "Jake" Irwin took over temporarily, but he was soon replaced by Chambers.

My platoon leader was 1st Lieutenant Ed Wheeler, a fine officer in his own right. Wheeler and I would develop a very good relationship, and he tried to keep me close by whenever we went into combat.

My platoon sergeant was Stanley D. "Ed" Kops, a tough old Marine from Hollywood, California. Kops, in fact, was at an age where he did not have to serve in a combat unit, but he chose to remain with Edson and the Raiders.

My squad leader was Corporal Homer "Spike" Edwards, a four-year veteran of the Marine Corps and something of a hell-raiser. How he kept his stripes I never knew.

I discovered several men, besides Bowers, in the platoon and the company as a whole, with whom I became close friends. Pfc. Richard T. "Mac" MacNeilly of Oneida, New York, was a scrounger. If you needed something, from a fountain pen to a pistol, he could probably rustle it up. Pfc. Ray Ruble hailed from New Jersey. Because he was built like a football lineman, we nicknamed him "Big Stoop." Alexander Stewart Jr. was another New Jersey guy, hailing from Carneys Point. We would become especially close. Michael Rihaly was from the Keystone State, like me, making his home in Merrittstown. He was our platoon BAR man and I was his assistant.

And no outfit is complete without a boisterous, hard-drinking, hard-fighting Irishman. In our platoon it was Private Patrick Henry O'Shanahan, a jolly, dependable fellow and a good man to have on your side in a bar fight, which he would prove in brawls from Wellington, New Zealand, to Los Angeles.

The battalion under Edson was broken down into four rifle companies, each consisting of a captain, 4 lieutenants, 130 men, and 2 Navy medical corpsmen. Our A, B, and C companies contained three platoons each, while D Company had just two, with 2nd platoon being under Wheeler and 1st platoon under 1st Lieutenant Robert Neuffer. Charlie and Dog companies also each had an attached weapons platoon. Ours was led by Gunnery Sergeant Elwood Gebhart.

Our rifle platoons were generally divided into eight-man squads, although some had as many as thirteen. These included the squad leader, two men with Browning Automatic rifles, and five men with Springfields. One man—the best marksman in the group—was designated as a sniper, and equipped with the eleven-inch-long Weaver M8 03A3 sniper scope.

There was an E Company commanded by Captain George Herring, which served as our weapons company. It consisted of two rifle platoons, a mortar platoon, a demolition platoon, and an anti-tank section. Since we were a light striking force, dependent on speed and stealth, our weapons company had eight light machine guns, three 60mm mortars, and two Boys .50-caliber anti-tank guns.

These were the very early days of the Second World War, when America had neither the manpower nor the resources to launch full-scale assaults on Japanese-held islands. Yet in light of the string of stunning defeats the Allies had suffered at the hands of the Japanese—Pearl Harbor, Singapore, Hong Kong, the Philippines, Guam, and Wake Island—home front morale demanded that we take the war to the enemy and not let him rest on those early victories and solidify his defenses. That's what the Raiders were all about, keeping the Jap off-balance by attacking him where he least expected it and where he might be most vulnerable, mainly inside his Pacific ring of conquests, where he thought himself to be secure. Some of these missions behind enemy lines might be swift in-and-out, what Edson called "stiletto"-type raids, requiring speed and surprise, while others could require conducting guerilla operations for long periods of time. Whatever the mission was, we Raiders were prepared to carry it out.

For that purpose, Edson was looking for young, physically fit Marines, preferably unmarried men, eager for action and willing to undertake hazardous duty. More than once, Edson would stand before us, holding up one of the distinctive stiletto knives we all carried, donated by a wealthy female admirer, and he'd snarl, "When we meet the Jap, he will show you no mercy, and you will show none to him. So, men. Do you have the guts to slit a Jap's throat?"

"Yes, sir," we shouted back lustily.

To his officers and NCOs, Edson hammered home the message that responsibility went with those bars or chevrons, and he encouraged them to make decisions under pressure. He was a believer in men showing initiative, regardless of their rank.

Of course, an extraordinary group of Marines had to be led by an extraordinary flock of officers, and Edson had a knack for selecting them.

Lieutenant Colonel Sam Griffith became Edson's executive officer. He was thirty-five when he came to the Raiders in the second week of March 1942, after having spent five months in England studying commando techniques. A native of Lewistown, Pennsylvania, Griffith was a 1929 Annapolis graduate and had served in Nicaragua, Cuba, and China.

On the company level, A Company was led by Captain Lew Walt, or "Silent Lew" as he was sometimes known, using one of the "tribal" names we Raiders sometimes gave each other. Walt originally had been a member of the Colorado National Guard, before joining the Marines. After serving in Shanghai and Guam, he found himself stationed at Quantico, where Edson noticed him and wooed him over to the Raiders. As a sort of good luck omen, Walt's birthday was February 16, the same birth date as the Raiders.

His executive officer was the capable 1st Lieutenant John Antonelli, who would command the company at Bloody Ridge.

Second Lieutenant Thomas F. Mullahey, who would distinguish himself as a Raider, led 2nd platoon under Walt and would also become a company commander.

Major Lloyd Nickerson, a native of Spokane, Washington, and a Marine Corps reservist, took command of Baker Company.

Charlie Company was led by a terrific guy, Major Ken Bailey. Broad-shouldered, six-foot-three, and Hollywood handsome, the Pawnee, Oklahoma, native had attended Colorado State University as a chemistry major, not to mention wrestler and captain of the football team. He later joined the Illinois National Guard and served with the 130th Infantry Regiment before joining the Marines as a 2nd lieutenant in 1935. One of his assignments in the Corps was aboard the battleship USS *Pennsylvania*. Bailey was thirty-one when he came to the Raiders.

Commanding Bailey's 2nd platoon was 2nd Lieutenant Clay A. Boyd, who would distinguish himself as a Raider.

Another officer who would prove vital to Edson was his assistant, 2nd

Lieutenant John Erskine. Erskine's tribal name, "Tiger," was misleading since he was a frail man, weighing in at 108 pounds. In fact, he had been rejected by Marine recruiters in 1941 because he failed to meet the minimum standards, being too short and too skinny and having lousy eyesight. What finally got him noticed was that he was the son of missionaries and grew up in Japan. He could read and speak the language fluently.

Our standard uniform was made of heavy cotton twill to soak up moisture from the rain and humidity of the jungles, as well as sweat, body oils, and accumulated dirt. We also wore the standard soft overseas cap, or "pisscutter," and a short-brimmed soft hat we dubbed the "Raider cap." Some men tucked their trousers into the tops of their low-cut, brown, rough suede boondockers, and others did not. We were given leggings but threw them away after our blistered feet, following rainy hikes, taught us that they prevented wet boots from drying. And we had our "782 gear," the light tan web belt, ammo pouches, backpack, canteen, and other personal items that were issued via the military's #782 Form.

Training began immediately. First, we refamiliarized ourselves with every weapon a Raider might be called upon to use, from the Colt .45 automatic to the BAR to the Boys .50-caliber anti-tank rifle, or "elephant gun." That also meant getting to know how to kill a man with a knife, be it our stiletto, which had the nasty habit of sometimes breaking when thrown, the Marine Corps's standard, broad-bladed KA-BAR, or the machete and bayonet.

Self-defense was taught by Colonel Anthony Biddle, a World War I veteran and expert on close combat. He left us slack-jawed and thoroughly impressed, when he surrounded himself by a circle of Raiders, all wielding unsheathed bayonets, and, bare-handed, disarmed them all. Edson, of course, frowned upon practicing with naked blades, so we trained using fencing foils and masks.

There were also lessons in the best use of camouflage and small unit combat tactics.

We were instructed to fight with what weapons and gear we could carry into battle, and not be dependent on artillery or air support. We worked eighteen hours a day, seven days a week learning about the art of combat, armed and unarmed.

Since our missions included probable landings behind Japanese lines, we spent many hours on the Potomac River training in the use of rubber boats, under the stern glare of Gunnery Sergeant Gerald B. Stackpole, an old China Marine and expert in rubber boat handling. A man of rabid discipline when it came to "his boats" and their handling, we dubbed him Admiral of the Condom Fleet. Bivouacking along the lazy, meandering Chopawamsic Creek as it made its way to the Potomac in Prince William and Stafford counties, the gunny would drill us relentlessly, both on handling the rubber boats and on their care and maintenance. We began to suspect that he worried more over his damned boats than he did about us.

Edson, knowing we might be subjected to long treks on foot, insisted on daily runs between our barracks and the camp's main area. But it was through hiking that "Red Mike" really weeded out the boys from the men. He seemed to take sadistic joy in long marches, generally with heavy packs and full combat gear. These jaunts included compass marches in the dark of night. Rain or shine, it made no difference to the man we began calling, among ourselves of course, "Eddie the Mole," for the way his oversized helmet sat on his undersized head, with the rim of the steel pot touching his shoulders.

Edson's marching goal for the battalion was seven miles per hour, and we once covered twenty-five miles in five hours, and then went straight into a mock battle. One of his favorite marches was the thirty-mile trek from Quantico to the Civil War battlefield at Manassas, returning the next day. Every mother's son of us cursed Edson as we puffed along behind him, yet we noted that, at every stop, the colonel, who was a good deal older than many of us, would walk along the line during the break, checking on our condition. Then he'd double-time back to the head of the column when it was time to move again. As we drew near our barracks on the return trip, tuckered out as we were, he'd bellow, "Double-time, march," for the final mile.

In fact, we ran an awful lot, including five miles every day before breakfast.

Edson was not constantly at the head of the column during these marches. He'd move around, from rear to front and everywhere in between, keeping an eye on his boys. During one of these grueling hikes, a new fellow in our platoon, Pfc. Joe Connolly, snarled to the man next to him, "The guy who dreamed up this hike ought to be taken out and hung up by his balls."

Connolly did not realize that "the guy who dreamed up this hike" was the same man he was speaking to, having never met Edson. But Edson did not reply. He just smiled.

On one late-night hike, we marched back into camp at 2 a.m., tired as hell, yet with enough spark to break loudly into song, rousing the whole damned place. Edson caught holy hell about it from his superiors the next day, but he let the remarks roll off. He knew we were developing a strong sense of spirit and unit pride, and that was all he cared about.

Edson believed in action over words, and if we performed, he rewarded us, not with speeches, but with regular leaves. Once, when he was especially proud of us, he arranged a dance and brought in four busloads of secretaries from the Pentagon. How he coaxed them into partying with a bunch of rowdy Raiders, we never learned.

Soon, however, the war demanded our presence, and orders came to pack up and ship out. But not all of us. Not at first, anyway. In late March, Edson was told to bring his battalion west, but he was to leave 9 officers and 233 men at Quantico. Sam Griffith was ordered to remain, and we men of D Company were also among those left behind. We were, understandably, disappointed, and we had no idea why this was being done. One rumor said it was lack of transport space. Others whispered that we were being deployed to the European Theater of Operations. Still other scuttlebutt said we were to be the "seeds" for a new Raider battalion. I told Bowers it was because our group were the last ones to join the Raiders, so we had more raw recruits straight from boot camp. Perhaps, I reasoned, Edson figured we needed more training. Whatever the explanation, we were left to cool our heels in Virginia.

The move began on April 1, with the Raiders boarding a train for a destination unknown to everyone except Edson and his top staff members. As the train rolled due south, speculation abounded. Most assumed the next stop was Florida, for more rubber boat training. But as the train's direction shifted westerly, the best bet was San Diego. The cross-country trek was somewhat uncomfortable, with Marines crammed into every car. However, that discomfort was alleviated to an extent by the baggage car, which had been converted into a galley that never closed. When this first contingent of Raiders arrived at San Diego, there was no time for leaves to see the town. Instead, the men spent their time doing calisthenics and preparing their gear for shipment overseas.

On April 6, Edson's Raiders clambered aboard the 21,000-ton attack transport USS *Zeilin*, named for Jacob Zeilin, a veteran of both the Mexican War and the Civil War, who became the Marines Corps's first general in 1874. The ship hoisted anchor that same day and steamed into the Pacific Ocean bound for Samoa.

While the first echelon was gliding toward the South Pacific, we who remained at Quantico continued to practice small unit tactics, self-defense, rubber boat "yachting" on the Potomac River, and making night landings on the banks of the Potomac and the Chesapeake Bay, using ten-man rubber boats launched from obsolete World War I destroyers. In one drill, we made a beach landing on a stretch of Maryland sand that the brass had dubbed "Solomon Island," never for one second imagining that within six months we'd be landing for real in the Solomon Islands. Hell, most of us didn't know where the Solomon Islands were, or had never even heard of the place. Nor could I foresee that I would be among the first fifty men to make that landing, the first U.S. ground offensive of the war.

Near the end of May, our orders came through at Quantico, and we boarded a west-bound train to join up with the rest of the battalion. The trip was boring except for when the train was chugging across the western prairies. There we amused ourselves by firing our rifles at jack-rabbits and prairie dogs spooked by the noisy locomotive and the rattling of the steel wheels on the rails. During our short layover at San Diego we busied ourselves gathering equipment and adding a few replacements for men who had dropped out. A few days later, we climbed the gangplank of the attack transport USS *Heywood*, an eight-thousand-ton ship built in 1919 by Bethlehem Steel. Learning that made me think of my dad and the injuries he had suffered while employed by that same firm. Having lifted anchor, we were soon off.

How excited I was! What a thrill for a boy straight out of the rural farmlands of Lancaster County. I had never seen an ocean, much less a ship of this size. This was truly a dream come true, I told myself, giving no thought to what lay at the other end of my journey.

We sailed on across the seemingly endless Pacific, our ship rising and falling gently on the rolling waves. Then on June 27, without explanation, the *Heywood*'s engines quit turning and we came to a dead stop smack-dab on the equator. At first we Marines wandered about, gawking at each other and wondering what the hell was happening. Then we found out. It was time for us to pay homage to King Neptune.

The U.S. Navy has this time-honored tradition of inducting guys crossing the equator for the first time, called "Polliwogs," into the "mysteries of the deep." The award, if you wish to call it that, of conducting that initiation, goes to men who have already undergone it, called "Shellbacks," who work under the guidance of King Neptune and his Royal Court. These latter include old salts portraying Davy Jones, Neptune's first assistant; Her Highness Amphitrite; the Royal Scribe; the Royal Doctor; the Royal Dentist; the Royal Baby; and others. The cost of admittance to this seagoing society was a price none of us would ever forget.

One by one, we Polliwogs were hauled before King Neptune, a sailor done up to look like the King of the Seas, complete with crown and trident. As we were presented to Neptune, he handed out "sentences" to be carried out by the Shellbacks. Every Polliwog got the same sentence, which began with us running a gauntlet that consisted of a greased tarp spread out on the deck over a cargo net. We had to crawl along the tarp, a distance of maybe ten yards, with Shellbacks striking us all the way. And just when we thought we'd reached the end, the sailors turned a fire hose on us, the force of the water driving us back.

Next came the Royal Bath, where we were dunked in water and struck about the head, none too lightly, every time we came up for air. We also had to say "Shellback" three times rapidly as we were being dunked.

Officers or enlisted men, it made no difference where the initiation was concerned. In fact, I think they treated the Polliwog officers worse than us enlisted guys.

The worst trial we had to endure, though, was when they brought us before the Royal Baby, a big, hairy, ugly son of a bitch, who lay down on his back. Eggs were then cracked on his hairy belly, and we Polliwogs had to lick the egg off of him. It damned near gagged me.

When the ordeal finally ended, the newly initiated Shellbacks, particularly we Raiders, decided it wasn't over until we said it was, so we laid into our tormentors. What followed was one hell of a deck fight, with flying fists and more than a few bloody noses and bruised faces, after which all was forgiven and the ship moved on. As we put the equator behind us, I vowed never to go through that again. Six months later, when we docked in New Zealand after Guadalcanal, I raced off to find the nearest tattoo artist and had a sailing ship, along with the date 6-27-42, tattooed on my right bicep.

Our first port of call was Tutuila, the largest island in American Samoa. Codenamed Strawstack, Tutuila lies 2,276 miles southwest of Pearl Harbor and 1,580 miles northeast of Auckland, New Zealand. Volcanic in origin, the island has steep ridges almost its entire twenty-one-mile length, with the highest peak being Mount Matafao at 2,141 feet.

Right in the center of the island, opening to the east, is Pago Pago (pronounced Pon-go Pon-go) Harbor, which was a scene straight out of a picture postcard. When our first echelon entered here on April 28, they did so in a driving rainstorm, with poor visibility. But we arrived in glistening sunlight on July 3, allowing us a breathtaking view of the crescent-shaped harbor's high, green walls of lush foliage, its fringed sparkling white sandy beaches surrounding the bluest water I had seen in my life.

"Beautiful, isn't it, Marlin?" Kenny Bowers said as we stood by the rail, taking in the sight. "I wish I could take a picture to send to my folks. I'll bet they never imagined a place like this existed."

"It's like all the South Seas stories I ever heard as a boy, all come to life," I replied.

The harbor, one of the finest in the entire Pacific, although not large enough for a fleet anchorage, began with a one-mile-wide entrance, flanked by Point Distress on the west shore and Point Breaker to the east. The harbor was two miles wide and three miles long, ending at the village on Pago Pago, set on a low, narrow isthmus, a belt of land that seemed to connect Tutuila's mountainous northern and southern portions. The water in the harbor, which is a volcanic crater, was said to be 36 to 150 feet deep.

About ten thousand people called Tutuila home, with about one thousand living there in Pago Pago, where we dropped anchor. The natural wildlife of the island was birds and lizards. Interestingly, none of the tropical diseases we would come to dread elsewhere, such as malaria, existed here. Instead, the people were plagued by tuberculosis, parasitic infections, and elephantiasis. This last, a mosquito-borne, unpreventable disease, caused extremities, like arms and legs and scrotums, to enlarge and harden, and would result in the United States withdrawing all of its forces by the end of 1943. But not before some three thousand Marines and sailors were infected, with the only cure being transfer to a cooler climate.

Debarking from the *Heywood*, we were trucked to a camp near Leone on the southwestern end of Tutuila, where we had a joyful reunion with the rest of the battalion. During the weeks they had been at the camp, Edson had run their asses ragged with training and mountain climbing. We now joined in this regimen, working from 5 a.m. until 10 p.m., or even until midnight, handling rubber boats and practicing such skills as judo, stalking, bayonet and knife fighting, demolition, first aid, and communications. For this last, Edson had found that our short-range radios were all but useless in the jungle, and even the long-range TBX with its three components—the transmitter, antenna, and generator, weighing a combined 120 pounds—was prone to difficulties.

Some of our weapons weren't much better. The Reising submachine gun, produced by Harrington and Richardson Arms Company in Worcester, Massachusetts, was shorter, lighter, more accurate, and less costly than the Thompson, but it was so adversely affected by the climate in the southwest Pacific that we began calling it the "Rusting" submachine gun. It was so undependable, in fact, that on Guadalcanal, Edson ordered all men who possessed one to throw it into the Lunga River.

Our men, myself included, liked the Browning Automatic Rifle, but it weighed a bulky seventeen pounds and had a hard recoil. Still, these did not get tossed into the Lunga, but came to serve the Raiders well in all of our actions.

Our training was tough and not without incident. One Raider died of an accidental gunshot wound and another man fell from a 150-foot cliff while we were mountain climbing.

But the rugged conditioning continued, trudging up and down what, at the time, seemed like every goddamned hill and mountain Edson could find. Every time we looked, it seemed that we were walking up a hill. Samoa was nothing but hills.

Edson loved it, even going so far as to place a wager with the local garrison commander that we could scale the island's highest peak, Mount Matafao, undetected and capture its secret radar installation in a predawn attack. Edson won his bet.

Another part of our training involved three British commandoes whom Edson called in to give us lessons on how to silently kill a man with a knife, or with bare hands. They illustrated their skills with the help of a triangular steel knife that could penetrate a fifty-cent coin. One of them also taught us jujitsu and demonstrated the use of a short bayonet in a new fighting procedure that called for parrying, slashing, and thrusting. It was this type of specialized training that set us apart from the rest of the Marine Corps.

It was difficult and laborious work, and not every man could take it. Samoa separated a few people from the Raiders.

Amid our rigorous training schedule, Edson did allow us some time for recreation, which included boxing matches, called "smokers." We also had plenty of good food and even beer, which our guys "requisitioned" while unloading ships in Pago Pago or Leone harbor. Our recreation also included enjoying the Samoan women, many of whom wore skirts called *lava lava*. To our delight, they also tended to walk around topless.

My future squad leader and close friend William "Wild Bill" Waltrip joined the Raiders on Samoa. Bill had come to Pago Pago four months earlier with the 2nd Marine Brigade, and ended up bouncing from one grimy job to another. He was on a shipboard work detail aboard *Heywood* shortly after we docked, when he spotted Lester "Leck" Malone, whom he had gone to school with back in Mattoon, Illinois. He called to his old friend and they had a glad reunion. Waltrip told him about being stuck doing crappy work details, and Malone told him about his assignment with the Raiders.

"They're still looking for guys," Malone told him. "Why not volunteer? You'll see some action, guaranteed."

Waltrip decided to take his friend's advice.

"Sure. Why the hell not," he replied.

"Hey," Malone said. "You hungry? I'll go grab us a couple of sandwiches from the galley and be right back."

Waltrip said sure, and Malone hurried off as Waltrip went back to work. Malone did not return. Still, Waltrip followed Malone's advice, volunteered for Raider duty, and was accepted. Since his previous assignment had been with the machine guns, he was placed in Easy Company.

"I was afraid I was never going to see anything," Waltrip later told me. "I might have been left sitting in Samoa for the next ten years. They always say never volunteer, but signing up with the Raiders was the best thing that I did."

Officially a Raider, Waltrip asked around for Malone, but no one had seen him. Two days out of Samoa, Waltrip was leaning on the ship rail watching the *Heywood*'s wake trail out behind the transport, when Malone walked up to him, his head bandaged. What had happened was that, after hurrying off for the sandwiches, Malone had failed to see cargo being loaded aboard the ship. He was struck on the side of the head by the boom from a crane. Coldcocked by the blow, he lay in sickbay for three days.

Our training on Samoa ended, and on July 7 we set sail for New Caledonia, a former French possession said to be sympathetic to the Axis Powers.

New Caledonia, third largest island in the South Pacific, after New Guinea and New Zealand, sits 2,360 miles from Pearl Harbor, 1,230 miles from Auckland, and, although it meant nothing to us at the time, 800 miles southeast of the Solomon Islands. Covering 8,453 square miles of ground, it is just slightly smaller than New Jersey.

Long and narrow, New Caledonia stretches for 248 miles and is 31 miles wide, with coastal plains covered mostly by coconut trees. These plains give way to two long, parallel mountain ranges that run the island's length, with razorback ridges and rugged, heavily eroded slopes. The mountainous landscape is slashed by deep gorges and ravines. Streams and small rivers flow from the peaks and across the coastal plains before emptying into the sea.

In the early days, many in the native population were cannibals. And though the French, who claimed the island in 1853 after a survey crew had been attacked, pretty much stamped it out, we were told some isolated tribes deep in the interior might still adhere to the practice.

In the early days of World War II, the official government of the island was pro-Vichy, supporting the puppet government of France set up after the German conquest, but a large segment of the population was not. By the time our forces landed on the island in January 1942, the Vichy officials had all left, but there were still seventeen thousand French civilians scattered about, and we, perhaps unjustly, never quite trusted them.

The island had been used by the French as a penal colony and at one time housed as many as forty thousand prisoners. About one hundred were still on the island when we arrived. There were also more than eight hundred so-called indentured servants, mostly from French Indochina. They were mostly used for general labor in the island's many mineral mines. These people lived under deplorable conditions in work camps, residing in wire cages that resembled chicken coops or rabbit warrens. Housed in these shacks or even caves, the workmen lived on one side while, across from them, were the women, who were mostly used as prostitutes to satisfy the workers. Some of my most horrific memories were of us taking truckloads of our garbage to the Nickel Mines, what today would be called a landfill, near the town of Nouméa. The trucks would first stop by the caves, and these poor bastards would descend like ants, climb aboard the trucks, and throw over the side anything they could use. It was a scene out of Dante's *Inferno*, and one I carry in my mind to this day.

We disembarked from the *Heywood* at Nouméa, a small city of about eleven thousand people, and capital of what had been called French Oceania. After climbing aboard waiting trucks, we were carried about twenty-five miles to our new home, a newly established base near St. Louis Mission. Naturally enough, we christened the place Camp St. Louis, and it would become our principal base of operations for the duration of our campaigns in the South Pacific.

Part of the reason for our seclusion so far from Nouméa, I suspect, was to limit our contact with what we assumed were the Vichy-loving local French population. This, the brass hoped, would lessen the chances of an unpleasant incident, such as us beating the shit out of them. Another reason, of course, was for training purposes, stationing us closer to the jungle and mountains and farther from civilization.

The training, which commenced upon reaching camp, was exactly what we had come to expect: hard work and long hours. But we toughed it out, and our unit pride grew fiercer with every successful exercise. On one occasion, we were marching back into camp, tired and haggard after an especially difficult training session, when we passed a few noncombatant, rear echelon assholes.

One of them chided us. "Well, well. Here come the Wugged Waiders."

One of our guys, a big Texan, spun toward the man, raised his Springfield, chambered a round, and aimed. Two other Raiders quickly stopped him, convinced that he intended to fire.

But it wasn't just non-Raiders who challenged our pride. Ever since Evans Carlson's symbolic slap to Edson's face when Red Mike transferred A Company to Carlson only to have him reject many of them, we'd held a long-standing hatred of the 2nd Raider Battalion. It was a loathing second only to our feelings for the Japanese. During leaves in Nouméa, the bad blood boiled over and we wrecked more than one bar in fights with those guys. On one memorable occasion, totally pissed off, we rounded up a few machine guns, and even a couple of mortars, with ammo, and headed for the main gate of the camp, an unruly mob. Our intent was to go to their camp, which was just a mile or so from Camp St. Louis, and wipe the bastards out once and for all. We were in deadly earnest, and to this day, I don't know what would have happened had Lieutenant Colonel Griffith not stormed out of the HQ hut and ordered us to stand down and return to our area.

He raged. "You crazy bastards! You can't do shit like that! Now, put those weapons down and get back your duties. That's an order, damnit."

We grumbled, but did as directed.

The high command soon wised up, and, from that point on, our two camps were placed many miles apart, sometimes on completely different islands.

Edson's regimen of hikes and field exercises continued. He drilled us relentlessly, and I will never forget him watching us with his cold, icy-blue eyes that never smiled, even when his mouth did. It is little wonder that war correspondent Richard Tregaskis, author of *Guadalcanal Diary*, who would follow us into battle on Tulagi and Guadalcanal, called Edson "the bravest, the most effective killing machine I have met in fifteen years."[1]

Through all of this, we knew our training would soon end. Sure enough, in late July we were ordered to pack up our gear. Trucked back to Nouméa, we found four waiting ships: USS *Little*, USS *Gregory*, USS *Colhoun*, and USS *McKean*. These ships were dubbed APDs (auxiliary personnel destroyers). They were four-stack destroyers of World War I vintage, which had been stripped of much of their armament and fitted with davits so each ship could hold four Higgins landing boats. In addition, one boiler and one stack had been removed to create a hold for combat troops and our gear. On the downside, the saltwater distillation equipment on these antiquated ships was inadequate; the galley, or mess hall, was small and cramped; and calling the heads "poor" was a compliment. The little ships rolled heavily even in moderate seas, turning the vessels into stinking scows, reeking of puke from seasickness. The ships were also classed as "high-speed" transports, but high-speed was in name only. They could carry 135 officers and men.

Despite their many shortcomings, we Raiders grew to love these little ships and their crews, and the swabbies returned the sentiment. We would work closely with them in the coming operation.

We now began training on the APDs, clambering down cargo nets into rubber boats that, even with the ships anchored, rose and fell as much as eight feet. This required us Raiders, loaded down with gear and ammo, to hover above the bobbing boat, then drop down into it or, if our timing was right, just step aboard. If we misjudged, we landed on a pile of equipment or, worse, plunked into the water, loaded down with nearly one hundred pounds of equipment. How we did not lose anyone, I will never know.

Then it came time for us to join the invasion fleet headed for God and Edson alone knew where. Departing New Caledonia, Edson left fifty men behind to watch over our camp, fifty men who had worked and trained as hard as any of us but would never share in the glory of the two most important actions of Edson's Raiders.

That was July 24. The rest of the fleet had sailed out of New Zealand two days earlier and were awaiting our arrival at the rendezvous point about four hundred miles from Fiji. As we entered the harbor at Fiji, my squad mates and I hung on the rail of the USS *Little*, gaping with awe.

"Holy shit, will ya look at that, Whitey?" Mike Rihaly said. The guys had begun calling me "Whitey" because my light blond hair almost looked white.

"It sure as hell is something," I replied.

And indeed, it was. Dubbed Task Force 62, our convoy contained eighty-two ships, including three aircraft carriers, the *Wasp*, the *Enterprise*, and the *Saratoga*, the battleship *North Carolina*, fourteen cruisers, thirty-one destroyers, nineteen transports, five minesweepers, five fueling ships, and our four APDs, which now took on the rampless landing craft called Higgins boats. These craft were old and well used, having been requisitioned from several different training bases. The military did have newer Higgins boats with ramps to ease landings, we later learned, but these were all earmarked for the Army and the invasion of North Africa. From July 28 until July 30, we used these vessels during practice landings on Koro Island, and even though we had to climb over the craft's gunwales to get out, landing proved to be a breeze after the unstable rubber boats we had been working with up to this point.

On July 31, the fleet raised anchor and we set off across the Coral Sea. The night was warm and overcast, punctuated by short bursts of moonlight. As the prows of our ships knifed through this body of water, I recalled that it was near this spot, just over two months earlier, that the United States and Japan had fought the first all-air naval action in history, where no gunfire had been exchanged and neither country's surface fleet had seen the other. It was a battlefield where the only monuments to the fallen would be the coral-encrusted remains of ships and aircraft lying on the bottom.

Because of the heat, some men slept in the *Little*'s lifeboats, while many more of us lay sprawled on the deck. This made walking in the dark something of a challenge since the ships were in total blackout after sunset, due to the threat of enemy submarines. In that manner, we were bound for the first amphibious landing by U.S. Marines since the Spanish-American War forty-five years earlier. But we still did not know where that might be.

But Edson, also on board the USS *Little*, knew our destination. Our target was the Solomon Islands, specifically the large island of Guadalcanal, which would be hit by the 1st Marines; the small islands of Gavutu and Tanambogo, which were to be seized by the 397 men of the 1st Paramarine Battalion; and Tulagi, which was our objective. We Raiders were assigned Tulagi instead of Gavutu and Tanambogo because it was thought to be the toughest nut of the three to crack. During the voyage, Edson frequently conversed with two coast watchers, Dick Horton and Henry Josslyn, who were intimately familiar with Tulagi and Guadalcanal.

On August 1, our second day at sea, Raiders on all four APDs gathered to hear about the island we would be attacking. Being on board the *Little* along with Edson, we got our briefing from the man himself.

We would be assaulting the Solomon Islands, where, Edson told us, the Japs were building an airfield that would threaten our supply lines to Australia.

One of the coast watchers, I forget which one, showed us maps and explained that the Solomons were the longest island chain in the entire South Pacific; 992 islands stretching for more than 900 miles and totaling 240,000 square miles. They consisted of two chains of islands separated by the 20- to 40-mile-wide New Georgia Sound, which we came to know as "The Slot." To me, looking at the map, the Solomon chain looked like a loaf of bread with a slice cut out of the middle.

Temperatures would range from the low seventies to high eighties, with high humidity and gusty southwest trade winds, the coast watcher said. Rainfall was about two hundred inches a year, mainly in the "rainy season" of November to March. Unlike in Samoa or New Caledonia, tropical diseases, especially malaria, dysentery, dengue fever, and fungal infections, were prevalent.

Then the map of the Solomons was taken away and another map put up instead, this one of a small clump of islands. Colonel Griffith took over the briefing.

"Our particular target is here," he said, tapping one of the islands with a pointer. "This is Tulagi, codenamed Ringbolt. It is just a quarter mile south of Florida Island," he added, indicating a larger landmass just above Tulagi, "and a stone's throw off are Gavutu and Tanambogo." The pointer struck against two smaller islands, linked together by a causeway, about three thousand yards due east of Tulagi.

The coast watcher now took over again.

"Tulagi is just a mile-and-a-quarter long, and half-a-mile wide, measured northwest to southeast," he told us. "The upper portion in particular has steep-sided coral ridges with two-hundred- to three-hundred-foot slopes. These are covered with trees and brush. Very rough to traverse. The extreme southeastern tip of the island, which your map indicates as Hill 281, is also rocky, and its face is studded with caves. Between these two high, rugged areas is a low saddle that cuts across the island. This is the government center. Tulagi was the capital of the Solomon Islands Protectorate from 1896 until our friendly Mr. Jap came calling earlier this year. So government buildings are here, as well as residences and wharves. You will find bungalows, villages, shops, a hotel, a cricket field, and even a small, what you Yanks would call a pitch and putt, golf course."

Griffith picked up the narration.

"The Japs use the island as a seaplane base," he said. "There are hills, ravines, and caves all over the place, which the Japs will occupy, so they may be tough to root out. The most prominent elevation in this part of the island, which is where we think most of the enemy will be concentrated, is Hill 281 at the southeastern end of Tulagi. There is a coral reef on the southwest side of the island, with a quarter mile gap right here." He tapped the map more than a mile west of the main settlement. "This is our landing area. Blue Beach. Once ashore, our goal will be to cut the island in two as quickly as possible. To our left lies the village of Sesopi. That is the objective of the 2/5, who will be coming ashore behind us. Once we've cut the island in half, we will wheel right and move in a southerly direction toward the government station, our left on Tulagi Harbor, our right on Sealark Channel. Our order of advance, from north to south, will be Baker, Dog, Able, and Charlie companies. We will then advance along the length of the island, killing the Japs as we go. Our jump-off date is August 7, and we expect to be on Tulagi by 0800. Questions?"

"Any ideas on the opposition?" Chambers asked.

"Jap forces are scattered between Tulagi, Gavutu, and Tanambogo," Griffith said. "We're told they are comprised of the detachments from the Kure 3rd Special Naval Landing Force, the enemy's version of Marines, and the 14th Construction Unit. The CO on Tulagi, we are told, is a Navy commander named Masaaki Suzuki. We do not know how many men he has on Tulagi, but it is at least three hundred to three hundred and fifty. Oh, we will also find sixteen float planes from the 25th Air Flotilla of the Yokosuka Air Unit moored just offshore."

"What kind of weapons do the Japs have?" another man asked.

"Machine guns, mortars," Griffith said. "No tanks and no big naval guns. Anyone else?"

Seeing no one, Edson spoke up.

"I've said this before, and I will say it again," he said. "Unlike the crap they're being fed back home, the Jap is not a comical-looking, buck-toothed guy wearing glasses with lenses the thickness of Coke bottle bottoms. He is not a lousy marksman armed with an inferior weapon and firing poor quality ammunition. The Japanese soldier is a worthy opponent to be respected. He is fearless, mainly because he does not expect to go home alive, so do not try to outguess him or act on something because you think you know what he would do. You don't. He does not think like you, and will do what you least expect. He is perfectly willing to die for his emperor. How many of you are willing to die for Eleanor?"

Everyone chuckled.

"Right," Edson said. "Remember that, and you might do OK. Just remember your training, work as a team, and listen to your officers."

Edson turned and left. I looked at Ken Bowers and he smiled. We both felt pretty confident now, but how would we be under fire?

We would soon find out.

CHAPTER THREE

THE BLOOD OATH

TULAGI

FRIDAY, AUGUST 7, 1942

Shortly after midnight, the cone-shaped silhouette of Savo Island slid silently past the starboard rail of our transport. Many of us saw it, for there was little sleep that night among the Raiders. Some men's thoughts were on the coming fight. "How will I do?" "Will I prove myself as a Raider and a man?" "Will I survive?"

But for most of us, our thoughts turned toward home, and we wondered when we'd see our families again, or if we'd see them again.

As Savo faded into the gloom off our fantail, the dark mass of Florida Island sat ominously off to port. In my imagination, I "saw" thousands of Japanese eyes peering at our convoy as they sharpened their bayonets and clicked banana clips into the feeder slots atop their Nambu machine guns.

The inky black water our ship was now slicing through was known as Sealark Channel, although in the days and weeks of naval clashes and air raids that were to come, it would take on the more funereal name of Iron Bottom Sound.

I felt a tap on my shoulder. It was my squad leader, Corporal Edwards.

"Better go below and try to grab a few more Zs, Whitey, we got a little time yet," he told me. "Wheeler wants us alert when we go ashore. Besides, it might be the last sleep you ever get."

"That's what I like about you, Spike," I said as I straightened up. "You've always got words of encouragement."

"That's me, Feather Merchant," he said and grinned, using the Corps slang for short fellows like me. "A regular Shirley Temple."

I went below, found my rack, and climbed in. As I recall, I fell asleep promptly.

Much of our journey after leaving Fiji had been over turbulent seas, causing these old tubs we were riding in to disappear in the troughs between waves, only to pop back up like corks on a fishing line. The result was that a good many Raiders went topside to make the voyage "by rail," so to speak, heaving their guts into the sea. I was fortunate. I didn't feel so much as a twinge of seasickness.

Most of the past six days since we left had been spent killing time. Poker, seven-card stud or eights-or-better, was popular, and for the high-roller, there was always a craps game going on somewhere. For those feeling athletic, or who just wished to hold on to their money, there were wrestling matches or just good, old-fashioned calisthenics, although the latter were usually done by platoons by order of Edson, who did not want us growing soft.

We also spent a lot of time just talking. Over the curling wisps of smoke from a Lucky Strike (my prewar green packs with the red circles had been replaced by white as "Lucky Strike goes to war,") we beat our gums about our homes, families, girlfriends, wives, jobs—anything except the battle waiting for us just beyond the horizon.

I enjoyed being on deck and out of the stuffy holds below. I spent a lot of time shooting the shit with my buddies and watching the fleet spread out around us. I thought about the other troop transports, and wondered about the guys on board, some of whom would not be sailing home ever again. Were they watching my transport and thinking the same thing about me?

The ship closest to us, some distance off our fantail, was the USS *George F. Elliott*, sister ship to the *Heywood* that had brought me to New Caledonia from the West Coast. Named for the tenth commandant of the Marines, she was also built by Bethlehem Steel, and carried men of the 1st Marines, including future author Robert Leckie, who, years after the war, would write the classic *Helmet for My Pillow*.

When not on deck, we were readying our gear for war, going over our maps, cleaning and oiling our weapons, sharpening our stilettos and KA-BARs, and stuffing as much ammo into our belts and pockets as we could lay our hands on. We were also issued our rations, about three days' worth; just enough to sustain us until the field kitchens could be landed and set up.

"Don't worry about the food," Edson growled to his company commanders. "Japs eat, too. We just have to go and get it."

Our main food was the C-ration, which came in a gold-colored can. The M-unit contained a canned entrée that was a mix of beef and pork seasoned with salt, various spices, and chopped onions. Initially it came in three varieties—a meat hash, a meat stew with vegetables (carrots and potatoes), and a meat stew with beans. Collectively, we lumped these all under the heading "the great unknown."

There was also a B-unit that generally contained five hardtack crackers, three sugar tablets, three dextrose tablets to give us energy (so the theory ran), and a packet of beverage mix, which could be instant coffee, powdered lemon drink, or bouillon soup powder. In later variations, orange drink powder was added.

A number of us had also taken to cutting strips of burlap and attaching them to our steel helmets to both disguise the helmet's shape and to reduce the chance of being betrayed by glare from a stray beam of light. The Japs would take note of this and call us the Tiger Cubs. (Three years later, after the Raiders were disbanded, and I was on Okinawa with the 22nd Marines, a Jap officer would regale his men with tales about some of us Marines who, on Guadalcanal, wore burlap bags on our helmets.)

———————

Shortly before the fleet reached the entrance to Sealark Channel, the naval task force silently split in two. The main body, now called Task Force X-Ray, peeled off to the right, passing Savo to the south, bound for Guadalcanal, specifically, a prominence of land where the Lunga River flowed into the channel. The area was called Lunga Point. Our group of ships, eight in all, dubbed Task Force Yoke, continued on, then also veered to starboard, passing Savo's northern shore, on our way to Tulagi, Gavutu, and Tanambogo.

The invasion of Tulagi was codenamed Operation Huddle, while the assault on Guadalcanal was Operation Watchtower. Interestingly, Guadalcanal had never been a part of Operation Watchtower at all until the command center at Pearl Harbor got a message from Captain Martin Clemens, a Brit who had been the colonial officer in the Solomons. Now a coast watcher, he reported that the Japanese were building an airstrip on the island. Clemens had observed twelve enemy ships drop anchor off Lunga Point and unload four heavy tractors, six road rollers, two electrical generators, an ice plant, two small locomotives, and twelve hopper cars, plus construction workers, largely Koreans, and four hundred combat troops. The airstrip was especially disturbing to our Pacific HQ. If put into operation, it would mean Japanese bombers could strike Allied bases at Efate in the New Hebrides, Espiritu Santo, and even Koumae Airfield on New Caledonia, and disrupt supply routes to Australia and New Zealand.

That report was what had brought us all here.

I awoke before reveille on August 7, dressed, and hurried topside for a look at Tulagi in the early dawn light. Initially, what greeted my eyes was a tranquil tropical scene, with a mountainous island, its sloping terrain coated by lush, jungle greenery. This seemingly lovely scene was marred, however, by the silent warships bobbing on the surface of the blue water, their crews at battle station as their gun turrets turned menacingly toward the island. Above, the rising sun illuminated a deep blue sky dotted with large clumps of billowy clouds. I wondered if the Japs had seen us yet.

Then the loudspeaker blared, "All Marines go below."

It was 0630. The bombardment was about to begin. I moved slowly, wanting to see some of the naval preparation for our assault. Yet even though I was prepared for it, I damned near jumped out of my skin as the twelve five-inch guns on six main turrets of the cruiser *San Juan* cut loose, the first of 280 shells the ship would lob ashore. The two destroyers in our task force, *Monssen* and *Buchanan*, joined in, sending their own five-inch shells streaking toward the small island.

Suddenly, the world around me had transformed into a deadly Fourth of July celebration. Added to this was the arrival of Dauntless dive-bombers and stubby Wildcat fighters from the carrier USS *Wasp*, which bombed and strafed suspected Japanese positions. Huge blasts from bombs and naval shells seemed to shake the island, sending palm trees, whole or in shards, tumbling into the air, as billows of smoke covered the land. As I watched, I thought the whole place might sink into the ocean, and there would be no need to land. And if by a miracle it should stay afloat, I was certain there would be little life remaining. How could there be after what seemed, at least to me, such terrible punishment, even though, by later war standards, this pre-invasion shellacking would seem puny.

I left the rail and made my way below.

As the racket outside continued, we were directed to the galley for what would become known as the "battle breakfast," a hearty helping of steak and eggs. This was generally accompanied by the inevitable comments about being fattened up for the kill.

Outside the bombardment roared with such intensity that we felt the concussion vibrating through the *Little*'s steel hull. Nothing in our training had prepared us for this kind of show of power, and my thoughts turned to Tulagi's inhabitants.

"I feel sorry for them," I muttered over my eggs.

"Who?" Alex Stewart inquired. "The Japs?"

"No, asshole," I replied. "The people who live on the island. They didn't ask for the Japs to take the place over, and they sure as hell didn't ask for us to come in and shell the shit out their homeland."

"One of the misfortunes of war," Big Stoop injected. "That's a common theme of conquered people since war began. Civilians get into the crosshairs. It's a fact of life."

"Yeah," I answered. "But it's a lousy fact if you're one of those in the crosshairs."

Ken Bowers looked at me from across the mess table.

"What do you think it'll be like when we go in, Whitey?" he asked me. "Do you think we'll meet stiff resistance?"

"Can't imagine we would," I said, trying to sound reassuring. "Listen to that racket. I doubt a cricket could survive that."

"Hope you're right," Bowers said. He looked troubled.

After breakfast we returned to our assigned holds to make final preparations, which meant collecting our gear that we were taking with us and stowing everything else in our seabags for delivery to us after the island was secured. Then came the call, "Marines, to your debarkation stations." We climbed into our backpacks, shouldered our weapons, and followed Wheeler topside. The Higgins boats had already been lowered into the water and were waiting for us at the bottom of large cargo nets that had been draped over the ship's sides. All around us the Navy gunners and flyboys kept plastering Tulagi. The same thing was happening twenty miles away across Sealark Channel at Guadalcanal, but we could not hear it over the din from our own task force.

Whistles blew and the order "Man the landing boats" rang out, and we began loading. As the APD sailors patted us on the back and added "good luck," we swung our right legs over the gunwale. It was important that each man use the same leg; otherwise we'd end up kicking each other in the ass. Then, swinging the left leg over, we began to crawl down the dangling nets, keeping our hands on the vertical ropes so as not to get our fingers stomped on by the man above. I climbed down as swiftly as I could while being careful not to lose my grip and either crash into the Higgins boat or plop into the sea. Finally reaching the boat, I waited for it to rise on a swell, then dropped in and quickly moved forward, away from the net and those men coming down behind me. The Higgins boat bobbed unsteadily beneath my feet.

After our boat loaded with its complement of thirty-six men, it motored away from the transport toward a preassigned rendezvous point where we circled in the water while the other boats finished taking on Marines. As we circled, we watched the pyrotechnics show on Tulagi, as shells exploded, hurling debris into the sky. Bowers stood beside me. He still looked troubled. Perhaps another discussion we had while we were still on shipboard that morning, watching the Navy plaster Tulagi, was still on his mind. Standing by the ship rail earlier, Bowers had turned to me.

"Whitey," he said. "Can we swear an oath to watch each other's backs?"

"Sure," I replied.

"I mean a blood oath," he continued. "You know. Blood brothers."

Without hesitation, I removed my KA-BAR, which I had honed to razor sharpness, from its sheath and drew it lightly across my right wrist. Bowers quickly did the same, and as the trickles of blood oozed up from our respective cuts, we joined wrists, allowing our life's blood to mingle as we promised to look out for each other. Bowers nodded his thanks.

As I recalled that earlier promise, the signal "Land the landing force" was flashed, and our boat churned toward the smoke-covered shore. We were supposed to jump off at 0800. It was 0740. We were twenty minutes ahead of schedule, a good omen, perhaps.

"Lock and load," Chambers, our company CO, ordered, and we loaded our weapons as we prepared for war. "When we get in, don't bunch up. Move up from the beach quickly to make way for the men coming in behind us."

Feeling the Higgins boat's engine vibrating through the landing craft, I watched the coast draw closer as spray from the jouncing bow blew back in our faces. Baker and Dog companies, led by Edson's XO, Lieutenant Colonel Griffith, would be the first ashore. In fact, we were to be the first Americans in World War II, regardless of theater of operation, to land on an enemy-held island, as America finally went on the offensive. I recall that I was surprisingly calm. I knew we had a great outfit, and I had a lot of confidence that we'd accomplish our mission, and that I'd be OK.

The boats bearing B and D companies approached Blue Beach in a line abreast, and we were ordered to fix bayonets. So far, no Japanese fire had greeted our approach, and the only gunfire came from the Lewis machine guns on our own boats, as our gunners swept the landing zone. One hundred yards offshore, the bottoms of the boats scraped on the coral reef with a jolt that sent us crashing into each other.

"Over the side," Jumpin' Joe yelled.

We swung over the boat's gunwales, plunging into what was armpit-deep water for most of the Raiders. But for us feather merchants, it was all we could do to keep our noses above the waves.

"Damn," I thought. "I didn't come nine thousand miles just to drown."

I bobbed up and down like a cork, sinking beneath the surface and then pushing myself back up when my feet touched bottom. In that fashion, I "ran" toward the shore.

Blue Beach had been selected by HQ because it was hoped the area would be lightly defended. In fact, it was undefended, which was fortunate for us, because even with no opposition, just getting to shore was a challenge. The coral underfoot was slimy and slippery, and men fell, cutting hands and knees and ripping uniforms on the jagged spires. We finally emerged, dripping wet and bloody from our cuts and scrapes, on the shore of Tulagi.

"Blue Beach my ass," I sputtered to Bowers as I stepped onto the shore. "There is no damned beach."

"Don't worry, Whitey," quipped Big Stoop, who was so large it looked as if he hadn't gotten wet above the waist. "You'll dry out."

The first thing that greeted our eyes upon landing was an old Church of England cemetery, made even more sad-looking by the recent addition of shell holes and downed trees. I heard someone yell something about it being "a helluva way to start a war, in a graveyard." I couldn't have agreed more.

"Fan out," Chambers called. "Form a defensive perimeter."

We did as ordered, moving inland about forty yards and spreading out, holding the landing beach until the rest of the battalion arrived.

By 0815 Edson's Raiders were standing on Tulagi, and Red Mike ordered us to move up the steeply sloping ridge that bisected the island. Since Charlie Company would be following the southern coast, they swung right and got into their jump-off positions first. The rest of us kept climbing. It was tough going. This part of Tulagi was covered by heavy brush and tangled jungle, and we had to hack pathways through the vegetation. About halfway up the slope, Able Company wheeled right and took up their position. The rest of us kept climbing, now with a much better understanding of Edson's insistence on hiking and physical endurance.

Cresting the ridge, Chambers ordered us to halt and deploy as Captain Nickerson led Baker Company past us. Their position would be the northern coastline of the island, moving along the coastal road toward a village dubbed Chinatown.

Once the entire battalion was in position, we struck out southeast toward where we knew the Japanese were waiting. Moving along the top of the ridge was not any easier than the climb up to reach it, and it took us three hours to advance a mile and a half. As we drew nearer the "civilized" portion of the island where the government station, golf course, and village were located, we saw increasing signs of the Japanese presence. In Chinatown, B Company found ample evidence that the enemy had fled in panic, including overturned furniture in huts and abandoned weapons and equipment.

Baker Company ran into some of Tulagi's civilians near what was called Carpenter's Wharf, and hustled them to the rear and out of the line of fire. Continuing to cautiously probe forward toward a stone jetty, they came under deadly Japanese fire from caves in the side of a cliff. Three men, all from 1st platoon, were killed in the initial fusillade, including Lieutenant Eugene Key and Navy corpsman Lieutenant (j.g.) Samuel Miles, a promising young doctor, who died trying to help Key and the other fallen Marine. One Raider, Private Thomas Church, took a Jap round in the front of his helmet that careened upward, then exited without touching his head. Sometimes those crazy things happened. B

Company's situation got pretty hot, and they were pinned down until Pfc. Vince Cassidy courageously managed to climb up on the cliff and lob grenades on the Japs. Throwing all he had, Cassidy was forced to climb up and down the slope repeatedly to replenish his grenade supply, but he finally silenced the sniper fire.

Around 4 p.m., as Dog Company approached the saddle or ravine that bisected the island, we also began encountering snipers, crazy men who tied themselves to their positions in the tops of trees, then fired at us after we passed them by. A rifle would crack and sometimes a man would moan as he was hit. Our Reising guns, BARs, and Springfields bucked heavily against our shoulders as we sprayed the treetops, watching the large palm fronds jump as they were struck by our rounds. But the bullets hit flesh, too, and the sniper would fall, sometimes lifelessly hanging by the vine he'd used to tie himself to the tree, gently swinging like a macabre Christmas tree ornament.

Coming across a house at the base of a steep hill, we searched it carefully. Unexpectedly, a Jap Type 99 Nambu machine gun opened up from a hillside directly in front of our squad, and we dove for the ground. Hugging the earth as close as I could, I heard the 7.7mm rounds zip over my head so close I felt I could stick my hand up and catch them. A couple of men fell around me, struck by the Jap's rounds. One man seemed to have been hit in the groin and was in obvious agony. I crawled over to him. It was Mike Blotter, a man in my squad.

"Corpsman," I yelled. Then to the man I said, "Hang on, Blotter. The corpsman is coming."

I cautiously made my way forward as bullets chipped away at the trees around me.

"Get that damned gun," Lieutenant Wheeler called out.

That would be no easy feat. The Jap gun was up a hill, the slope of which was so steep the Japs had actually carved steps into its side.

"On me," Spike Edwards said, and our squad cautiously followed, keeping our heads low.

Ken Bowers was lying right behind me.

"Let's go," I shouted to him.

As I moved, I noticed that Mike Rihaly had not budged. Crouching low, I hurried over to him, Nambu slugs kicking up the dust behind me. He lay curled up on the ground, cradling the BAR, frozen by fear. I nudged him with my foot.

"Rihaly," I said.

"We're gonna get killed," he wailed. "We're all gonna get killed."

"Rihaly," I hissed harshly. "Pull yourself together. We're moving. We gotta take out that Nip gun."

"We're gonna get killed," Mike cried again.

"Whitey," Edwards yelled. "Grab that weapon."

Rihaly refused to move, so, as assistant BAR man, I slung my Springfield over my shoulder and picked up the sixteen-pound weapon, stripped Rihaly of his ammo belt, and followed the squad.

Working our way cautiously up the hill, we spotted the Jap gun, secured in a dugout and protected by felled logs. But the position was hastily prepared, and it had no roof, so I could catch an occasional glimpse of the gunner. We opened fire, intent on keeping the Jap's head down. I cut loose with a sustained burst from the BAR. I loved this weapon. It laid down a tremendous amount of fire in a short period of time, five hundred to six hundred rounds per minute. The main drawback was that it ate up my twenty-round box of clips at a fearful pace. After emptying one magazine, I rammed another home and continued firing. The BAR's bolt remained open after the last round, so when you reloaded, you were "hot." There was no bolt to cock first. No round that needed to be fed into the chamber. The weapon was ready to go instantly, and that could mean the difference between life and death.

As I slipped a new clip into the Browning's receiver, I glanced at Bowers, who was bringing up the rear of our seven-man squad, just behind Irv Reynolds, a new man who had joined us in New Caledonia. I winked. Bowers smiled, as we all kept moving forward together.

"Let's go!" Edward yelled again, and we rose up and charged ahead, up the slope.

"Bowers, let's run for it," I heard Reynolds call out from behind me.

Wilfred Hunt, our assistant squad leader, and I were in the lead when the machine gun chattered again and we were once more forced to hug the ground. However, I noticed that every time the Jap gunner had to reload one of his thirty-round banana clips, which attached to the top of the Type 99 Nambu, his right arm was visible. Taking aim, I waited for him to empty his magazine and reload.

He did. Up went the hand with a fresh clip, giving me a clear shot. I squeezed the trigger and emptied the magazine. My rounds exploded into the logs and earth all around the Jap position. The Jap yelped as his hand above the wrist seemed to vanish, and he dropped from sight. Hunt leaped up, stiletto drawn, and charged into the gun position, where he knifed the wounded man. Later, I learned that I had been nominated for a Navy Cross for this action, but it was Hunt who would receive it. As a decorated war hero, he would be returned to the States to take part in war bond drives, riding around the country on trains for a couple of months. (The Marines may not have thought I deserved a medal, but Lieutenant Wheeler appreciated me. Years later, Wheeler, then a lieutenant general, told me I was the best BAR man he ever had. That was good enough for me.)

The Jap gun knocked out, the way was now clear for us to continue. I turned to face the rear, looking for Bowers. I spotted him lying on the ground in an unnatural tangle of arms and legs. I raced to his side, and kneeling down next to his body, I saw blood on his face and yelled "Corpsman!"

But Kenneth Bowers would not need a corpsman. The Jap bullet had punched through the front of his helmet and caught him right in the forehead. His lifeless eyes looked up at me, but his face was strangely peaceful.

"Dear God," I moaned, thinking of our blood oath to watch out for each other. "I'm sorry, Kenny."

Irv Reynolds, who had grabbed Ken's rifle after he was hit and followed the attack up the hill, now approached.

"I saw him get it," Reynolds told me. "He gave one violent jerk and fell. He didn't make a sound. I doubt he had time to know what hit him. Too bad. I liked him."

I just nodded as I knelt there on the ground. A corpsman arrived, checked the body, then took one of Ken's identity tags and moved on. Death was that commonplace.

But there was no time to mourn the loss of my best friend. That time would come later. Now we had to move on. I patted my dead friend on the shoulder one last time and rose to my feet. Bowers would be buried here on Tulagi by the old cricket field until 1948, when he was returned to his hometown of Nazareth and interred with full military honors. His town would honor his memory by naming its VFW post after him.

As we worked our way closer to the saddle, the battalion was called to a halt. This was what was called Phase Line A. It was our first objective. It was around 11 a.m. Our company CO, Jumpin' Joe Chambers, was summoned to an officers' conference with Edson while we waited.

From our vantage point, we could see Jap planes over Guadalcanal, as they bombed and strafed the 1st Marines' positions and the ships anchored off Lunga Point.

As we sat watching that far-off spectacle, a Jap patrol suddenly appeared and opened fire on us. Bullets whistled and hummed through the air all around our heads, striking trees and nipping off vines, as D Company hit the dirt and began shooting back. The racket was tremendous and our return fire much too heavy for the enemy, who rose up and began falling back. We never eased off our triggers, and one by one, the Japanese dropped until none remained alive. Chambers, upon hearing the clatter, left the meeting and hurried over to see what the fuss was all about. Seeing that everything was under control, he returned to the conference, where he was reamed out by Edson for leaving the meeting without permission. We thought this treatment was overly harsh.

Now it was the Navy's turn to strike the enemy, as their five-inch shells, and ones of lesser caliber, came screaming in and exploded ahead of us. Their mission was to soften up the enemy for our next advance.

"Get 'em, Navy," we silently urged as we watched the explosions blossoming up from in front of us. "Get the bastards."

They might have gotten some, but not enough, because we were still drawing sniper fire. Over on our left, in B Company, Pfc. John Holladay was taking shelter behind a fallen tree with First Sergeant Brice Maddox. Holladay, who hailed from Florence, South Carolina, loved to strum his guitar and often regaled us with songs, his favorite being "John Henry." Hell, he knew all twenty-seven verses. Like the rest of us, Baker Company men were taking hits. Johnny Holladay was about the best marksman I ever knew, and he had lovingly named his trusty Springfield "Old Lucifer."

As the sniper fire pinned men down, Holladay took careful aim on a nearby tree and squeezed off a round. Nothing seemed to happen.

"You missed," Maddox informed him. "Better try again."

Holladay lowered Old Lucifer and glanced at Maddox.

"Top," he replied. "Old Lucifer don't lie. He'll fall in a minute." Sure enough, moments later, the sniper's body plunged from amid the palm fronds and crashed to the ground. Holladay grinned to his friend.[1]

A signal came for us to attack, and the battalion surged ahead. We had gone just a few a yards when the Japanese raked us with everything they had. Men fell as we scrambled for cover, trying to pull the earth over our heads.

On our right, Able Company charged across the golf course, dribbling casualties as they ran. Their goal was a short ridge out in front of them, but the Japanese, barricaded as they were in houses and secure in bunkers at the foot of the ridge, laid down a murderous fire. The company was forced to fall back, linking up with us near the Residency, the former home of the island's governor, which we had taken without a shot a short time earlier.

On the far right, Charlie Company swarmed toward the small, knobby prominence dubbed Hill 208, but they came under well-aimed machine gun fire from a Japanese bunker. C Company's commander, Major Ken Bailey, led his men in an attack on the bunker. Bailey somehow managed to crawl on top of the gun position, where he attempted to kick open the gun ports so his Raiders could stuff explosives inside. Just then six bayonet-wielding Japs burst out of the bunker, intent on killing Bailey. Bailey raised his Reising gun, John Wayne style, and mowed them all down with one long burst of fire. A Jap inside the bunker stuck a rifle out of a port and fired, his bullet plunking Bailey in the thigh. It was a serious enough wound that Bailey had to be dragged to the rear for medical treatment. Bailey was down, but he refused to stay down, and soon he and Platoon Sergeant Robert Jernigan were off again. Bailey, limping badly and in pain, wanted to scope out the Jap positions. That was when a sniper fired at him, but struck Jernigan.

With a corpsman tending the wounded Jernigan, Bailey and Lieutenant "Spike" Ryder, leader of C Company's weapons platoon, returned to the fray and were charging a Jap bunker when an unexpected explosion sent them both sprawling. Wounded, they, along with Jernigan, were finally evacuated to the battalion aid station, and Colonel Griffith took over temporary command of Charlie Company.

We of Dog Company had earlier seized the large bungalow called the Residency, which we were told had been the home of the island's governor. We lucked out and took it without a fight, and this structure would become Edson's HQ while we were on the island. Chambers came forward a short time later and ordered up our mortar section. He was directing their fire at a Jap strongpoint off to the right when an explosion rocked us all, and sent Chambers sprawling. We were certain the source was one of our own weapons; either a badly made 6omm shell had detonated prematurely, or a fired round had struck one of the tree branches overhead. Whatever the cause, several men had been injured, including Chambers, who had a broken right wrist and injuries to his left wrist and right leg. Chambers, who would win the Congressional Medal of Honor on Iwo Jima three years later, was for now out of action.

To Dog Company's immediate right, Captain Lew Walt was charging ahead of A Company across the pitch and putt golf course when someone yelled for him to watch out for a sniper just ahead. Walt saw a Jap soldier lying prone and sighting along his Arisaka rifle not forty yards ahead of him. Silent Lew dropped to the ground, he recalled, as the man fired. The bullet passed just inches above him. Frozen, he watched the man reload and raise his rifle again. Just as the Jap prepared to fire a second time, he was struck by blasts from two Raiders, one wielding a Reising and the other a BAR. Even as he died, though, he squeezed the trigger, his round just missing Walt.

Shortly after that incident, Walt led A Company forward toward the series of ridges that comprised Hill 281 and came under fire from Japanese barricaded in houses and bunkers at the base of the hill. Able's assault bogged down.

In fact, all of our forward movement stopped. We had approached what can best be described as a shovel-shaped ravine. The flat ground had been used by the Brits as a cricket field, but it was the three high sides that gave us the headaches. They were honeycombed with caves dug into the limestone, some fortified with sandbags and almost all linked inside by tunnels. The Japs were defending each one of these caves, and they poured down a murderous fire upon us. We flopped to the ground and took what cover we could.

As the sun began to set, Edson knew, as did we all, that there was not enough time for us to organize and launch a new assault. Too tired to dig foxholes, we simply braced ourselves for the inevitable counterattacks we knew would come with the darkness. I had to piss, and so, like every Raider around me did that day, I emptied my bladder into my pants. I wasn't about to stand up. Settling in, we took a little solace in the fact that the 2/5, having mopped up the other end of the island, had dug in to our rear. We had fought and bled a lot today. Behind us, in plain sight, were dead comrades, one of whom, and I knew exactly which one, was Ken Bowers.

It was a tense night. Out in front of us, Japs taunted us by rattling bamboo stalks and shouting "We drink American blood" and "You die tonight." Then there were the moans and cries of the wounded emanating from the darkness. Off in the distance, the faint sound of battle drifted across the dark water, proof that the Paramarines were also getting no sleep over on Gavutu and Tanambogo.

Wary of infiltrators, we made sure our passwords included anything containing numerous "L's" like "lollipop" and "Laura Lee," since we were told by our language officer, "Tiger" Erskine, that the Jap had difficulty prouncing American words with too many "L's." Edson had an incident where he and Lieutenant Sweeney of E Company were inspecting the lines when they were challenged by an alert Raider.

"It's Red Mike," Edson simply replied.

The man refused to believe him, and told him to talk some more.

"Lucky Strike, Lilly Thistle, Lola's Thighs," Edson said. "Is that enough, son?" [2]

The Japanese counterattacks—there would be four of them—began around 2200, or 10 p.m., with a large, frontal Banzai charge aimed largely at Able and Charlie companies to our right. The volume of fire coming from A and C companies' positions was deafening. The night was lit up by muzzle flashes and burning tracers arcing back and forth. Somehow, the enemy found a small gap between A and C company lines and burst through, coming to within seventy-five yards of Edson's command post. Fighting there was hand-to-hand, knives and bayonets at close quarters. Some of Red Mike's intellignce staff members were killed before the Japs were annihilated. The assault was finally driven back by the liberal expenditure of machine gun rounds and grenades.

Firing now broke out to our left as another attack materialized out of the darkness.

Then they came at us, dark figures, rushing forward, bayonet-tipped rifles at the ready, shouting insults or simply "Banzai." Tracers crisscrossed through the blackness. I blazed away with my BAR, spraying my front left to right with short bursts, not knowing if I was hitting anything or not. In war, it's often hard to tell. Then, just as suddenly as they appeared, the live Japs were gone and only the dead remained, dotting the ground ahead of us. These attacks made me wonder just how good the Japanese were at night fighting. In almost every case, we had heard them coming. They talked, shouted insults, and just made one helluva lot of noise.

The next morning, dead Japanese were scattered everywhere, but so were dead Raiders. I glanced around at our guys and was happy to find that Stewart, Ruble, and the rest had survived the hellish night.

Some did not. The story went around about a young private first class in Charlie Company named Ed Ahrens, who saw several Japanese approach his position in the night, including an officer gripping a sword. Ahrens cut lose with his BAR, chopping the enemy down as they rushed him. He was shot once and bayoneted several times as Japs overran his foxhole. Lew Walt, inspecting his line the next morning, found Ahrens, badly wounded but alive. Beside the wounded Marine lay the dead officer and a sergeant, with eleven more dead Japanese sprawled on the ground in front of his position. Ahrens was clutching the dead officer's Samurai sword. Walt called for a corpsman, picked up Ahrens, and carried him toward the rear. As he laid him down and the corpsman administered morphine, Ahrens held up the sword and gave it to Walt as a souvenir.

"Those yellow bastards tried to come over me last night," he said before passing out. "I guess they didn't know I was a Marine."[3]

Edson put Ahrens in for the Medal of Honor, but it was downgraded to the Navy Cross. And Ahrens would be killed in action before receiving it.

That's the stuff we Raiders were made of.

The second day's fight was a long, slow, grinding process of rooting the Japanese out of the caves and bunkers at the base of the ridge of Hill 281. Since we had no flamethrowers, bazookas, or Bangalore torpedoes, our only recourse was grenades and TNT-loaded satchel charges. Consisting of eight blocks of high explosives and two priming assemblies, tucked inside a canvas shoulder bag, just one satchel charge lobbed inside a cave entrance was enough to send the enemy off to see his ancestors. Having picked our way slowly around and above a cave, we would lower one man, generally the lightest guy, via a rope, down the slope toward the cave's mouth. Then he would yank the two pull cords that armed the charge and swing it into the cave, tossing it as far back as possible. He then hugged the face of the cliff tightly as the charge detonated, the cave mouth belching smoke and debris.

One of our favorite guys for lowering was scrawny, 108-pound "Tiger" Erskine. Initially, we'd drop him over the side so he could try to talk the Japanese out of the caves, but they preferred dying where they were to surrender. And that's what they did.

At one cave, a dozen or so of the enemy charged out screaming and yelling in a suicide attack. We opened fire, our slugs hammering into them, dropping them in bloody pools on the ground. Those we did not kill killed themselves right in front of us. There is a grotesque horror in watching a man activate a grenade and then clutch it to his chest, blowing himself apart before your astonished eyes. Others chose to kill themselves more privately, ending their lives inside their caves as we closed in. At one cave, the three men inside fired at us until they were down to their last three rounds. Then one man shot his two comrades and finished himself off.

I will never understand that type of fanaticism.

A few opted to fight on with determination. A Raider would take a grenade, yank the pin, and toss it into the cave, only to see it come flying back out at him. In response, when we tossed the next grenade, we yanked the pin, let the spoon fly off, counted to three, then tossed. Even then, some Jap would catch the damned thing and try to hurl it back.

Blustery Angus Goss found out the dangers of satchel charges. The crusty thirty-two-year-old sergeant, who led our demolition platoon, rigged up a short-fused charge and lobbed it into a Jap-held cave dug into the hillside by the cricket field. His eyes opened wide with surprise as the sizzling charge came flying back at him. The force of the explosion sent him crashing into a wooden shack that stood nearby, where he lay, cut up and bleeding, his pants blown clean off.

Regaining his feet, Goss raged. "God damnit!" he yelled, and staggered back toward the cave, his blazing Reising gun sweeping the entrance. Reaching the cave mouth, he sprayed the interior. When we looked inside the cave later, we found twelve dead Japanese. Why the Japs inside didn't blast him as he staggered toward them, I'll never know. It was suggested that they couldn't believe their eyes as they watched him run toward them. Goss was nominated for the Medal of Honor by Edson, but as so often happened, it was downgraded to the Navy Cross.

Gradually, the gunfire and explosions died away, and by 3 p.m., Edson had declared Tulagi secured. That did not mean all of the Japs on the island were dead. Stragglers would be flushed from caves for the next several days, but much of that was done by the 2/5, which now passed through our lines and continued up Hill 281.

Exhausted, we went into bivouac by the cricket field. I thought about Kenny Bowers and hoped his body had been retrieved and properly taken care of. I thought about his family back home in Nazareth. I wondered how long it would be before they were notified. I was suddenly very sad, not to mention a bit guilty. Why did I survive and he did not? We both ran the same risks. It was just that the fatal bullet found him and not me. War was all one big crapshoot. You tossed your dice, and some guys rolled a natural and others craps. That's just the way it was.

I turned my attention to Sealark Channel, where another Jap air raid was plastering the 'Canal. A huge billowy cloud of black smoke rose from one ship as a bomb or torpedo struck her. I would later learn this was the transport *George F. Elliott*, the same ship I had recently contemplated, sailing so gracefully off our stern as we were en route to the Solomons. She would burn for much of the day before being scuttled and sent below, the first ship to dot the bottom of Iron Bottom Sound.

Then, with the shooting ended, came the hunt for souvenirs: knives, medals, uniform patches, Jap flags, and whatever else we could scrounge. Our three days of rations we'd brought ashore were dwindling, so we smoked Japanese cigarettes, drank Jap beer, and hoarded canned seaweed, crabmeat, or sliced beef in soy sauce. These latter would come in handy.

Meanwhile, fighting on Tanambogo and Gavutu raged on. We could hear the gunfire and explosions on the tiny islands just three thousand yards from Tulagi's eastern point.

With the darkness came the rain, a steady, soaking rain, as if God was trying to wash away the blood that stained Tulagi.

Around midnight, Sergeant Gene Martin came by, making a buddy check, to be sure all was quiet.

"Everything OK here, Whitey?" Martin inquired.

"Sure thing, Sarge," I replied. "The rain's stopped, so I'm snug as a bug. A very wet bug."

He chuckled and moved on.

The company was dug in on both sides of a path that bordered the cricket field. The path, in fact, cut clear across the island, severing Tulagi in two as it passed through the ravine. The caves in the walls of the ravine that we had been clearing of defenders all day long now yawned empty, including one in particular that had been especially troublesome. We finally sealed it with a huge charge of TNT. At least, we thought it had been sealed.

Martin dozed, for how long even he did not recall. Then he awoke to the strong smell of rice powder. Gazing out of his hastily scratched foxhole, still bleary-eyed, he spotted a Jap soldier standing so close he could have reached out and touched the man. Four more stood nearby, all with their backs to Martin. He noticed that one appeared to be an officer, as he was grasping a sword in his hand. A second man held a machine gun. Gripping his Reising gun more tightly, Martin recalled that the safety was on. Switching it off, he knew, would alert the Japs since the Reising made a distinctive click. Slowly covering the switch with one hand to muffle it, he quietly raised the submachine gun. He carefully switched off the safety. No one heard it. Then he yelled, "They're Japs! Give 'em hell," and opened fire.

That got our instant attention, and all of D Company began shooting. I'm sure some of us didn't even know where to fire and who to fire at, but we squeezed our triggers nonetheless. I emptied two clips of the

BAR at the dark forms as bullets, interspersed with blazing tracer rounds flashed across our company area. One Jap, possibly looking to escape the fusillade, stepped on Lieutenant Wheeler in the dark. Wheeler turned and shot the man.

Then it was over as suddenly as it began. Next morning, we found the enemy corpses lying all around us. They had escaped from the fortified cave and, in looking for a place to set up their machine gun, had walked clean through our company area and then wandered back. Anyone who saw them initially probably just thought they were fellow Raiders.

Sergeant Martin kept the Jap sword.

Few men got back to sleep after that. I found that I had little trouble sleeping, even under the most adverse conditions, so I must have been dozing when a distant rumble reached my ears, jolting me awake.

"What the . . . ?" I mumbled, sitting up, wrapped in the cocoon of my rain-soaked poncho.

"Out there," Alex Stewart, my foxhole buddy, whispered, pointing toward the blackness of the channel. "Someone's catching hell."

He was right. Far off across the dark water, the skies lit up in the reddish-orange glow of muzzle flashes. Seconds later, the deep boom of large-caliber naval guns came rolling out of the darkness. Sometimes a huge ball of light would appear as some ship took a direct hit.

"Damn," I muttered to myself, wondering what the hell was going on out on that expanse of black water.

"What time is it?" I asked Stewart.

"Hell if I know," he said. "0200 maybe."

We continued watching the flashes and hearing the faint roar of guns and explosions. It was like having nickel seats to a Joe Louis fight.

"I wonder who's winning," I mused.

"We are," Alex said.

"We damned well better be," I told him. "Or the Japs will come back to the island in force, and we might be eating sukiyaki for lunch."

Not too far from my foxhole, my future squad leader and good buddy Bill Waltrip was also watching the battle.

"It was really something," he later recalled. "Those ships would blow up, and the big flashes of light from the naval guns. It was really something to watch. Of course, we had no idea what was going on out there."

What we were watching was the second half of the Battle of Savo Island. Navy warships, expecting a Japanese response to our landings, were guarding the western appoaches to Sealark Channel. The fleet had been divided in half, with one flotilla cruising the southern entrance and the other half the northern entrance, with Savo Island in between. To give the fleet, which consisted of five heavy cruisers, advance warning, two of our destroyers patrolled the approaches to the west of Savo. Incredibly, the Jap fleet sailed, unseen, between the two picket destroyers and entered the channel, heading for the southern group. Around 1:30 a.m. they opened fire on our ships, making short work of them. Within twenty minutes, the cruiser USS *Chicago* was limping away, heavily damaged, and another, the HMS *Canberra*, was a smoldering, sinking wreck. The Japs then turned and headed for the northern group.

During the fight, lookouts with the northern fleet had seen the flashes and the searchlights sweeping the water, but, hard to believe, they raised no alarm. Just as hard to believe was the fact that no one thought to warn the northern ship commanders, all of whom were asleep. They got a rude awakening around 1:47 a.m. when Jap searchlights lit them up like Main Street in Los Angeles. Within half an hour, three U.S. cruisers, the *Quincy*, the *Vincennes*, and the *Astoria*, would be sunk or sinking.

The Battle of Savo Island or, as we Marines called it, the Battle of the Five Sitting Ducks, was the U.S. Navy's worst defeat in its history. Four cruisers sunk and one crippled, while the Jap ships barely got their paint jobs scratched. Just over one thousand American sailors died, compared to fifty-eight Japanese.

But that wasn't the worst of it, as we Marines were to find out the next day.

Miraculously, the Japanese fleet, after polishing off our warships, turned and left, sparing the many freighters and cargo ships anchored nervously off Lunga Point. Most of these ships still had their cargo

holds more than half-full. But the defeat at Savo Island had spooked
the Navy. Fearful for its few remaining carriers, the Navy's commander,
Admiral Richmond Kelly Turner, wanted to bug the hell out by 6:30
a.m. The Marines' CO, General Alexander Vandegrift, practically had
to beg Turner to stick with it longer to get more supplies landed. Turner
did, but only until midday, when we Marines stood on shore watching
in total disbelief as the United States Navy turned tail and scooted off
into the sunset with a whole lot of our much needed material, especially
food, ammo, and medical supplies, still on board.

As Americans, we would've been embarrassed had we not been so
pissed off.

"They're leaving us bare-assed," Vandegrift is said to have complained. "Plain old bare-assed." [4]

Vandegrift had raged in front of everyone he could, but to no avail.
The Navy had left us to the tender mercies of the Japanese, who could,
and would, sit offshore in their ships and fly over at will in their bombers, and plaster the crap out of us. In the days to come, Marines stood
helplessly on shore watching ships unload enemy troops, and there was
not a damned thing we could do about it.

Edson was royally pissed as well. We had come ashore carrying just
three days' rations, with the promise that they'd last us until the field
kitchens could be brought on shore and set up and a proper mess begun.
We had captured Japanese rations, of course, including bags of rice that
tasted like shit, even if you could overlook the small bugs and worms
that had infested them. We'd boil the rice in our helmets to kill the
insects, but nothing could improve the flavor.

But, even bad as it was, none of that would last us very long. There
were fewer Japanese defending the island than there were Marines
who'd landed to take it, so even with us eating two meager meals a day,
it was soon gone. All we had left was the coconuts; we cracked open the
tough shells with our KABARs and scooped out the meat before it
hardened, then drank the milk. Tender is the only way I can describe
the taste of coconut milk.

We scoured the length and breadth of the island, pathetically pick-ing up shells to see if they were intact. Most were empty, their contents already devoured by hungry Raiders. By the time we left Tulagi three weeks later, we had eaten up every last coconut on the island.

We had plenty of drinking water, though. By the grace of God, it rained almost every night, so we dug holes and layered them with our ponchos to catch the rainfall.

But food was not our immediate problem. In the two days of heavy fighting on Tulagi, about 40 Marines had died and 350 Japanese had been killed. Our job now was to get these bodies under the ground as quickly as we could. In the tropical heat, the bodies bloated up so they resembled sausages. The stench of decay seemed to be everywhere, and a lot of guys heaved their guts. Dead Japs and parts of dead Japs had to be dragged out of caves. We pulled 35 torn bodies out of one cave, and 30 out of another.

Our own dead were buried with care. Graves were dug using entrenching tools, and the dead were reverently wrapped inside pon-chos and their names recorded for notification of next of kin and re-trieval for later reburial. The Japanese got no such luxury. Their corpses were rolled or tossed into shell craters and buried en masse. Others were tossed into shacks and the shacks set on fire, the smell of burning hair and flesh now mingling with the stink of death and decay. This had to be a scene straight out of Dante's *Inferno*. Through all of this, we could still hear the distant gunfire as the feisty bastards of the Paramarines subdued the last defenders on Tanambogo and Gavutu.

The burial detail seemed to have no end. Even after the bodies were buried, the smell clung to the place for days.

On August 12, war correspondent Richard Tregaskis landed on Tulagi, coming in at the harbor on a Higgins boat. He arrived wet and soggy after nearly being sunk by a roving Jap submarine that fired on his boat. He was met by a contingent of brass and went off with them to talk about the fighting at Tulagi. This would be his first meeting with Edson, but certainly not his last. In his book *Guadalcanal Diary*, Tre-gaskis wrote that Edson was "a wiry man with a lean, hard face" who "talked rapidly, spitting out words like bullets." He recalled Edson's "eyes were cold as steel" and that they never smiled "even when he was being pleasant."

Later, Edson escorted Tregaskis to the cricket field area, where they explored the many caves we had taken just days before. As they walked along together, I couldn't help but notice how the writer's tall, gangly form—he stood six feet, seven inches—towered well above Edson's five feet, nine inches. Tregaskis's nostrils flared as they reacted to the stench of death that seeped out of the cave openings. He stepped gingerly over some as yet unburied Japs, their bodies bloated and turned black from the tropical sun and heat.

After his grisly tour, Tregaskis spoke to a few officers, then headed back for the jetty, his next stops being Gavutu and Tanambogo.

Over the next few days, we finished the burial details, but that did not end our duties. Edson, still expecting the Japs to try to retake the island, sent intelligence-gathering patrols across the 125 yards of water that separated Tulagi from the much larger Florida Island. We tended to agree with Edson, seeing Tulagi as a possible second Wake Island, with an isolated garrison of Marines besieged and eventually overrun by superior numbers of the enemy.

Patrol duties rotated, and D Company's turn soon came. Having reached Florida Island on rubber boats, we cautiously picked our way inland. Out of the jungle came a handful of natives, jabbering and indicating we were to follow them. Since no one spoke the language, we did so, but carefully, alert for a possible ambush. We assumed that the natives, after years of British rule, would be sympathetic to the Allies, but we could never be certain.

They led us into a village where we found a wounded Marine corporal and a Navy lieutenant who was barely alive.

"Thank God," the corporal said when he saw us. "I'd given up hope of ever seeing an American again."

He explained that he and the lieutenant had been aboard the cruiser USS *Quincy* the night of the Japanese attack at Savo Island.

"Japs were all over us before we knew what hit us," he said. "The ship was caught in a cross fire between three Jap cruisers, and we got hit over and over again. It was horrible. Then we took at least one torpedo. By the time I got topside, the dead were everywhere. It looked like a butcher shop. The decks were slippery with blood. The ship was listing heavily to port and going down by the bow when I jumped over the side." He stopped to regain his composure. "As I swam away, I spotted the lieutenant and got him on board some floating wreckage. I got us as far from the ship as I could, then I watched her go down, burning and hissing steam as she disappeared. I don't know how many guys got off. I know the *Quincy*'s CO, Captain Moore, got killed."

He lapsed into silence.

Meanwhile, we did what we could for the Navy lieutenant, but it was not enough. He soon died, and we buried him outside the village, after first collecting his identification tags. We took the corporal back with us, where he remained until we evacuated Tulagi.

Then, of course, there was *Reveille Charlie*, a Jap destroyer that would sail into the channel each morning and lob a few shells at us. He'd pull so close to the island that I could watch the crew scurry about on deck, wheeling their guns toward us. *Reveille Charlie* did no real damage, and in fact, most of his shells passed clear over the island, exploding in the water on the other side, doing far more harm to the fish than to us. One, in fact, smashed one of our PBY Catalina flying boats that had been moored in the harbor after being disabled. What unnerved me most about *Reveille Charlie* was that our position was on high ground, and I distinctly heard the shells make a clicking sound as they passed above my head. Other than that, *Charlie* was a just a pain in the ass, and a constant reminder that we were powerless against the enemy. Not that we didn't try to retaliate. Our weapons platoon fired their 6omm mortars at him. They never came close to hitting the ship, but there was a bit of satisfaction on our part as we watched our shots burst in the water near him, love notes from us Raiders to Tojo, saying "wishing you were here."

On occasion some of our B-17 Flying Fortress bombers would drone overhead and drop their loads on the Jap ships out in the harbor shelling our positions, but trying to strike a moving ship from a bomber makes any hits just a matter of sheer luck, and I don't think any Jap ships were damaged. The Navy did smash a few enemy transports that had been unloading troops and supplies on the 'Canal, and the burning wrecks were beached just offshore.

By the end of August, we Raiders were in piss-poor shape. Due to the food shortage, we were down to two sparse meals per day, and at those, we had to battle the flies that swarmed around our plates. The trick was to wave them away and gulp quickly, swallowing our food and as few flies as possible.

Dysentery made the rounds, giving men the "trots," and the dampness—it rained almost every day—caused many guys to contract a fungal infection we called "the creeping crud" or, more simply, "the crud." We had no clean clothes—they were still in our duffel bags on the ships that had sailed away—and what we did wear seemed to be constantly damp.

Malaria started to appear, signaling its presence by chills that made one's teeth chatter, interspersed with bouts of high fever, weakness, and the sweats. To combat this, or at least lessen the effects, the bedpan commandoes of the medical unit passed out Atabrine, little yellow pills that tasted bitter but reduced nausea. However, the tablets also caused ringing in the ears and turned our skin, and even our eyeballs, a sickly shade of yellow. But their worst side effect, at least according to the scuttlebutt making the rounds, was that they left a man impotent. Needless to say, even though the rumor was not true, there was a great reluctance to take these little pills—but we did not have much of a choice. Most of the world's supply of quinine, the other effective antimalarial drug, was in Japanese hands.

So we sat on Tulagi and waited, for what we did not know. Near the end of August, the 2/5 was taken off Tulagi and transferred to Guadal-canal. A few of our guys were sent along to guard a group of Japanese prisoners. One of these was Bob Youngdeer, a member of the Eastern Cherokee tribe, who was in Charlie Company. After delivering the prisoners, Youngdeer and the others were assigned to help watch the stockade, which they were somewhat surprised to find held mostly Korean laborers.

Youngdeer was still there on August 21 when the Japanese attacked at Alligator Creek, an event that for years was mistakenly called the Battle of the Tenaru River. A detachment of Japanese, led by Colonel Kiyonao Ichiki, hurled themselves against Marine defenses in a disas-trous series of attacks that left their unit all but wiped out and their commander dead. As the battle raged, and the outcome was in doubt, the Marines guarding the POWs were ordered to kill the prisoners in case the Japs broke through the Marine lines.

But our lines held, and in the aftermath of that attack, Youngdeer was assigned to a burial detail to dispose of the more than seven hun-dred dead Japs that lay in heaps along the creek and on the sandbar where the creek met the channel.

On August 30, our turn came. Our four lovely APDs, *Little*, *Greg-ory*, *Colhoun*, and *McKean*, showed up offshore and began taking us on board, bound for Guadalcanal.

Overall, about 347 Japanese died on Tulagi, three became prisoners of war, and it is believed as many as forty swam to Florida Island. Thirty-nine Raiders were killed, and forty-two wounded, which was 9 percent of our force. Most of these men, including Ken Bowers, fell in the first twenty-four hours. Nine Raiders won the Navy Cross.

As I climbed on board the *Colhoun*, I thought how wonderful it was to get off that damned, smelly little island, where we'd left behind so many of our friends.

I did not know then that this would come close to being the last day of my life.

CHAPTER FOUR

THE PERFECT RAID

TASIMBOKO
TUESDAY, SEPTEMBER 8, 1942

A s I watched the windlass reel in the USS *Colhoun*'s anchor, one of the swabbies manning the hose that washed mud off the heavy chain as it clanked aboard turned to me.

"You fellas had a pretty rough time there, didn't you, Marine?" the young man asked, jerking his head in the direction of Tulagi.

If it had been another sailor on another ship asking me such an obviously stupid question, I would have gotten pissed and snapped him off, telling him yes, and it was the damned Navy's bugout that contributed so mightily to our hardships. But this sailor was a crewman on one of our APDs, and we had formed a close attachment to them, and they to us, so his inquiry did not offend me. I knew he was sincerely concerned.

"Yeah," I replied. "Pretty rough. I lost my best friend."

"That's too bad," he said, and I knew he meant it. "We hated leaving you guys stuck there, but we were ordered out. We were pissed as hell."

"That's nice of you to say," I told him, and he returned to his duties.

I didn't have the heart to tell him that the 1st Marines on the 'Canal had taken to calling themselves the 1st Marooned Division. I didn't want to hurt his feelings.

As I watched our APDs leave Tulagi behind, my thoughts turned to the large mass of jungle and mountains that sat broodingly twenty miles off our bow and drew closer with each turn of the *Colhoun*'s twin screws.

Volcanic in origin, Guadalcanal is a big island, one of the largest in the Solomon chain, eight hundred miles in length and thirty-four wide. It's ringed by a coastal plain, which ranges between three and ten miles in depth, and is sliced by a profusion of streams, creeks, and rivers, flowing down from the mountainous heartland. A few hundred yards in from the beach, the gentle plain becomes an endless ripple of steep-sided ridges of varying heights, blanketed mostly with kunai grass that grows to between three and ten feet in height. The greenish-brown ridges stand out naked against the tropical rain forest that laps around their bases.

The beaches that the 1st Marines had stormed on August 7 are ten to twenty yards wide at high tide, ending at the tree line. Beyond the trees, a two-lane government-built dirt road etched the coastline. Single-lane log bridges, many laid in by the Japanese, spanned most of the waterways, including the Lunga, Ilu, Tenaru, and Matanikau rivers and Kukum, Alligator, and Block 4 creeks. Our Seabees later bridged these waterways with pontoon spans, since most log bridges had three-ton weight limits and could not stand up to our heavier equipment.

When the Marines splashed ashore on Cactus, the codename for Guadalcanal, the Jap ground troops, caught with their pants down, hightailed it into the jungle, so the gyrenes met no resistance. Since then, with our Navy gone following their drubbing at Savo Island, the Japanese had begun reinforcing Guadalcanal. Landing barges bulging with troops boldly disembarked their human cargo within sight of the Marines, who could do nothing but spit nails and watch.

Things got a little easier on August 20 when the first of our aircraft— Marine fighters, dive-bombers, and torpedo planes—arrived from the escort carrier USS *Long Island*. This force, meager at first, constituted what became known as the Cactus Air Force. They immediately proceeded to make life hell for the Japanese, as they bombed and strafed enemy shipping in "The Slot," our nickname for that stretch of water between Guadalcanal and the enemy base on Bougainville. Suffering heavy losses in barges and men, the Japanese high command began using high-speed destroyers as troop transports, landing six hundred to eight hundred men at night to avoid our planes, and then shelling Marine positions before departing back for their main anchorage at Rabaul in New Britain.

That was what awaited us on Guadalcanal, whose cloud-shrouded mountain peaks rose picturesquely against the sky. It's little wonder that the Marines, choked off from supplies with our Navy gone, began referring to Operation Watchtower, codename for the invasion, as Operation Shoestring.

But before we could experience the "luxuries" of Guadalcanal, we first had to get there safely, which I almost did not.

As we approached our anchorage at Kukum Point, the booming of naval guns, which had been faint when we left Tulagi, swelled in volume. A few of our Navy ships, taking advantage of daylight, when our planes could keep enemy surface vessels at bay, were shelling targets inland. I could see the pinpricks of light flashing amid the green of the jungle, announcing where a shell had exploded. By dusk, of course, our ships would be gone, and the Japanese would sail into Iron Bottom Sound to take their turn at pounding us.

Standing at the ship's rail with my comrades, I watched the USS *Little* drop anchor nearby. Nets went over the side, and the men of A Company began clambering down to waiting Higgins boats. Then the throbbing of the *Colhoun*'s engines ceased, and her crew began dropping cargo nets over the gunwales on the port side. The men of Easy Company, which included Bill Waltrip, lugging their mortar tubes and machine guns, went first, disappearing over the side toward the boats bobbing in the blue water below. As the last of them swung over the gunwale, Dog Company lined up next. Lieutenant Bill Sperling, Chambers's XO who had taken over the company after "Jumpin' Joe" was wounded, watched the Higgins boats approach the *Colhoun* to pick us up.

"OK," he shouted. "Let's go."

He swung over the gunwale and was gone, followed by rank after rank of Marines, four or five at a time.

In the midst of this unloading process, the ship sounded "battle stations" and crewmen ran for their weapons. Now the deep *pom pom pom* of 40mm and 20mm anti-aircraft fire began to roar all around us, filling the sky with rivers of flaming tracers. Then I saw what they were shooting at. Eighteen Japanese Mitsubishi G4M bombers, which we called "Bettys," were approaching, some up high, some less than a hundred feet above the water. Because the Bettys had no armor plating to protect their seven-man crews, the twin-engine planes bore in on us rapidly, at more than 250 miles per hour, making them hard for our gunners to lock in on.

We Raiders kept unloading the ship as rapidly as possible, streaming down the nets in a human tide of khaki. Speed was important, especially to me, as I was in the last line of men awaiting their turn to leave what had suddenly become a large, stationary target. As I drew closer and closer to the nets, I cast nervous glances over my shoulder. I saw one Betty, its right wing trailing black smoke, bank to the left. Then its non-sealing gas tanks exploded, tearing the bomber apart and sending it into the water in a shower of jagged pieces.

Some of our guys were already on the beach, scrambling like hell for the cover of the tree line. Bill Waltrip was still in his boat, anxiously watching the sky as the craft raced toward shore.

"Can't this scow go any faster," he heard one of his squad mates ask.

"He has it opened up all the way," Waltrip replied, not taking his eyes off the Jap planes. "What do ya want? Egg in your beer?"

Finally I was at the gunwale and I swung over the side. As I descended the net, I heard a loud roar overhead as a Betty buzzed the *Colhoun*. Then the ship heaved and jolted as at least four bombs struck her on the starboard side. Sailors on the deck were tossed into the sea like rag dolls, some alive and kicking as they splashed into the sea, and others dead. Many sailors on board were killed outright. The *Colhoun*, suddenly converted into ripped and burning scrap metal, began settling fast, with me hanging on to the cargo net, two-thirds of the way down her port side.

"Let go, Whitey, let go," my friends called from the bobbing Higgins boat below. "Move it, Whitey! We gotta get the hell out of here."

The *Colhoun*, it was later determined, had been hit by two planes. A bomb from the first Betty struck the searchlight platform, the explosion sealing off the after engine room and starting a river of fire that followed a stream of spilled diesel fuel. Bombs from a second plane, finished her off. Two of the 20mm guns and one of her four-inch batteries were blown off the ship entirely, splashing into the sea around her, and an oil pump from the aft engine room was hurled through the bulkhead and into the forward engine room. The deckhouse was also struck, killing everyone inside.

I did not know all that then, of course. All I knew was that I could feel the *Colhoun* shudder as she began her downward plunge, and I realized she'd take me with her in a few moments if I didn't get my ass off of this damned net. I also knew the Higgins boat had to get away or be dragged down by the suction from the sinking APD, leaving me hanging if necessary. "God help me," I thought, and let go of the net. I dropped into the boat, caught in part by my friends. The instant my boondockers clumped down on the deck, the pilot threw the boat into gear and pulled away from the *Colhoun* as fast as his 225-horsepower engine could push us.

As the Higgins boat scurried to safety, I turned and watched the final moments of the *Colhoun*. Burning furiously, she settled rapidly stern first, a plume of angry black smoke mingling with white clouds of steam as the roaring flames were doused by the cold water of Iron Bottom Sound. With the churning sea boiling and sizzling all around her, the *Colhoun*, commissioned in 1918, finished her illustrious career by disappearing beneath the waves just two minutes after she had been hit. She carried fifty-one members of her crew along to her watery grave. Only bobbing bits of debris, some of it human, remained on the surface to mark where the valiant little ship had stood just moments earlier. It was so tragic.

We joined the effort to fish survivors, many horribly burned or otherwise wounded, out of the water. I thought about the smiling young sailor who had spoken to me earlier in the day and wondered if he had made it. If he did, I never saw him again.

Coming ashore on Guadalcanal was an entirely different experience from wading in on Tulagi. Instead of damned near drowning or being sliced and diced on razor-sharp coral when I went over the side of the Higgins boat, I now landed on soft sand and walked to shore without getting wet above the knees. The Higgins boats had a draft of just two feet, six inches, so they could just about run us up onto dry sand.

We landed at Kukum, about a thousand yards west of the sandbar created by the Lunga River where it flowed into Iron Bottom Sound. Once on land, we moved west, past what prior to our August 7 invasion had been a Japanese bivouac. We then turned south, tramping along the west bank of the Lunga.

The Lunga Perimeter, the name for the area the Marines had secured, was five miles long and three miles wide, stretching from Alligator Creek in the east to a ridge overlooking the Matanikau River a few miles away, on the west flank.

Our destination was a coconut grove fifteen hundred yards inland from Kukum, one of three in the area owned by Lever Brothers, who harvested the copra to make soaps and beauty products. This proved to be an ideal campground. The stately thirty- to forty-foot-tall trees, planted fifteen to twenty feet apart, not only provided welcome shade from the tropical sun that baked the 'Canal, but also made sure the ground stayed devoid of vegetation. Beyond the plantation, the landscape of the coastal plain was mostly fields of the ever-present kunai grass, dotted by small, wooded patches before one entered the foreboding jungle beyond.

Directly to the east, just across the wide but shallow Lunga River, was the western edge of the 3,778-foot-long runway of the airstrip that we were here to defend. With the airfield in Japanese hands, the Allied lifeline to Australia and New Zealand, just 1,905 air miles away, was threatened.

Our reason for landing here had been to take and hold the airfield. We had done the former. Now we were preparing to do the latter.

The airstrip had been named Henderson Field after a Marine flier, Major Lofton Henderson, who had been killed at the Battle of Midway three months earlier while leading his dive-bomber squadron in an attack against the Japanese carrier *Hiryu*. Built in the middle of what had been a large pasture, where some of the island's estimated ten thousand natives grazed their cattle, the airfield was unfinished when the 1st Marines arrived. Luckily the Japs, when they fled, had kindly left behind six road rollers, four generators, six trucks, fifty carts, seventy-five shovels, and explosives, allowing our guys to easily finish the job.

Life on Guadalcanal was a world better than on Tulagi. For one thing, we had more food. With our planes on the island to help defend them, Navy transports had begun making in-and-out daylight supply runs. We spent many leisure hours swimming in the sound off Kukum or bathing in the cool, clean waters of the Lunga, which was said to have crocodiles, although I never ran into one. For many of us, a dip in the river was preferable to the beach at Kukum, mainly because getting to the sea took more effort. One had to maneuver around barbed wire entanglements and possible booby traps to reach the water, which sometimes was coated with an oil slick from damaged or sunken ships. The sound also had the occasional shark.

Evenings were spent enjoying the "cocktail hour," during which we drank canned grapefruit juice to which we added several squeezes of toothpaste followed by a dose of medicinal alcohol covertly provided by medical staffers, who were led by our battalion surgeon, Dr. Robert W. "Doc" Skinner, whom, to my delight, I discovered was from Lancaster County, just like me. Whether this was with or without Skinner's blessing we did not know, nor did we care. Edson, however, was frequently displeased with our tendency to drink and carry on.

He scolded us. "You men are not here to have fun and get drunk. There is a lot of work to do. Remember, the Jap will fight to the death. He is good and he is determined."[1]

We still drank when we could.

Naturally, Guadalcanal also had some definite disadvantages. Rain, a heavy, soaking downpour, fell frequently, flooding foxholes and turning some company streets into flowing waterways. Palm trees transformed into waterfalls as rainwater collected among them, then cascaded down from their leafy canopies. And it wasn't even monsoon season yet.

Land crabs were another pain in the ass, constantly invading our foxholes and tents and skittering about underfoot. Overnight, some Marines killed them with their KABARs and tossed them outside their foxholes. Next morning, they'd compare piles of dead crabs with their buddies to see who'd had the most nighttime visitors.

But most of all, it was the ever-present Japanese who were our biggest concern. Noontime bombings—you could set your watch by them—were daily occurrences. In fact, noon became known as "Tojo Time." At first we Raiders, not used to this type of thing on Tulagi, scrambled for our foxholes, generally dug right next to our pup tents, whenever the Japanese bombers droned overhead. However, we soon began shrugging it off, realizing that it was Henderson Field they were after and not us.

These air raids often ignited grass fires, which sometimes swept across the Perimeter, and we'd hear the *blam, blam, blam* of exploding small arms rounds and mortar shells as an ammo dump went up. Fuel drums at Henderson were detonated by the flames and bombs, and angry black smoke billowed into the sky. On the night of September 2, a Jap bomb landed on one of our dive-bombers parked along the airstrip. The exploding SBD set off an adjacent ammo dump, filling the sky with a spectacular Fourth of July show from bursting 90mm shells. Watching the aerial display provided us with a modest bit of entertainment.

Luckily, we had some warning when Jap aircraft were approaching, thanks to Martin Clemens's network of coast watchers strung up and down the islands rimming The Slot. These alerts gave our interceptors time to get airborne and prepare a greeting. Watching our fighters tangle with Jap Zeroes and Bettys high overhead became a popular spectator sport. We'd hold our breath when one of our planes was hit, waiting for the telltale sign of a blossoming parachute to let us know the pilot was all right. And we'd cheer like hell when a Japanese plane spiraled toward the sea, trailing heavy smoke, or came down in pieces after exploding in the air.

The same sort of warning was seldom present when it came to the Jap Navy.

After dark, the enemy's warships ruled the waters off Guadalcanal. Night after night, ships ranging in size from destroyers to battleships, steaming in pitch-blackness down The Slot from Rabaul—we called this the Tokyo Express—would sit offshore and blast the hell out of our meager foothold. As the shells, sometimes fourteen-inch rounds weighing fourteen hundred pounds apiece and airmailed from a Kongo-class battleship, erupted around us, the cry "Condition red" rang out. We ran like hell for shelter as the earth rumbled and bucked beneath our feet and palm trees were converted into matchsticks.

Another certainty of the night was a single plane that would fly over the island, dropping a bomb or a flare, just to harass us and prevent us from sleeping. This annoying character was bestowed with several names, most commonly "Louie the Louse" or "Washing Machine Charlie."

Sometimes Jap submarines under the general name of "Oscar" would surface offshore and lob in a few shells before disappearing again.

Thus was life on Guadalcanal.

––––––––––––

In early September, headquarters caught wind of a possible Japanese landing on Savo Island. The job of verifying the report was handed over to Edson, who, on September 4, dispatched Able and Baker companies to undertake a reconnaissance of the small, conical island at the entrance to Iron Bottom Sound. Accompanied by coast watcher Dick Horton, they began loading onto Higgins boats and were shuttled out to the APDs *Little* and *Gregory*. En route to Savo, there was a tense moment when a lookout thought he had spotted a Japanese submarine, but blessedly it turned out to be a false sighting.

The APDs dropped anchor off Panuila on Savo's northern shore. Their Higgins boats were lowered, and A and B companies crammed on board for the ride to the beach. The Raiders fully expected to come under fire as their boats drew near to the sand, but all they met when they reached the shore was loincloth-wearing natives.

"You lookim, Jap-an man?" Horton asked the leader, using Pidgin English.

The leader blabbered out a reply, in essence saying that there were no Japanese on the island. Relieved, but still wanting to check out the situation for themselves, the two companies began a reconnaissance hike. A Company trekked along Savo's eastern shore, while Baker took the western coastline. Combined, they scouted the entire eighteen miles of beach that circled the island. On the Iron Bottom Sound side of the march, A Company came across beaches strewn with debris from the August 8 naval battle, including life jackets, oil drums, lifeboats, rafts, and, saddest of all, salt-encrusted articles of clothing, stiffened by the sun. They found the remains of a dead sailor, whom they buried just off the beach after taking his identification tags.

Having confirmed that there were no Japs on Savo, the Raiders reboarded their Higgins boats and returned to the *Little* and the *Gregory*. Ten hours after Able and Baker companies left, half a dozen Daihatsu-class Type A Jap landing barges approached the western beach of Savo. Some of these steel-hulled, double-keeled boats, each capable of carrying as many as seventy men, had been damaged by Henderson Field fighters during the perilous run down The Slot from Bougainville. Other barges in this little flotilla had been sunk, with the loss of all on board. This throwing of men onto Guadalcanal in small chunks was a persistent flaw in the Japanese attempt to retake the island. The troops who landed were always too few in number and too ill-equipped to do the job required of them. The reason for this careless response to our landing was that the Imperial Headquarters in Tokyo, as well as the commanders at Rabaul, assumed that there were only between 2,000 and 3,000 Marines on the 'Canal, when in fact we had about 12,500 men.

That haphazard strategy is what would cost Colonel Ichiki and his men so dearly on August 21 at Alligator Creek, and would continue to plague the man now assigned the task of bringing Guadalcanal back under the flag of the Rising Sun, Major General Kiyotake Kawaguchi.

Forty-nine-year-old Kawaguchi, commander of the 35th Infantry Brigade, had seen great success early in the war, leading his men to victory in Indonesia and the Philippines. During the fighting in the Philippines, Kawaguchi made enemies of some of his more powerful colleagues when he strenuously objected to the executions of former Philippine government officials. His defeat in the upcoming fighting on Guadalcanal, partly through his own errors and partly through faulty intelligence supplied to him, would result in his removal from command and eventual posting in a backwater area, where he would languish for the rest of the war.

We didn't know this at the time, of course. Nor did we know that the enemy force being assembled consisted of more than six thousand men, hard-fighting veterans who had never been defeated in combat, plucked from Lieutenant General Harukichi Hyakutake's victorious 17th Army.

This force included Kawaguchi's 35th Brigade, stationed on Palau, the 4th Aoba Infantry Regiment, then in the Philippines, and the ill-fated 28th Infantry Regiment under Colonel Kiyonao Ichiki, which three months earlier had been the force selected to overrun Midway Island, but instead was sent to Guam after the Japanese Navy's defeat in June.

These scattered units were dispatched to Guadalcanal independently, landing in dribs and drabs on beaches eighteen miles east of our perimeter. First to arrive was an advanced element of Ichiki's detachment under command of the colonel himself. Instantly striking westward, they were spotted by native scouts, who spread the alarm. At Koli Point on August 19, Japanese and Marine patrols brushed against each other, emitting a shower of sparks like flint smacking against steel.

Two days later Ichiki's main body confronted elements of the 1st Marine Division across the sluggish brown water of Alligator Creek. Shortly after midnight on August 21, without prior reconnaissance, Ichiki bravely but foolishly sent his 917-man force splashing across the meandering stream. Met by a solid wall of rifle and machine gun fire, the Japanese fell in windrows, their blood turning the muddy water red as it flowed toward the sea. At the broad sandbar at the mouth of the creek, twisted, mangled bodies lay so tightly packed that one could have walked across the sandbar without touching the ground.

Through the charge and the mop-up that followed with the daylight, only 128 of Ichiki's men lived to fade back into the jungle. The rest, including Ichiki, whose body was never found, or at least never identified, lay sprawled like broken dolls, now starting to swell and putrefy under the rising tropical sun. Called by history "the Battle of the Tenaru" or "the Battle of the Ilu," when in fact it was neither, the fight was over.

Even as Marines buried Ichiki's dead, the rest of the force meant to retake the 'Canal was en route down The Slot, which pointed, dagger-like, directly at Guadalcanal.

That's how the six barges came to nuzzle up on the beach at Savo. They carried about four hundred men and had halted to make repairs and to hide from our planes until dark. With the setting of the sun, they made the final run to Taivu Point, eighteen miles east of the Marine lines. Had these men landed on Savo a few hours earlier, our A and B companies would have had a helluva fight on their hands.

As it was, both Raider companies still came close to annihilation.

Returning to the 'Canal, the *Little* and the *Gregory* stopped off at Kukum, and the Raiders began the job of climbing down cargo nets into landing boats to be ferried ashore. Then new orders arrived. My friend Bill Waltrip, whose machine gun squad had been attached to the Savo expedition, later told me, "We were told to stay on board because there was another patrol planned for the next day."

Edson intended to use them on a hit-and-run raid on Cape Esperance, a main base for the Japanese resupply and reinforcement effort, located at the island's extreme northwestern tip. With Kawaguchi's force being the exception, almost everything coming down The Slot from Bougainville en route to the 'Canal was off-loaded at Cape Esperance. Unfortunately for Edson, but fortunately for the men of A and B companies, as things turned out, half the Raiders had already left their ships. Learning that, Edson countermanded his order, and the unloading of A and B companies was completed. That done, the two APDs were ordered to patrol off Lunga Point.

At about 1 a.m. their radar picked up blips that proved to be three Jap destroyers, *Yudachi*, *Hatsuyuki*, and *Murakumo*. The ships had dropped off some of Kawaguchi's troops at Taivu Point, near the village of Tasimboko, and then stopped to shell Marine positions on shore. The skippers aboard the two APDs, lurking in the dark some distance away, were unsure if it was best to steal away into the night or to attack the enemy, who certainly outgunned them. The decision was made for them when one of our PBY Catalina flying boats dropped a flare. Intending to illuminate the Japs so our shore batteries could find the range, the Catalina instead lit up *Little* and *Gregory*. Spotting them easily, the enemy quickly spun their turrets and opened fire on the two APDs. *Little* and *Gregory* were no match for the newer Japanese destroyers. Salvo after salvo slammed into the small ships, and both soon slid beneath the waters of Iron Bottom Sound. This was bad enough for the APDs, which we lovingly called Green Dragons since they had recently been painted green to help hide them against the backdrop of the tropical islands. But what pissed us Raiders off even more was when the Jap skippers ran their ships through the mass of survivors bobbing on the dark water, running many down, then ordering their machine gunners to fire on the rest.

In the end, eleven of the *Gregory's* crew were killed and twenty-six wounded, and the *Little* lost twenty-two killed and forty-four wounded. Two hundred thirty-eight men were pulled from the water come daylight.

The loss could have been much greater. Had A and B companies remained on board as Edson had wanted, Raider losses would have been severe.

"If we'd stayed on board that night, we'd have been dead ducks," Waltrip told me.

As it was, the Jap cruelty toward the sailors bobbing helplessly in the dark waters of the sound generated a bloodlust within us. We wanted revenge, and revenge we would soon have.

———————

It was not until September 7 that General Vandegrift finally got the word that there was more enemy activity to our east, at Taivu Point, than there was at Cape Esperance. In part, this news came from one of our P-400 Airacobra fighters, sometimes referred to as "Klunkers" by the men familiar with the aircraft. Flying to the east of the Marine position, the pilot radioed, "Japanese landing many troops near Tasimboko." He then dropped down to bomb and strafe the area.

But most of the information about what was occurring in the jungles near Tasimboko came from coast watcher Martin Clemens's network of informants, one of whom was forty-two-year-old Jacob Vouza. A retired native constable, Vouza met his first American on August 7 when he rescued a downed pilot from the carrier USS *Wasp* and guided the man safely back to the Marine lines.

Vouza lived in Tasimboko, so he had witnessed the first elements of Kawaguchi's troops—the Ichiki detachment—land on August 19. Trying to get word back to Clemens, Vouza was captured by Ichiki's men, who found a small American flag hidden in his loincloth. In retaliation, the Japanese bound Vouza, then beat him with rifle butts, before using him for bayonet practice, running him through in his chest, stomach, arms, and face. A Jap officer next delivered what he doubtless thought was the coup de grâce by slashing Vouza with a sword across the throat, before leaving him to die. Unfortunately for them, the Japanese did not take the time to make sure that Vouza did, indeed, die. A tough bastard, he chewed through the grass ropes that held him, then staggered and finally crawled his way to Marine lines. There, bleeding from no less than seven serious wounds, and nearly choking on his own blood, Vouza managed to relay the message to Clemens, although he passed in and out of consciousness several times while making his report. Because Ichiki's men had botched the job of killing Vouza, the Marines were waiting for them when they reached Alligator Creek on August 21.

As for Vouza, whom even Clemens thought would not survive, he recovered and proved he was a man who did not forget Japanese savagery. I once saw him walking through our camp, a severed enemy head dangling from each hand, suspended by the hair clutched in his fists.

(Vandegrift put Vouza in for the Silver Star, and he was also awarded the Legion of Merit for his work in helping Carlson's Raiders later in the campaign. Vouza was bestowed the rank of honorary Marine Corps sergeant major. The British also recognized his service, in 1957, by naming him a member of the Order of the British Empire, and he was knighted by Queen Elizabeth II in 1979. Vouza died in 1984, and a statue to his memory stands before the police station in the modern city of Honiara on Guadalcanal.)

In the days following the Ichiki disaster, the Japanese poured in more reinforcements. Clemens's natives reported this, although some of their details were incorrect. The Japs around Tasimboko, one spotter said, were ill-equipped and half-starved. In truth, they were well rested and fresh. What the native had seen was most likely the shattered remnants of Ichiki's men, which he mistook for incoming reinforcements.

Vandegrift needed to do something to counter the Japanese landings, and on September 7 he called Edson to his HQ tent and briefed him on the situation. At this point, Edson commanded 833 men, 605 Raiders and 228 'Chutes of the 1st Paramarines, whose commander, Major Richard H. Williams, had been hit on Gavutu.

We Raiders were always a little skeptical of Edson's obvious delight in volunteering us for special missions, and that day was no exception, when he returned from the meeting with that cold, lopsided smile on his lips. It was a grin we all knew well, because whenever he wore it, we knew we were in for trouble.

And yet we were eager to see some action, having done nothing more than a little patrolling and a lot of ducking shells from the Tokyo Express since we secured Tulagi on August 9. We were especially chomping at the bit after the tragedy that befell our Navy comrades aboard the *Little* and the *Gregory.*

The information Edson had received was skimpy at best. He was told that the Japs at Taivu Point numbered "several hundred" and that, as noted above, they were ill-fed and under-equipped. The raid was a risky one, and everyone knew it. Tasimboko was out of range of even our heaviest pieces of artillery. Limited air support would be available, and then only if there were no Jap planes over Henderson. Our force would be transported on two APDs, the *Manley* and the *McKean*, and two "Yippies," YP-289 and YP-346. These latter were former California tuna boats pressed into service by the Navy and converted to troop transports. Using these boats meant that, besides showing how unprepared America was for war, we could pretty much rule out the element of surprise. Their engines made one helluva racket while spewing a torrent of glowing orange sparks out of their funnels and into the sky for all to see. Colonel Griffith commented that the Yippies "announced their presence to all but the blind and deaf." [2] Another problem was landing boats. There were only enough Higgins boats to ferry ashore two companies at a time, so the initial landing force would be in grave danger until the boats returned to the fleet to load up the next wave and bring them ashore.

With all of those factors working against us, Vandegrift asked Edson, "Do you think you can accomplish your mission?" Edson, it was said, simply smiled.

We got the word to get ready for action at about 4 p.m., and began moving out of our camp an hour later.

"I wonder what Eddie the Mole has lined up for us this time," I huffed to Alex Stewart as we tramped along the coastal road toward the anchorage at Kukum, carrying full combat gear.

"Not much," my friend replied. "Knowing Edson, we're probably just gonna hit Tokyo."

"If we do," I said with a chuckle, "I'll bet we win."

By 8 p.m. we were boarding the little invasion fleet. Baker Company would sail on the *McKean*, along with Edson, and Able Company would board the *Manley*. Colonel Griffith, with Charlie Company and what was left of Dog Company, would be crammed aboard the YP boats. There was not enough room for the Paramarines and Easy Company, so they would have to come up as soon as one of the APDs could sail back to Kukum and fetch them.

I say "what was left of Dog Company," because by this time, we were down to just forty-six men. We had suffered some losses on Tulagi, of course, but by and large, our ranks were depleted because Edson had decided to bolster his A, B, and C companies with "replacements" from D Company.

While we were en route, Edson received a new dispatch upping the number of Japs around Taivu Point to as many as three thousand. He mulled over this new information, then decided to proceed as planned. He had the utmost confidence that we could do the job.

In point of fact, this raid had all the potential of becoming a first-rate disaster. We were landing beyond Tasimboko, which put the Japs between us and the Marine lines at Lunga Point, some eighteen miles to the west. If we ran into a large Japanese force, and they managed to somehow cut us off, our forces on the island were too weak to mount any serious relief operation. We'd be SOL (shit out of luck). This was not a happy thought to dwell upon.

Around midnight, our little fleet steamed out into Sealark Channel, far enough so as not to be spotted from shore. Our goal was to surprise the Japs, so the smoking lamp was lit, meaning we could not enjoy a cigarette on deck, which was silly considering that the Yippies were both belching clouds of flaming embers high into the night.

As if we weren't miserable enough because of the no-smoking order, the sky opened up and rain cascaded down on us in bucket loads. Those of us who tried to get some sleep had a choice of either the steaming hot holds belowdecks or the rain-swept world above. And if the rain did not make us wet enough, the ships rolled on choppy seas that sent waves of cold water, whipped by a stiff, chilly wind, washing across the decks. The only cheery part of this trip was that the waves washed away the vomit of men who were becoming violently seasick.

War correspondent Richard Tregaskis was one of the seventy men jammed aboard our Yippie, YP-346, along with Griffith. He later noted in his book that the YP's skipper was a West Coast tuna captain named Joaquin S. Theodore. Being a lowly private, I naturally enough never met the man, but Tregaskis remarked that, although American, Theodore was of Portuguese descent and his use of English was awkward, reflecting his heritage.

"Tal your men I don't like to smoke it on deck," was one comment Tregaskis recalled. [3]

By 5 a.m., still being subjected to heavy rain, our ships came to a halt four thousand yards east of Tasimboko. Landing preparations were soon under way. The shoreline of Guadalcanal stood broodingly about one thousand yards off our bow as the first four Higgins boats, carrying Charlie and Baker companies, churned their way toward the beach. At 5:20 a.m., the boats reached the sand, and the first Raiders jumped over the sides and hastily dug in to secure the landing zone for the rest of us. They expected a counterattack at any moment and clutched their weapons tightly as their eyes scanned the jungle entanglements.

Shortly after 6 a.m., as A Company and we men of Dog readied ourselves to go ashore, someone cried, "Oh my God! Look!"

We followed his pointing arm and our blood ran cold. Steaming our way were several ships, including transports, destroyers, and at least one cruiser.

"Japs," I heard Stewart whisper hoarsely. "Our ass is grass."

We agreed, but then heaved a deep sigh of relief when we saw that one of the destroyers was flying the Stars and Stripes. The ships turned out to be the transports *Beatrix* and *Fuller*, escorted by a cruiser and four destroyers, bringing supplies to Lunga Point. Feeling reprieved, we continued unloading.

On shore, our initial shock and dismay had been shared by our enemies. As we later learned, they were waiting to attack us and try to push us back into the sea when they, too, spotted the mysterious vessels. In their case, however, they were correct in the assumption that the ships were hostile; only they mistook their coincidental arrival and ours as part of a single, large offensive operation. Their mistake was further reinforced by four P-400s that now zoomed in, wings knifing through the air. These began to drop three-hundred-pound bombs and strafe the Japanese defenses with a torrent of machine gun fire from the two .30-calibers mounted in each ship's nose. Unprepared for the massive numbers of Americans they believed were heading their way, the Japanese filtered back into the jungle, abandoning Tasimboko, at least for now.

At around 8 a.m., my feet touched the sand as D and A companies reached the shore. On the beach, we found several of our comrades brandishing Jap flags, articles of clothing, blankets, and personal items. These had been "liberated" from Japanese knapsacks that had been discovered, some lined up neatly just inside the tree line and others stacked under trees. Contents told us that they were the property of men belonging to the Sendai Division's 2nd Field Artillery Brigade. The looting was stopped by Edson when he came up in the second wave.

"This isn't a goddamned picnic," he bellowed. "Get off the beach and keep your eyes peeled for the Japs. After they're all dead, then you can souvenir hunt."

While the battalion readied to move out, our company CO since Tulagi, Bill Sperling, shouted, "D Company! Dig in here."

Our understrength company had been attached to Charlie Company, commanded by Captain Bob Thomas, filling in for the wounded Ken Bailey. Our job was to secure the beach landing area until the APDs could return to Kukum and bring up the 'Chutes and E Company, which would be at around noon. As we began entrenching, the *Manley* and the *McKean* turned their bows to the west for the nearly two-hour trip back to Kukum, while Edson and the bulk of the Raiders struck out for Tasimboko. The two APDs made one brief stop in order to lob a few five-inch shells at Tasimboko. We could hear the muffled drumbeat as their rounds burst among the bamboo and rattan huts.

Edson pushed the Raiders forward with Captain Floyd Nickerson's Baker Company on the right, moving along a coastal road that paralleled the beach just inside the tree line, while Captain John Antonelli's Able Company swung southwest, deeper into the jungle. Together, the two companies were to envelop Tasimboko. This was Antonelli's first time in company command—he was filling in for Lew Walt who was down with malaria—and the twenty-five-year-old proved to be an able leader.

To maintain contact with the two companies, Edson relied on his runner, Corporal Walter Burak. A Greensburg, Pennsylvania, fellow, Burak stood five-foot-nine, just like Edson, and tipped the scales at 190 pounds. With that physique, it should come as no surprise to know he loved football and played as a running back in high school.

Walt was the nicest guy you'd ever want to meet. As a football player at Quantico, if he knocked an opposing player flat during a play, once that play was completed he'd help the man up and even apologize. A strong Catholic, Walt didn't drink, smoke, or swear. Nor did he whore around on liberty, or spend three days in the brig living on piss and punk (bread and water) like so many of us seemed to do all too frequently. This made him stick out like a sore thumb among us hard-living Raiders, but we respected Walt for his beliefs, and if we poked fun at him, it was done purely in good-natured jest.

In combat, if Walt was sent back to HQ with a message from Edson, he never failed to return without bringing along needed supplies such as ammo or medical stores.

But despite Burak's best efforts, A and B companies were frequently out of communication due to the difficult nature of the terrain.

When it came to maintaining radio contact with Vandegrift back at Lunga Point, Edson relied on the cumbersome TBX. This heavy radio came in three sections. The transmitter/receiver was carried by Corporal Fred Serral, while Pfc. David Tabor handled the accessory pack and Pfc. Herschel "Bull" Sterling lugged the twenty-four-foot collapsible antenna and the hand-operated electrical generator. The three units combined weighed 120 pounds and proved an absolute bitch to move, so there was plenty of cussing during our advance on Tasimboko, when the radio had to be relocated thity-seven times. Rather than disassemble the antenna, Sterling wisely chose to drag it through the jungle with each shift in position. The signal, both voice and key, from the TBX could not reach Lunga due to the heavy foliage, so Serral kept in contact with Sergeant James "Horse Collar" Smith, still on board the *Manley*. Smith then relayed the message to Lunga. The reverse was true for messages from Vandegrift to Edson.

As we drew closer to Tasimboko, evidence of a Japanese force of considerable strength quickly became evident. Baker Company, which Edson and Tregaskis accompanied, stumbled across an intact 37mm field gun, abandoned along the coastal road, squatting just at the edge of the beach, its silent muzzle aimed at our ships offshore. The Marines found more knapsacks, slit trenches, foxholes, and about a thousand dull gray life preservers. There was also a pile of empty clamshells and uneaten meals still on cook fires.

"I'm thinking they've gone up for breakfast and knocked things off here," Edson told Tregaskis as they surveyed the shells. [4]

As B Company moved unopposed toward Tasimboko and God only knew how many Japs, it all seemed too easy. I'm sure more than one Raider was thinking of the August 12 patrol made by Colonel Frank Goettge near the Matanikau River. After being told by a prisoner that there were Japs at the Matanikau who were willing to surrender, Goettge took twenty-five men, plus the POW, with him to check it out. It was an ambush. Only three men returned. Goettge was not among them.

Overhead, the P-400s returned, this time in company with three Dauntless dive-bombers. The aircraft began working over the village and the *ca-rump ca-rump* of their bombs reached our ears as we silently cheered on the Marine flyboys.

Closing on the village, B Company stumbled across a second intact 37mm gun. God must have been watching out for us. Had these two weapons, both pointing toward the sea, been used against our incoming Higgins boats, it might have been a slaughter. But the timely arrival of the mysterious ships had spooked the Japanese and saved us a difficult and bloody landing.

The company now began to receive some sporadic fire from the Japanese, whose resolve had returned after the mystery ships had moved on and they saw that they were up against a much smaller force than they'd feared. This slowed our advance since Edson, never one to worry, now began to fret over the danger our battalion was in should the Japs appear in large numbers. He was unaware, of course, that Kawaguchi's main body was even then slogging west through the jungle, intent on striking Henderson Field, and that turning back now would mean a delay in the Japanese general's delicate timetable.

Tasimboko was a village of about eighteen huts set astride a coastal trail and near a shallow ford of the Kema River. With Japanese in front of him, Lieutenant John Sweeney, lately moved from Easy Company to become a B Company platoon leader, was at point during the advance. Now he swung his men deeper into the jungle, crossing the Kema upriver, through chest-deep water. Peering warily ahead, Sweeney spotted something that made his blood run cold: a 75mm M41 field piece. This gun, standing menacingly in a small clearing, was similar to our 75mm pack howitzer in that it could be broken down into six two-hundred-pound units and carried by animals or men. Beyond this first gun loomed a second, and even as Sweeney watched, a three-man gun crew raced to the weapon. Rifles cracked as the Raiders fired at the Japanese, but they reached the gun safely, wheeled it around, loaded it, and fired. The detonation resounded loudly in the tangled jungle. They quickly loaded and fired again, the shells creasing the air low over the Raiders' heads. Explosions ripped around and among the platoon, and twenty-three-year-old Corporal Bill Carney was killed. One exploding round brought down a large tree branch that pinned Pfc. Ken Brubaker, while nearby, another man screamed in agony. This was Corporal Maurice Pion, whose left arm was hanging by bloody shreds.

"Corpsman" was the call, and two of these brave men, Alfred W. Cleveland and Karl Coleman, hurried forward. Working under fire, and using a penknife as a scalpel, they removed Pion's shattered limb and bound up the stump. Pion would survive his wounding, thanks to the courage of our corpsmen, and Coleman would earn the Navy Cross here at Tasimboko.

As the corpsmen labored over Pion, Pfc. Andrew Klejnot, Springfield cradled in his arms, wormed his way forward through the underbrush. Finding a good firing position, Andy leveled his rifle, sighted in, held his breath, let it out slowly, and squeezed the trigger. His slug drilled one of the Japanese gunners through the head and he dropped from view. The other two men spun in Klejnot's direction, but Andy, who had learned his marksmanship skills well back at Quantico, calmly sighted in again, fired, and dropped a second man. The third decided now was not the time to die for his emperor, and fled into the jungle.

Baker Company moved forward. Resistance was stiffening as Edson drew closer to the village. Enemy fire, like at Tulagi, came from well-emplaced Nambu machine guns. These had to be slowly and cautiously outflanked, one by one, after which a few well-tossed grenades settled the issue. Some 90mm mortar rounds began raining down on the Raiders as well, bursting among the trees, further slowing their advance as they were forced to hit the ground in order to avoid the shrapnel that cut through the air with a whirring sound.

Our commander had been led to believe that the Japanese at Tasimboko were mostly supply and service personnel, which was partially true. But also left as a rear guard were veterans of the 10th Company, 124th Infantry. Edson radioed that he was up against about a thousand Japanese soldiers. He requested a second landing and more air support. Colonel Gerald Thomas, Vandegrift's chief of operations, refused, saying Henderson was under heavy rain with poor visibility, which had temporarily grounded any further air support. Instead he told Edson to re-embark his force and pull out. Edson declined the offer and we stayed where we were.

The situation improved around noon. The 'Chutes and Easy

Company arrived, and we all hurried westward to assist in the taking of Tasimboko. The rain back at Henderson had let up by now, and a pair of P-400s were soon droning overhead, bombing and strafing the Jap defenses.

Antonelli's A Company, with whom Colonel Griffith was traveling, was still groping and hacking its way through the dense jungle. Thanks to poor maps, Antonelli was not sure where he was, and was further confounded when he discovered they'd have to slog through the waist-deep, smelly muck of an uncharted swamp. Guiding on the sounds of battle somewhere off to his right, Antonelli finally came across the trail he was seeking. He and his men now hurried toward Tasimboko.

Sweeney, meanwhile, was just outside the village, his advance snagged for the past hour by one especially troublesome and well-placed machine gun pillbox. Looking around, he spotted Corporal Ben Howland.

"Howland," he shouted, and signaled that the NCO was to join him.

Howland made his way from his position to where Sweeney awaited him, rounds from the Japanese gun sending up little sand geysers all around him.

"Take your squad and find a way to outflank this son of a bitch," Sweeney ordered. "We'll try to keep him distracted on this end."

Howland nodded, then made his way back and gathered his eight-man squad, and they crawled off into some underbrush. Sweeney gave Howland time to work his way into position, then he shouted, "Ba-ka! Ba-ka!"

In reply, the machine gunner sprayed Sweeney's position with a hail of 7.7mm fire that caused Sweeney to duck low behind the trunk of a fallen palm tree.

"Ba-Ka! Ba-Ka!" he called again when the firing died down, and again another long burst of fire was sent his way, bullets chewing up the tree trunk.

"Holy shit, Captain," yelled a Raider who was nearby and trying to pull the ground over his head as the enemy gunner hosed Sweeney's position. "What the hell does that mean?"

"I learned it from Tiger Erskine," Sweeney replied, head low.

"Yeah, but what's it mean?" the man urged.

"I'm not sure," Sweeney replied. "I think I'm calling him a son of a turtle."[5]

Sweeney kept up the taunts until Howland's squad had a clean shot, then two BAR men opened fire and wiped out the gun crew in a hailstorm of .30-caliber slugs.

At about this time, seven grueling hours after they had entered the jungle, Able Company attacked the Japs' right flank, startling the defenders and sending them scurrying for the underbrush. The way into Tasimboko was now open.

What we found in the village left us slack-jawed. It was a major Japanese supply base meant to sustain a very sizeable force. We came across mountains of hundred-pound bags of swamp seed (Marine slang for rice) and crates of food stacked ten feet high, containing tins of crab meat and sliced beef, which we ruefully referred to as monkey meat, packed in soy sauce. We found cartons of British cigarettes bearing Dutch East Indies tax stamps, over half a million rounds of small arms ammo, mortar, and artillery shells, Japanese lager beer in dark brown bottles (twenty-one cases to be exact), and lots of medical supplies, including opium and blood coagulants.

We also began rifling the dead for whatever we could find, which included documents, currency, flags, and even photos of loved ones back home. Some of the more stalwart Raiders searched Japanese mouths for gold teeth and, finding them, cut them out using their stilettos or KABARs. It's funny how in war, men do things they would never consider doing under normal conditions.

As had happened when we first landed, the all-businesslike Edson put a quick stop to the looting.

"Knock it off, damnit," he bellowed. "Knock it off. Destroy everything! Now!"

We went about doing as ordered with an almost sadistic glee. Rice bags were slashed open, their contents allowed to spill onto the ground.

Then the rice was saturated with gasoline or we simply pissed on it. After stuffing our pockets with whatever tins of food we could carry—many of us recalled how hungry we had been on Tulagi—cases of rations and other supplies were tossed into huts and the huts set on fire. But not all of the supplies went up in flames.

"No, damnit," Sergeant Pete Pettus shouted to some Raiders who were about to toss medical supplies into a blazing structure. "Take that shit back with us. We may need it."

Captured enemy rifles and machine guns were smashed and ammunition tossed into the sea. A long-range radio transmitter was also consigned to the salt water and its generator battered into junk. Some rubber boats we'd discovered were slashed and their outboard motors destroyed. Hundreds of anti-tank mines were tossed into Iron Bottom Sound, as were the breech blocks for the captured artillery. The guns themselves were attached to Higgins boats and dragged out into deep water. Someone found a 75mm gun sight manufactured in England, and we picked up scores of American weapons, including Thompson submachine guns, and American-made ammunition with Dutch labeling. The idea that our own stuff was being used against us really pissed us off.

Richard Tregaskis, more discerning about what he took than us gyrenes, picked up Japanese documents that revealed Kawaguchi's order of battle and his overall mission. At the time, we had no idea how valuable those pieces of paper would be for us.

About the only thing we kept aside from the medical supplies, food, practical personal items, and as much "liberated" beer as we could carry, were 81mm mortar shells, for use in our own tubes, and a couple of Nambu machine guns and ammo.

One treasure we captured was a trunk containing a neatly pressed white officer's uniform. This belonged to General Kawaguchi, who, it was later learned, planned to wear it when he accepted our surrender of Guadalcanal. [6]

As we reveled in our spree of destruction, Edson radioed Lunga

Point, "Am destroying Tasimboko and as much property as possible. Will re-embark about 1530 unless you desire we remain here until tomorrow."

The reply was from Vandegrift himself.

"Re-embark and return to Kukum," it read. "Well done."

Our vandalism completed, we stood back and admired our work. All around us, Tasimboko was ablaze as crackling flames consumed the supplies whose loss would be so devastating to Kawaguchi and his men. We watched showers of sparks rise into the sky amid heavy clouds of black smoke.

War correspondent Robert Miller, who traveled with Tregaskis, spoke for us all when he wrote, "Just finished a first rate act of arson. It was fun."[7]

By 3:30 that afternoon, we were climbing back aboard our APDs and Yippies, for the two-hour trip back to Kukum. A few Japanese filtered among the burning huts and sent sporadic and ineffectual fire our way. Their shots were returned by some of our men. I recall helping to load the badly wounded Pion, the stump of his arm heavily bandaged, onto a Higgins boat on the beach. As our ships sailed west, a pillar of thick smoke continued to smudge the sky above where Tasimboko had once stood. By 8 p.m. we were back in our camp.

We lost two Raiders killed—I helped to bury one man by a coconut tree—and six wounded. By our count, twenty-seven Japanese soldiers lay dead among the ruins of Tasimboko. It had been an almost perfect raid, exactly the type of operation which we had been recruited and trained to execute. And, as it turned out, it would prove to be the only such mission the 1st Raiders would ever conduct.

––––––––––––––––

Kawaguchi took the loss of Tasimboko very hard. Like his garrison at the village, he initially was led to beleive that there was a second American invasion force landing in his rear. He radioed his headquarters, alerting them of his predicament. Rabaul responded by dispatching a force consisting of cruisers and destroyers, intent on inflicting a second Savo Island defeat on our Navy. They arrived off Taivu just hours after we left, and found nothing. In lieu of sinking our ships, they contented themselves with shelling the remains of the village where they thought American Marines might be located. Unfortunately, the village had been reoccupied by Kawaguchi's small Tasimboko garrison, so the only thing the Japanese naval shells killed was a few of their own comrades.

The Japanese fleet did score one success, however. After shelling Tasimboko, they steamed to Tulagi, still seeking our fleet. The Japs found what they thought was an American destroyer, and opened fire. Their shells scored several hits, and the ship began sinking. Content, the enemy left.

What the Japs had found was not a destroyer, but YP-346, our own Yippy commanded by Captain Theodore. Badly wounded, Theodore managed to keep his boat from sinking by running the burning Yippy aground on Tulagi. Considering I had been on the YP-346 a few hours earlier, it was my second close call in about a week.

At the time, of course, we had no idea of the ramifications our raid would have on our enemy and, ultimately, on us. We had dealt Kawaguchi what would become a crippling blow. He had lost his entire base of supplies and was now faced with two choices. He either had to succeed by defeating us Marines on the 'Canal, or undertake a retreat through the jungle, with not enough food or medical supplies for his troops. This succeed-or-perish fate would hinge upon one battle, one grand assault that would make or break the Battle for Guadalcanal on both sides.

Ironically, when Kawaguchi made that do-or-die attempt, it would be launched against us, the very men who had created his dilemma. And it would be decided on a bleak hilltop that would forever be known as Edson's Ridge or, perhaps more appropriately, Bloody Ridge.

CHAPTER FIVE

"THIS IS WHERE THEY'LL HIT"

LUNGA RIDGE
THURSDAY–FRIDAY, SEPTEMBER 10–11, 1942

I was lounging by my tent in the Lever Brothers coconut grove that had been our home since we arrived on Guadalcanal from Tulagi on August 30. The palm trees towering above our heads were a godsend as the blazing sun baked the airfield and grassy plains.

As we had been told to expect, malaria had started making its way through the ranks as early as Tulagi, infecting many, including myself. But other maladies now began to appear as well, such as dysentery, dengue fever, and fungal infections that we derisively called "jungle rot" or "the crud." Every morning, the list of men falling out for sick call grew longer.

The natives seemed less vulnerable to the ailments that plagued us, but they were susceptible to leprosy, yaws—an infection of the skin, bones, and joints that is spread by contact with infected lesions—and hookworm.

At 11:50 a.m. on this day, just like every other day, Jap planes arrived like clockwork over Henderson Field. You could almost set your watch by the bastards. Twenty-five Mitsubishi Betty bombers escorted by fifteen Zero fighters, flying down from Rabaul, had unleashed their loads over our perimeter, their explosives tearing apart the morning calm. We hit the air raid shelters, of course, at the first cry of "Condition Red," but no bombs were aimed at us today. This gave Alex Stewart, Dick MacNeilly, and me a chance to watch the show overhead as a dozen of our Wildcats rose to meet the intruders.

"Go get 'em, Marines," Mac mumbled as we watched the small dots that were our planes close with the larger specks of the Japanese bombers.

As I scrutinized the aerial battle, I thought about the Marines manning those planes. I often walked around Henderson Field, just to see all the activity going on. I watched Wildcats and Dauntless dive-bombers being refueled and rearmed, with ground crew guys feeding long belts of .50-caliber ammo into the wing-mounted guns, ammo that could be used up in about twenty seconds of sustained firing.

Ammunition and fuel dumps were scattered about, hidden under camouflage netting, while the hulks of planes destroyed on the ground, or scrapped due to heavy damage, were massed at the edge of the field, where their usable parts could be salvaged.

The pilots lived in an area referred to as "Mosquito Gulch," although I'm not so certain their location was any worse than ours in that regard. As officers, they got to sleep on cots or straw mats left behind by the Japanese. This allowed them to avoid the black, malodorous mud that the frequent rains left behind.

Their food was pretty much the same as ours: Spam, canned hash, captured Jap rice, and dehydrated potatoes.

Out on the airfield, by the runway, stood a rickety wooden structure erected by the Japs. We called it "the Pagoda," and it served as a command center for air operations. When enemy planes approached, a captured Rising Sun flag was hoisted over the Pagoda, alerting pilots to scramble.

This went through my mind as the tussle raged overhead, with aircraft twisting and turning high up among the billowing clouds. The whine and roar of engines was punctuated by the faint but distinct hammering of machine guns, and occasionally, one of the specks exploded in the air and spun down in fragments, or corkscrewed intact, into the waiting waters of Iron Bottom Sound, trailing oily black smoke as it fell. We hoped it was one of theirs.

Then the fight was over. Oftentimes these engagements were relatively brief, just a few minutes, at least so far as we mud crushers were concerned. I'm sure for the men in the cockpits they seemed interminable. After the sky cleared of aircraft, we returned to our previous activity of lounging around in the warm, moist air, cooled by the slight breeze wafting in from the sea.

As we lay there, shooting the shit about women, the Corps, and the land crabs that infested our camp, my platoon sergeant, Stanley Kops, approached.

"Whitey," he bellowed. "Patrol! Grab your weapon and ammo and double-time to the colonel's tent."

That quick he was gone.

"What the hell?" I moaned, rising to my feet.

"Give our regards to the Mole," Mac sighed, his eyes closed as he reclined on the ground.

"Up yours," I muttered, then grabbed my Springfield and web gear and headed to Edson's HQ area.

At Edson's tent, I found the colonel surrounded by staff officers, plus Lieutenant Colonel Sam Griffith, his XO, and Walt Burak, Edson's runner. I noticed three other Marine enlisted men clustered around Sergeant "Horse Collar" Smith and I joined them.

"The colonel is going to make a personal reconnaissance of that ridge," Horse Collar told us. He pointed toward a grassy hogback rise that poked up from the jungle about fifteen hundred yards south of where we were standing, overlooking both our camp and Henderson Field. "We're going along to provide protection in case any of those little yellow bastards are up there ahead of us."

That sat well with us Raiders as we were itching for a chance to get at the Japanese again, and we shortly set out for the ridge that would soon forever bear our commander's name.

All this time, Kawaguchi's force was still hacking its way toward our perimeter. Having initially advanced as one large body, when the column reached Koli Point, the individual strike units began peeling off, one by one. Marching along the coast road were the 1st and 3rd battalions of the 124th Regiment under, respectively, Major Yukichi Kokusho and Lieutenant Colonel Kusukichi Watanabe. Marching with them was the late Colonel Ichiki's Second Echelon, which included the survivors of the decimated First Echelon. It must have brought back harsh memories for these men as they followed practically the same path they had traveled eighteen days earlier as they followed their late commander to Alligator Creek. The rest, led by Kawaguchi himself, swung in a southwesterly direction, deeper into the jungle, in a sweeping motion intended to bring them up on the ridge's southern slope. Well to our west, near Kamimbo Bay, the remainder of the 124th Regiment, under Colonel Akinosuka Oka, was landing, intent on attacking that side of our fragile perimeter. Kawaguchi intended for these separate wings to launch a coordinated attack from three different directions that would crush the Marines between them. He was convinced that his force was more than sufficient to drive what he believed was only a few thousand isolated Marines back into the ocean.

All of this was heading our way, and when it came, all that would stand between success for Kawaguchi and the fall of Henderson Field would be Edson's Raiders.

W e're movin' out," Griffith said, and our small party started across the grassy plain, Raiders walking at point to either flank, our senses on the alert.

As we drew closer to the ridge, the ground began a gentle ascent. With me on the right flank, our group advanced along a well-used footpath, one of many that connected the coastal areas to the inland villages, worn into the earth from decades, if not centuries, of use. The grass-covered coral hogback that would soon be forever known as Bloody Ridge was about 2,000 yards in length and rose to about 150 feet above the airfield at its highest point. Except for scattered clumps of brush and a few small, spindly trees, the ridge stood virtually bare above the surrounding jungle. Seven hundred yards to the east, the Lunga River sliced through the jungle, paralleling most of the ridge before sharply veering off to the northwest. In the near distance to the west, Japanese-held Mount Austin, Mambula to the natives, rose 1,514 feet above the surrounding sea of green rain forest.

The ridge itself was not straight. Rather, it bowed to the east between its highest point, Hill 120, located roughly halfway along its length, and Hill 100 at the southern tip of the ridge, about six hundred yards beyond. The crest of the ridge dipped slightly between these two hills, forming a saddle. East and west, the ridge sloped steeply into the jungle. The foot trail we were on was etched along the entire crest, north to south.

Edson called a halt atop Hill 120. The sun blazed down on us. Sweat flowed down from under my helmet, stinging my eyes. Gripping my '03 Springfield, I dropped to one knee, eyes darting left and right, vigilant for any movement in the jungle at the foot of the hill, or in the tall kunai grass around us.

Edson stood tall, boldly gazing around the barren ridge like a land baron inspecting his property. I noticed him nodding to himself, his oversized helmet bobbing atop his undersized head. Red Mike, as we often called him, knew that the Japanese troops whose supplies we'd left smoldering at Tasimboko were somewhere out in the jungle beyond the ridge, making their way toward the airfield.

"This is the place," Edson said, almost as if he was talking to himself. "This is where they'll hit."

Addressing the others in his staff, he said, "General Vandegrift believes the Japs coming at us from Taivu will not risk the unknown of the jungle but will stick close to the coast and attack in the same area those Japs did a few weeks ago near the Tenaru. He simply can't believe the Japs might come from this direction. I don't share the general's conclusion. Based on the Jap documents we picked up at Tasimboko, I'm convinced the enemy will see this ridge as a tailor-made attack route."

Edson walked away from the group a short distance, striding in my direction, scanning the surrounding terrain with his binoculars. Then he dropped to a knee directly beside me. This made me more nervous than a June bride on her wedding night. I recalled how, in our first interview after I had volunteered for the Raiders, Edson had rejected me for my lack of swimming prowess. Yet a few days later, my orders to report for Raider training came through. I was overjoyed, but assumed it was an error. So I reported and kept my mouth shut. Now here he was, kneeling by my side, and I was certain he'd recognize me as the fellow he sent packing and say, "Hey! What the hell are you doing here?"

Instead, he said, "Tell me, Private. What did you think about this ground for a battle?"

What did I think of it? What the hell was I supposed to say?

"I think it'll be just fine, sir," I replied.

"I think you're right," Edson replied, then clapped me on the shoulder and rose. He rejoined his staff.

"The private thinks this is a good place for a battle, and I agree," Edson said. "We'll move the battalion up in the morning, along with the 'Chutes. That will give us just over eight hundred men. That's not enough to cover this entire area in a solid defensive line, but we'll have to make due."

Pointing to Hill 100, he said, "I want B Company to emplace around that hill. We'll have to put Charlie Company down in the jungle between the base of the ridge and the Lunga. A Company will be their reserve, a few hundred yards to the rear. We'll supplement those companies with machine gun sections from Easy Company. Dog Company and the rest of Easy will dig in here as a reserve and to protect HQ, which I will set up just to the rear here. The 'Chutes will deploy on the east side of the ridge."

"What about artillery support?" Griffith asked.

"The 11th Marines have been directed to set up their 105s at the base of the ridge, between us and Henderson Field," Edson said. "We won't have a lot of time to get ready so we must work fast. I want commo wire strung and as much barbed wire as we can lay hands on. I also want extra ammo and grenades brought up here, and a supply line established in case we need more."

Edson's fortifying the ridge was done pretty much on his own initiative, based on his belief that his thinking and General Kawaguchi's were identical. Both Edson and Colonel Gerald Thomas, Vandegrift's operations officer, who also believed as Edson did, failed to convince the commanding general that the ridge was a natural attack route. So, employing a new tactic, Thomas talked Vandegrift into the move by convincing his commander that the ridge was a good place for the Raiders to rest up from their exertions at Tasimboko.

We now headed back for the coconut grove, where Stewart and Mac grilled me about what was up. All I told them was that we were moving to the ridge the next day in case Japs attacked from that direction. Not long after, orders came for me to again report to Edson's HQ tent.

"I want you to spend the night with the Paramarines, Whitey," Griffith told me when I arrived. "When we move up to the ridge tomorrow, you show Captain Torgeson where the colonel wants him to place his men."

Returning to my squad area, I grabbed my pack, weapon, and web gear and headed off. After reporting to Captain Henry L. Torgeson, the Paramarines' acting commander, I found a patch of ground to call home for the remainder of the day and night, and settled in.

"What's going on?" several 'Chutes asked me.

"Don't know," I replied, not altogether truthfully. "I just know we're moving up tomorrow."

The next morning, Edson addressed the men, saying, "We're shifting our bivouac up to the ridge. It will be a rest area for us and will get us out of the Jap bombers' V-ring."

He told them to get ready and that we'd be leaving shortly after breakfast.

"And grab any spools of barbed wire you might come across," Edson added as if as an afterthought.

None of the men were fooled by Edson's remark about a "rest area," especially after the crack about toting along the barbed wire. We knew that a "rest area" was the last place Red Mike would pick out for us.

For our meager breakfast of soggy rice and dehydrated potatoes, we derisively thanked the Navy, which, after their drubbing at Savo Island, would race in each day with small convoys, off-load what supplies they could as quickly as possible, and then get the hell out again before the Japs found them. Having finished our sad meal, we shrugged into our packs and prepared to move.

"Pfc. Groft! Front and center," Torgeson bellowed.

Dutifully, I hustled forward.

"Take us to the ridge, son," he ordered.

I led off, and they followed.

Leading an entire battalion of Marines up the ridge made me feel like General MacArthur, and my chest puffed out with pride. The column passed through the 105mm smoke wagons of the 11th Marines, whom we called "Don Pedro's Canoneers" after their commander, Colonel Pedro de Valle. The weapons were set in sandbag revetments and under camouflage netting. Nearby we dropped our packs in a pile, keeping only what we needed: poncho, ammo, mess gear, and canteens. We hoped the artillerymen would not loot the packs, but we did not want to be burdened with more gear than necessary. This was yet another troublesome indication to any man who believed we were heading into a rest area, although I doubt any but the most knuckleheaded of knuckleheads still bought that line.

Cresting the ridge, I continued to lead the column forward, angling to the left and moving down the steep, grassy eastern slope. Reaching the spot Edson had pointed out yesterday, about two hundred yards forward of Hill 120, I signaled a stop and the battalion halted. Turning to Torgeson, I said, "You're to deploy your men in a defensive position and dig in here, sir."

Torgeson surveyed the ground, then turned to me.

"Well done, Private," he said.

"Permission to rejoin my company, sir?" I replied.

He nodded, we saluted, and I left.

Trudging back up the slope, I found Dog Company, the twenty-five of us who were left since Edson began using us as a replacement pool for his other companies, digging in around the base of Hill 120. Or, at any rate, trying to dig in. The hard coral core just beneath the ridge's dirt surface was like concrete. With few entrenching tools—most of our shovels and axes had still been aboard the transports when they bugged out on August 8—we were forced to chop away at the earth with bayonets, KABARs, or whatever else we had. No one managed to scrape a hole deeper than ten inches.

"We're moving to a rest area," Stewart said as he worked, trying to mimic Edson's voice. "Rest area. I'm laughing."

After hacking no more than a shallow dent in the ground, I gave up. Instead, I located a comfy spot in the tall grass, spread out my poncho, and claimed it as my own. Others felt the same way.

"Screw it," Stewart mumbled a few yards to my right. He had barely managed to scrape away a few inches of the hard earth. Like me, he finally surrendered to nature.

Edson set up his HQ just beyond the crest of Hill 120, a shallow trench without sandbags, wire, or a roof. From here, he would direct the most important battle of his and our lifetimes.

Everywhere around the ridge, we Raiders were preparing for the defense. Men hammered steel rods into the ground then strung single strands of barbed wire around and between them. We'd have loved to string more, lots more, but only eighteen rolls had been brought ashore on August 7, so there simply wasn't enough. Machine gunners, especially those down below in the jungle, from what I was told later, were clearing fields of fire, but in a precise manner so that approaching enemy soldiers might mistake these killing lanes for trails.

Then I noticed Edson and Sergeant Pete Pettus, his intelligence chief, along with the 11th Marines commander, Colonel de Valle; de Valle's executive officer; and some forward observers, moving about the ridge. They were surveying the ground, walking around, pointing, recording measurements, and plotting concentration points to help the men manning the heavies to zero in their guns. After they had charted what seemed like every inch of the ridge, de Valle and his XO bore their information rearward. The forward observers remained with us, digging in as best they could. If we had any doubts that something big was heading our way, the sight of the arty spotters painstakingly plotting our position dispelled them.

Preparing our defenses was hot work, and men began peeling off shirts and helmets, as sweat flowed from every pore on our bodies. Quickly we had discovered that the ridge was the complete opposite of our beloved coconut grove. This was a sweltering place. Devoid of the meagerest shade, the open ground was like a broiler oven under the tropical sun, and the cool breezes that fanned us in the grove as they blew in from Iron Bottom Sound did not reach us up here.

Then there were the Japanese.

If Edson thought moving us to the ridge would, as he said, remove us from the "V-ring" of enemy bombers hammering Henderson Field and the Marine perimeter, it was one of his rare miscalculations. At noon, "Tojo Time," right on the button, twenty-seven Bettys escorted by fifteen Zeroes droned overhead in their now-familiar V formations, toting five-hundred-pound high explosives and fragmentation bombs, "daisy cutters" we called them. Down on the airfield, three of our Dauntless dive-bombers were blown all to hell, and the main radio station was knocked out, along with some gas stores. Our F4Fs overzealously claimed six Bettys, when in fact only one was lost, as was one enemy fighter.

However, on this raid, all of the bombs weren't destined for Henderson Field; they included a special delivery from Kawaguchi to us. As the bombers winged overhead and the whine of bombs coming down rattled louder and louder, we scrambled for cover on a barren ridge that afforded little. We tried to flatten our bodies as explosions tore across the ridge, jarring the earth and sending a hot wind over us as the concussion pressed us down like an invisible hand.

When the planes left, here on the ridge and in the jungle below, eleven Marines were dead and fourteen wounded, their moans and screams of pain reaching our ears. Behind me, Edson surveyed the smoldering terrain. To him, the bombers had confirmed Japanese intentions.

"They're coming," he told his officers, in his low, gruff voice. "We must hold this ridge at all costs. If we don't, we'll be the ones roaming the jungle and eating raw coconuts instead of the Japs."

———————

As we continued making our preparations, out in the jungle, Kawaguchi's plan, devised with typical Japanese complexity that took into account no variables that might throw off the rigid timetable, was unraveling. The Japanese columns slogged their way toward the ridge which, due to its shape they called the *mukade gata*, or "centipede," much the same way a mouse weaves through a maze, going first one way, then another.

To begin with, Kawaguchi failed to anticipate the difficulty of moving a large body of men and heavy equipment through trackless jungle. Perhaps even more egregious, Kawaguchi had almost no communication with other units within his command, making any attempts to launch a concerted assault nearly impossible. Inaccurate maps and a lousy compass, coupled with the thick rain forest of huge trees with twisting roots and laced with rattan vines, caused the Japanese to wander off course. Being forced to laboriously hack their way through heavy tangles of vegetation cost them precious time.

The four enemy columns were advancing along their different paths, yet on September 10, three of them accidentally collided. The result was a monstrous traffic jam that slowed things down for hours as units sorted themselves out. Meanwhile, one battalion not involved in the congestion, III/124, went missing in the jungle and would not emerge for two days. Kawaguchi continued leading I/124 and II/4 southwest while Kuma Battalion trudged toward Alligator Creek.

To a man, the Japanese were tired and hungry. No one had anticipated the difficulty of moving over narrow trails, hampered by thick vines, deep mud, gnarled tree roots, swamps, steep ravines with slopes as slippery as ice, and stagnant streams. The march was worsened as handcarts used to tote gear broke down, forcing mortars and ammo to be lugged by hand.

Artillery units, dragging along what few guns Kawaguchi was able to bring, fared even worse. Wheels sank hub-deep into mud at each river and stream crossing and had to be manhandled out with the greatest of effort. Rubber tires on ammunition carts blew and axles bent, meaning shells had to be physically carried by hand. It was sweaty, backbreaking work, and most of Kawaguchi's precious artillery was soon lying abandoned along the way, where much of it lies rusting to this day.

Time and miles were added onto an already long and painful trek, as open fields encountered along the way had to be either detoured around or else crossed only at night. Once they had crossed, the Japanese had to be careful to leave no visible trail in the field that might be spotted by one of our flyboys.

As of September 11, one day short of the enemy's attack date, reports coming to Edson from Clemens's scouts said the Japanese were still five miles to our east, and moving at a snail's pace.

Back on our ridge, Edson knew there was no way he was going to be able to put together a continuous defensive line with the number of men he had on hand. As distasteful as it was, he had been forced to place men in the jungle between the ridge and the Lunga, knowing they ran a serious risk of being overrun. It was into this vulnerable spot that Edson ordered Captain Bob Thomas's Charlie Company to dig in. Strung out for eight hundred yards between the Lunga and a long, narrow lagoon at the base of the ridge the existence of which no one had known about because the foliage had hidden it from view, Charlie Company's three platoons entrenched themselves behind a single strand of barbed wire. Unable to make a solid line due to the undergrowth, the company became a network of isolated strongpoints, with overlapping fields of fire cut among the foliage to provide mutual support. Worse, if they had to pull back to the ridge, which seemed likely, the only way back was across the lagoon via a single log bridge formed by a felled tree. This slippery path could become a deadly bottleneck. In fact, Bob Youngdeer, a surefooted Eastern Cherokee, recalled how he had slipped off of the log and into the muck while moving into position. That was a bad sign.

Two hundred yards behind Charlie Company, its right flank on the Lunga, was Captain John Antonelli's A Company, with one platoon of the 1st Pioneers, on loan from Vandegrift, some distance behind them. As Antonelli's men settled in uneasily, one Raider asked Sergeant Joe Buntin how they would get out if they were overrun.

"Stay where you are," Buntin replied. "The word is nobody moves, just die in your holes."[1]

It was a sobering thought.

From the eastern edge of the lagoon and stretching up and over the crest of the ridge was Major Lloyd Nickerson's Baker Company, temporarily under the command of Captain Louis Monville since Nickerson was at the base hospital with severe stomach cramps. Monville, in fact, would become a victim of heatstroke before the day was out, passing the command to Captain John Sweeney, B Company's lone remaining officer.

All in all, at least ninety Raiders were out of action due to illness or wounds suffered at Tulagi and Tasimboko. They'd be sorely missed in this upcoming fight.

We twenty-five men of Dog Company were strung along the forward slope of Hill 120, near Edson's advance headquarters and close to where Doc Skinner was setting up the aid station. Our company straddled the footpath that ran along the crest of the ridge, so my position on the extreme left placed me on the eastern slope of the ridge, with the right of the paratroopers a few hundred yards ahead of me and to my left. On Dog's right flank was stretched what remained of Easy Company after the subtraction of its machine gun platoons, now on assignment with A, B, and C companies.

Even though we held the high ground, we were still in a lousy position because we were so badly understrength. Edson was well aware that the Japanese, if they sat back and studied the situation, would realize they could easily outflank us, and that would be it for us all. Our eastern flank was wide open, protected only by the dense jungle. To our west, beyond the Lunga, we Marines were spread even thinner than on the ridge. Our defenses west of the river consisted basically of three outposts manned by a Pioneer battalion, the 1st Amphibious Tractor Battalion, and the 3/5 (3rd Battalion, 5th Marines). These three units were separated by at least a thousand yards. If Kawaguchi focused his strength there, he could punch through our lines and right into the heart of the Marine perimeter with little effort. Thankfully, he was unaware of our weak spots.

To be realistic, the odds were weighed heavily against us.

As the day wore on, Edson had hot food brought up. String beans, Vienna sausages, and coffee were delivered to all of the men, including those down in the jungle. As we settled in for the night, our bellies satisfied, Alex Stewart looked around our position on the ridge.

"Do you know what this reminds me of?" he asked.

"Do I wanna know?" I replied.

"It reminds me of the pictures I've seen in a book about Custer's Last Stand," he said. "A sloping, grassy hill overlooking the Little Bighorn River."

"Custer's Last Stand," said MacNeilly, who was dug in beyond Alex. "Do you happen to remember how that story ended?"

"Yeah," he whined. "But I can't help it. It's what it reminds me of."

"Shut up, Alex," I quipped and threw a string bean at him.

"How many Japs do you think are coming our way?" Alex persisted.

"How the hell do I know?" I replied, fishing a cigarette from my battered pack of Lucky Strikes and lighting one up. "But you can bet Edson has a pretty good idea."

"You think they'll try to come through us?" he asked.

"Bound to," I said.

"They'd better," Mac complained. "Otherwise I'm wasting a lot of good energy being nervous."

Next thing I knew, Lieutenant Ed Wheeler, recently appointed to replace Bill Sperling as commander of what was left of D Company, was kneeling in the grass behind us.

"You boys OK here?" he asked.

"Yes, sir," I replied.

"By the way, Whitey," Wheeler said to me, "Sergeant Cafarella is taking a contact patrol into the jungle at dawn tomorrow. The colonel needs to know what's out there, so stand by. I'm assigning two men to the patrol, you and Mo Cooley. So be ready."

"Yes, sir," I said, and he left.

The patrol idea left me somewhat nervous, but I liked Cafarella, who, with a reshuffling of the battalion that would come next spring, would be awarded the exalted rank of gunnery sergeant.

The sun went down and cast us into pitch-darkness. All around, the night sounds of the jungle—chattering monkeys, squawking birds, and similar denizen noises—reached our ears. It was nerve-wracking enough for those of us on the ridge, and I wondered how the guys down below were making out, when every rustle of the leaves could be a Jap infiltrator.

As we dug in, waiting for the enemy, Bob Youngdeer took the battle's first prisoner when he spotted a Jap soldier in the river, waving a white flag. Youngdeer fished the man out of the water and packed him off to the rear. What intelligence he could give our interrogators, we never found out.

Interestingly, while Youngdeer was preparing for battle west of the ridge, on the eastern side, his brother, Jesse Youngdeer, was doing the same. He was a member of the Paramarines, I discovered later.

Around midnight the mournful drone of an airplane engine grew louder and louder in the blackness above us. It was Washing Machine Charlie intent on interrupting our sleep. Tonight, Charlie lit up our ridge with green flares the light of which pierced the night. We squinted as the harsh, painful glow assaulted our eyes, which had grown accustomed to the all but absolute darkness. An hour or so after Charlie departed on his way back to Bougainville, a Japanese cruiser and three destroyers glided into Iron Bottom Sound, yet another nightly ritual since our Navy had fled for safer waters. When they turned their guns on the island, their shells were soon whining through the dark with the sound of tearing fabric. I don't know if they were shooting at the ridge, since their rounds fell off to the east, blowing up trees and, hopefully, some of those damned loud birds.

Between these interruptions, we Raiders got what sleep we could, knowing full well that this night's rest could be our last.

CHAPTER SIX

"THEY'LL BE BACK"

BLOODY RIDGE
SATURDAY–SUNDAY, SEPTEMBER 12–13, 1942

Dawn comes slowly in the jungle, and as the first hints of light began painting the eastern sky, I awakened from a fitful sleep. Rising from my blanket spread out amid the damp kunai grass, I saw Sergeant Joseph Cafarella and the rest of the patrol assembling near Edson's forward HQ , just beyond the crest of the main hill to our company's immediate rear. Having draped an ammo bandolier, each pouch stuffed with two five-round stripper clips, diagonally across my body, I plopped my helmet on my head. Swinging the '03 Springfield onto my shoulder, I headed toward the assembly point. Passing Stewart, who was still softly snoring, I grinned as I resisted an impulse to boot him in the behind.

Arriving at the assembly area, I nodded good morning to the others as Cafarella counted noses.

"We're missing someone," he said.

We looked around.

"Cooley," I said.

"Go get him, Whitey," Cafarella ordered.

I had a good idea where to find Mo Cooley. He was one of the few men who bothered to challenge the cementlike ground in order to erect a lean-to using his shelter half, with one end weighted down by rocks and the other propped up on two spindly sticks. The angled shelter would provide some shade from the blazing sun come daylight. Locating the lean-to, I found Cooley sitting upright, swatting his own arms and legs, a wild look in his eyes.

"Mo," I said. "Patrol. Get your ass in gear. The Sarge is waiting."

"I ain't goin' out," he blurted, wild-eyed.

"What the hell do you mean you 'ain't goin' out'?" I shot back. "Cafarella'll have your ass for breakfast."

"There's Jap beetles all over the place," he said crazily, still slapping his body. "I ain't coming out."

"Damnit, Cooley," I said. "Quit goldbricking."

"Can't you see the bastards, Whitey?" he screeched imploringly. "They're all over."

"Get your shit together, Mo," I said, grabbing the front of his shirt and trying to sound firm. "There's nuthin' there."

"I can't. I can't," he mumbled over and over, still swatting.

"Bullshit," I muttered.

Letting go of him, I stood there somberly and watched Cooley cower under his shelter half, smacking insects seen only in his own mind. Cooley had always been somewhat erratic as far back as our training days at Quantico. One morning Mike Rihaly returned to our squad tent from a trip to the latrines looking bruised and disheveled, a cut on his one cheek.

"What the hell happened to you?" I inquired of my friend.

"That bastard Cooley jumped me in the head because he said I was in his way, which I wasn't," he complained. "He sucker punched me. That guy's nuts."

A surge of anger swept through me. Cooley had always rubbed me the wrong way, from the beginning, so I stormed out of the tent and entered the head. Cooley was still there, combing his hair in the mirror and grinning like a man who didn't have a care in the world, which he didn't until I strode up.

"This is for pickin' on Rihaly," I said, and swung a right that connected with his jaw. He was more resilient than I had guessed, and he came back swinging. We got into it right there in the head. During the brief scuffle, Cooley got in a few good belts to my jaw, but I landed a solid left on his chin, followed by a quick right cross. The combination left Cooley on the floor.

"From now on, you leave my friends alone," I warned him. Then I turned and walked out, leaving Cooley sitting on the deck, moaning and trying to refocus his eyes.

"I took care of Cooley," I announced when I returned to our barracks.

Rihaly took a look at the bruises forming on my face and said, "Looks like he took care of you, too."

"He got in a lucky punch or two," I conceded with a smile.

After that day, Cooley never bothered me or my buddies again.

Now I returned to the patrol, where Cafarella raised an eyebrow in my direction.

"Better get someone else, Joe," I told him. "Cooley's gone Asiatic." I explained.

"We go as is," Cafarella said. "Saddle up."

The sergeant led us down the east slope of the ridge, through the Paramarines' line, and into the rain forest beyond. We entered the underbrush, weapons at the ready. Pushing deeper into the vegetation, we hoped to effectively blend in with our surroundings. The Raiders were the first Marines to utilize camouflage uniforms, albeit homemade ones created by blotching our standard-issue fatigues with black dye and brown paint. As I mentioned earlier, many of us also covered our steel helmets with burlap to eliminate glare, especially moonlight at night, earning us the nickname "Tiger Cubs" from the Japanese.

Even though our little group included a two-man .30-caliber machine gun crew detached from Easy Company, we were not a combat patrol. Our job was to find the enemy and report back. Nothing more.

Picking our way through the dense undergrowth while trying to make the minimum of noise was slow work. About two hours into the patrol and just over a mile out from the ridge, we came to a dry riverbed. After cautiously crossing it in spaced intervals, we had labored about another fifty or sixty yards, brambles tugging at our clothes, when the flat crack of a Japanese Arisaka rifle split the jungle stillness. I flinched as a bullet twittered past my ear. More shots followed, snapping small branches and sending bark flying from trees where the rounds struck. We hit the dirt, horrified. The gunfire was coming, not from in front of us, but to our left and rear. Somehow, we had passed the Japs!

"Back to the riverbed," Cafarella whispered harshly, and we ran as fast as we could, retracing our footsteps as lead slugs chewed up the vegetation and hummed through the air around us. Reaching the riverbed, we dove in, hugging the embankment for cover. We fired a few rounds into the jungle, not because we saw anything to shoot at, but for the sake of our own morale and in hopes of making the Japs hesitate before attempting to charge us. The machine gunner began setting up his weapon, but Cafarella stopped him.

"No. No. If we stay, we're dead," he said.

Then he scanned the jungle to our rear.

"We have a better chance if we split up," Cafarella said. "Every man for himself. Back to the ridge! Go."

The patrol scattered, followed by Japanese bullets and shrieks of outrage at our escape. I chose to run stooped over, north along the dry riverbed, the bank of which afforded me a modicum of cover from the bullets that plucked leaves from the trees above my head. When I reached a spot where the jungle to my left seemed thickest, I ducked into it. The dense underbrush tore at my clothes as I ran, and heavy vines painfully slapped my face, but I kept moving, blindly plunging through the trees. Finally the ground began sloping up, and I realized I had hit the base of the ridge. Bursting out of the forest and into the grassy openness, I froze and my heart leaped into my throat. A short distance ahead of me stood a paratrooper sighting along the barrel of his .30-caliber Johnson rifle, its menacing-looking muzzle pointed directly at my head.

"Don't shoot," I blurted out.

The 'Chute recognized me, lowered his rifle, and grinned. Around me, the rest of my patrol was now emerging from the bush.

"Thank God you have great fire discipline," I told the 'Chute, and headed up the ridge.

The entire patrol returned safely. First thing I did was report to Lieutenant Wheeler, who welcomed me back and mentioned that Cooley had been sent to the rear. I nodded and turned away. Reaching my so-called foxhole, I collapsed on my blanket, breathing heavily. Lying down, I took off my helmet and used it for a pillow. I closed my eyes for a few seconds. When I opened them again, Ray Ruble was standing over me.

"You OK, Whitey?" he asked.

"I don't know what the Corps record is for cross-country running through dense jungle, Big Stoop," I puffed, still catching my breath. "But I may've just broken it."

I told him and my other buddies what had happened. Sergeant Kops came by, listened briefly, then said, "Full alert tonight, guys. Good job, Whitey."

Throughout the day, more patrols were sent out, and men coming back reported hearing Japanese voices and the sounds of vines and limbs being chopped. Several patrols made contact, and small arms fire periodically echoed from the jungle, getting closer and closer to the ridge with each skirmish.

They would come tonight, and every man knew it.

———————

With the Jap main body closing the distance on our ridge, preparations were rushed and the battalion was put on 100 percent alert. We gingerly strung all the barbed wire we could beg, borrow, or steal, then looked to our personal defenses, making sure our ammo bandoliers were fully loaded and laying in a supply of hand grenades.

At ten minutes before noon, the Japanese bombers were back, twenty-five Bettys and fifteen Zeroes, raking the Marine positions on Henderson Field and our naked ridge. We Raiders tried to pull the earth over our heads as the bombs whistled down, exploded, and sent jagged shards of hot steel buzzing by just inches above us. Our fighters, already on patrol, dove among the enemy planes, guns blazing. Jap aircraft fell, some streaming black smoke, others in fireballs, their death dives ending in Iron Bottom Sound, where they sank, sizzling, into the depths. Passing through the enemy formations, the Wildcats pulled out of their dives and roared back up into the fray, their guns again spitting out streams of lead, and more enemy planes fell. When the smoke cleared, five bombers and one Zero would not return to Rabaul. On our ridge, four Marines were dead and fourteen had been wounded.

Few among us doubted that when the Japanese infantry came at us, they'd come after dark. Fighting at night, the enemy knew, maximized that element of surprise the Japs were so fond of, while minimizing our firepower, especially air support. Also, their Navy had total command of the offshore waters after dark, completely offsetting the meager artillery support Kawaguchi could expect from whatever of his own guns his troops managed to manhandle through the jungle. But mostly, the Japanese were just so damned confident of their night-fighting ability, which they saw as superior to any other army's, that they never even contemplated a day assault.

We might have been less confident of our own position had we known that Admiral Robert L. Ghormley, commander of the southwest Pacific area, had warned Vandegrift that the Japanese were bent on retaking Guadalcanal, and that our Navy did not have the ships to adequately resupply or, if worse came to worst, evacuate us. He suggested to Vandegrift that he might want to consider surrendering our forces to the Japs if we were faced with imminent destruction. Ghormley, in effect, was writing us all off. Luckily, Vandegrift and Edson, when the latter was told of Ghormley's suggestion, did not share the admiral's viewpoint, and agreed that we'd take to the jungles and conduct guerilla operations if need be.

Over the years I have often wondered about the effect our surrender of Guadalcanal would have had, not just on us, but the entire nation, which had already had to stomach a long line of American defeats, from Pearl Harbor to Corregidor.

———————————

As we prepared our defense on the ridge, blissfully ignorant of how dire our situation truly was, Edson moved along the line, inspecting positions, directing defenses, and confirming machine gun emplacements and mortar positions.

Amid the growing tension, one pleasant diversion we had that day was the return of Major Ken Bailey, the popular Charlie Company CO from Pawnee, Oklahoma, who had been hit on Tulagi. He walked among us, accepting handshakes and "welcome back" slaps on the back, a totally likeable guy, for an officer. Back at Quantico, just before we shipped off to the West Coast and war, Bailey had gotten married and brought his beautiful young bride into camp and introduced us all to her. Her name was Elizabeth, and she sure as hell was a looker. Bailey would feign indignation at our wolf whistles and "hubba-hubbas" when, in fact, he was pleased by our approval.

"I'll think of you guys tonight," he told us, and winked.

Not a man among us didn't envy him.

But just as wonderful as it was to have Bailey back, even more welcome was what he brought along with him: sacks of mail, the first we'd had in three months. As the sun squatted low over the western horizon, we hastily ripped open envelopes and read and reread our cherished letters from home, temporarily casting aside thoughts of what the rapidly approaching darkness might bring. We'd heard that Edson, not a man to sit idly around while waiting to be jumped by the enemy, had said that if the Japs didn't attack us tonight, we would strike them in the morning. He had a pretty good idea where to find them, as did we all. Out in that darkening jungle, we knew the Japanese were gathering thicker than Baptists at a tent rally.

Since cook fires were out of the question, the dinner menu that night consisted of biscuits removed from C-ration kits, washed down with a few sips of tepid water from our canteens. Our mess hall was our individual fighting position.

Just before dark, Lieutenant Wheeler again made his way along our company line, stopping by each man.

"We've gotta hold here, Whitey," he said to me. "There's nothing between us and Henderson, and if they get through us and grab the field, we're duck shit."

"I understand, sir," I grimly replied. "How many Japs does the colonel think there are?"

"Could be as many as four thousand," Wheeler replied.

I was glad Wheeler could not see the expression on my face. In fact, I was glad I couldn't see it. It might have scared me even worse.

"Stay in your hole," Wheeler continued. "Make every shot count. The colonel will make every effort to keep us supplied with ammo and grenades. But we stay right here, no matter what. Pulling back is not an option."

I nodded in the gloom.

"Good luck, Whitey," he said, patting my shoulder. "I'm proud to serve with you."

"You, too, sir," I replied, and he was gone.

I looked toward Stewart, who was the only other Marine I could still clearly see in the darkening gloom.

"Heaven help us," I said.

Alex could only nod.

Night settles in the jungle like a black cloak seen nowhere else. Even your hand before your face can't be seen, let alone a friend nineteen feet away. So just before he faded from sight altogether in the encroaching blackness, I said, "I'll see you in the morning, Alex."

If he nodded in acknowledgment, I couldn't see it.

I was amazingly calm I guess because mentally I had prepared myself to die if it was the Lord's will. I rolled onto my side and thought of my family, my brothers and sisters and my parents. Then I prayed to God for our country and the Corps, and asked that He give me the strength to face the enemy with courage. I was certain I would not be walking off this ridge, and I'm sure most of the other fellas felt the same way. But whether I was to live or die, I was determined to do my duty.

I did not want to die, but I also wasn't really afraid of death. As I had done on Tulagi, and as I would do again on New Georgia and, much later, Okinawa, I remained within myself and didn't give in to panic. That's the way it always was with me. Some guys would lose it, like Mo Cooley had earlier that day and my friend Mike Rihaly had that first day on Tulagi, but I just didn't worry.

Relaxing in the blackness, I affixed my bayonet to the end of my rifle and settled down to wait.

Initially, the night possessed a death-like stillness, with only the thump of our hearts to remind us we were alive. Even the jungle, constantly alive with the cawing of birds and chattering of monkeys, lay silent, as if it, too, were waiting.

Though there were more than eight hundred men on the ridge and in the jungle below, each man was now alone in the blackness of the night with his own thoughts, fears, and concerns, cut off from the man next to him as if a curtain had been lowered.

When the fight began, it was almost a relief.

———————

The Japanese assault opened at about 11:30 p.m., not from the jungle, but from the sea, as a green flare arced into the sky to light up the night. The five-thousand-ton cruiser *Sendai*, accompanied by destroyers *Shikinami*, *Fubuki*, and *Suzukaze*, had quietly steamed into Iron Bottom Sound. The cruiser opened up on the ridge with her seven 5.5-inch guns, followed by the destroyers, each mounting six 5-inch main guns in three turrets. The shelling was terrific, with the incoming rounds sounding like an approaching locomotive. Five high explosive shells landed near Edson's CP, but to his good fortune, four were duds and the fifth exploded harmlessly. A number of Jap shells, in fact, passed clean over our ridge to crash among the enemy infantry assembling in the jungle.

Harsh fingers of light next swept the ridge, as *Sendai* switched on her spotlights. Star shells were soon bursting overhead, illuminating the ridge with a nightmarish glare. We stayed low as the ground beneath us shook and red-hot shrapnel zipped past our ears. The barrage lasted about twenty minutes, although it seemed like two hours.

Kawaguchi joined this cacophony of battle as he opened fire on our ridge with his meager artillery, consisting of a 75mm Type 41 mountain gun, and a couple of rapid-fire Type 94 37mm pieces, each capable of firing thirty rounds per minute.

Then the Japanese infantry came on, and as they did, a sweet scent rose from the jungle and reached our nostrils on the slight breeze, the smell of the chrysanthemum soap used by the soldiers. It was a smell we would come to know well.

Kawaguchi had wanted his three center battalions to be in position by two o'clock that afternoon, but only the 1st Battalion, 124th Regiment succeeded in making that timetable. Of the other two, 3rd Battalion of the 124th would not be in position until 10 p.m., just before the attack began, and 2nd Battalion, 4th Regiment, would not jump into the fight for another hour after that. In fact, these units were still trying to get organized even as the naval barrage was under way. The Jap commanders attempted to home in on the searchlights and exploding shells, but many still drifted off course in the tangle of the jungle, generally leading their men into the low area between the ridge and Lunga. Kawaguchi, however, didn't seem to be worried, convinced as he was that our ridge was the weakest portion of the Marine perimeter and might even be undefended. We would teach him otherwise.

At first the Japanese approached stealthily, probing for our lines. Bob Youngdeer, posted by the Lunga's eastern bank, heard men sloshing through the water as enemy troops waded toward his position. The Raiders held their fire. The Japanese were less restrained, and the sharp, flat crack of their bolt-action rifles erupted in the night. The Marines, when they responded, tossed grenades so as not to give away their posts. The grenades' sharp booming reached our ears up on the ridge, and we gripped our own weapons with added resolve.

Charlie Company took the brunt of the onslaught, and we could hear the gunfire erupting in the dark jungle and see the twinkling of muzzle flashes at the foot of the ridge to our right. At least seven hundred men under Major Yukichi Kokusko rushed forward, many slapping their rifle butts and yelling "U.S. Marine be dead tomorrow" in their stilted English.

Their assault jammed up at the barbed wire, and Charlie Company's machine guns took cruel advantage, chopping down the attackers. Grenades bursting among the massed infantrymen added to the carnage, as enemy bodies stacked up. Atop the ridge, we watched and heard the battle below intensify. Beneath the dark canopy of palms around the base of the ridges, rifles cracked, machine guns chattered, grenades burst, and men yelled and screamed.

Attacking such a thin line, it didn't take long for the Japanese to break through C Company. Hitting the spot where Charlie Company's left and Baker's right almost, but not quite, met, the Japs folded B Company's flank back toward the ridge like a gate swinging open, scattering C Company's end platoon. Our main line of resistance suddenly had a gaping hole, and the way was open for the Japanese to surge through the shattered C Company and up the slope of the ridge. Luckily, the confusion and intermingling of enemy units that had plagued the Japs from the outset resulted in a total command breakdown, making it impossible for them to press their advantage.

Elsewhere along the C Company line, closer to the Lunga, Japanese wandered along "paths" cut by our machine gun crews. The .30-cals opened up, scything down the approaching enemy like stalks of wheat. Those Raiders not squeezing a machine gun trigger were busily yanking pins from grenades and heaving them, the two weapons blending their horrific voices in a hellish serenade.

But the Japanese hurt us as well. A machine gun squad led by Neil Champoux of Canadaigua, New York, was swamped by Japs. Champoux was killed and his men scattered into the jungle. As Japanese continued pushing through our porous defenses, Raiders were cut off when enemy soldiers charged past them, not seeing the Americans crouching in the darkness. This happened to Pfc. John W. Mielke, an Easy Company machine gun ammo carrier temporarily attached to C Company, and Pfc. Ed Proffitt. As the enemy advanced past them, they kept low, feigning death to avoid being discovered and killed. As beads of sweat stung his eyes, from a combined mixture of heat and fear, Mielke noticed that Proffitt was holding down the spoon, or arming lever, of a live grenade. Alarmed, as well he should have been, Mielke fished a piece of string from his pocket, carefully took the grenade from Proffitt, and wrapped the string around it, securing the spoon.[1]

Pfc. Martin "Jeeper" Heitz, who had been pinked by a Japanese bullet four days earlier at Tasimboko, also heard the enemy advancing toward him. Squeezing his trigger, he opened fire with his machine gun and was greeted by screams and moans emanating from the night as his rounds found flesh. A number of Japanese charged his position, forcing Jeeper and his men to be displaced. They hustled to the log bridge spanning the lagoon, only to find that, as feared, it had become clogged by retreating men. Balanced precariously on the log, Raiders hastily crossed the slimy bridge until all were over. Japanese soon followed, several being shot off the log and plunging into the murky water, as Marines conducted a fighting retreat.[2]

Joe Rushton, a BAR man, had been cut off by the Jap push. Lying quietly in the underbrush, cradling his Browning, he heard several of the enemy pass him by. Then came a moment of cold panic as a Jap soldier stepped on his leg. The next sound Joe heard was that of a Samurai sword being drawn from its scabbard. Joe whirled around quickly. A Jap soldier opened fire with his submachine gun, hitting Joe in an arm and a leg. Keeping his wits about him despite the painful wounds, a frightened and enraged Rushton rolled to his left and opened up with his BAR, emptying his twenty-round clip in all directions.

A grenade tossed by an unseen Raider thudded onto the ground nearby and exploded, its shrapnel striking everyone around, including Joe, who took a shard in the behind. Lying amid several Japanese corpses, their blood mingling with his own, Joe played possum. Praying softly, he listened as wounded comrades lying in the darkness around him were bayoneted. When he at last dared to move, Joe crawled a short distance in the direction of the ridge, guided by a strand of communication wire. Pulling himself painfully along, he came across his assistant BAR man, Pfc. Kenneth E. Ritter. Ritter had been badly wounded in the back, by the same burst of submachine gun fire that had hit Joe, and was barely conscious. Unable to leave his friend, Joe grasped Ritter by the left arm and began laboriously dragging him through the brush as Japanese voices pierced the darkness.

Bob Youngdeer's squad had been left isolated as the Japanese tide flowed past them. Out in the night, they heard the sound of Japanese sliding back the bolts on their weapons and then spraying the underbrush. The Raiders dared not return fire, for fear of giving away their positions, so they tossed grenades instead. Then came the horrific sound of wounded Raiders being tortured and killed by enemy soldiers using swords and bayonets.

"The sound of someone being worked over out there in the darkness remains with me to this day," Youngdeer would recall. "The whole battalion could hear their screams."[3]

He was correct. Up on the ridge, the sounds of helpless men being mercilessly murdered was far worse than the sounds of battle, where our men at least had the chance to fight back. The screams filled each one of us with a deep sense of outrage and helplessness, and a yearning for revenge on the animals committing those atrocities.

At Hill 100 on the southern end of the ridge, Bill Waltrip hunched behind his machine gun, listening to the sounds of battle in the black jungle below him while watching for any signs that the Japanese had gained the ridge to his front. However, the only men climbing the ridge and passing through Raider lines were wounded and bewildered survivors from C Company.

"We didn't see a lot of action that first night," Bill would later tell me. "A lot of it was to my left, down in the jungle where Charlie Company was posted."

Baker Company's biggest worry this night was short rounds fired from the smoke wagons of the 11th Marines, who now began adding the weight of their metal to the fight. We in Dog Company had the same concerns. We could hear the 105mm shells tearing through the blackness above our heads and crashing amid dense foliage below the ridge, where Japanese soldiers lurked in heavy numbers. Occasionally, a short round would announce its arrival as an explosion blossomed near our position.

"Lift your aim, you damned cannon jockeys!" I heard MacNeilly's curse coming from somewhere to my right.

But the incoming shells weren't all Marine short rounds. Just after midnight, the *Sendai* and her escorts again started pounding our ridge, and we who were not busy fighting for our lives in the jungle flattened ourselves instinctively as the unseen Jap shells whooshed in at us. Our five-inch coastal guns on the beach fired back, which didn't seem to faze the Japanese, who continued to hammer the battle area for nearly an hour.

Although the Japanese had by now almost fully occupied C Company's former position, they were, to our good fortune, in such a state of confusion that they failed to capitalize on that success. In the absolute darkness of the jungle, unit commanders could not find their men, who, in turn, could not find their own comrades other than the few immediately around them. Sometimes they ended up fighting alongside total strangers.

In fact, only the 2,506 men of the III/124 saw action that night. The other units either got into position too late to take part or drifted totally off course. Adding to the enemy's failure, the diversionary attacks that were to be launched along Alligator Creek to the east never materialized.

With command in such a shambles, Kawaguchi's attacks could not be coordinated, and those assaults that did take place were conducted in short rushes by small groups of soldiers. Most amazing of all was that, despite the gunfire, yelling, explosions, and colored bursting flares overhead, some Japanese units never found the ridge at all that night. The great assault Kawaguchi planned had, in the end, dissolved into little more than a deadly barroom brawl.

Kawaguchi had lost any semblance of control, and he would later

write, "Due to the devilish jungle, the brigade was scattered all over and
was completely beyond my control. In my whole life I have never felt so
disappointed and helpless."[4]

As the first blush of dawn began to streak the eastern sky, the fight
in the jungle blackness slowly ebbed, but the bleeding wasn't over.
Bob Youngdeer and Sergeant Lawrence Holdren, whom we all called
"Pappy" since he was a veteran of Belleau Wood in 1918, began looking
for survivors amid a hellish landscape strewn with bloodied and mangled bodies. The two had begun dragging back one Marine who was
obviously dying, when Youngdeer heard a voice calling, "Anyone from
C Company out there?"

Following the voice, he located Pfc. Charlie Everett of Meadville,
Mississippi, whom the Japanese had beaten, bayoneted, and left for
dead. During the height of the struggle, Everett, a machine gunner with
Neil Champoux's section, had, like his buddies, laid low after Champoux's death and the overrunning of his gun position. Trying to make
his way back to the ridge, Everett was fired on by a Japanese machine
gun. Having yanked the pin from a grenade, he lobbed the pineapple.
The resulting blast took out the enemy gunners, but not before their final
burst hit Everett in both legs and shot his left hand completely off. In
severe pain and unable to move his legs, Everett crawled into the underbrush, where he applied a tourniquet around his left wrist. Then he lay
still, his shoes filling with blood from his leg wounds. Now Youngdeer
and Pappy Holdren found Everett, who was in shock and weak from loss
of blood. Having located a blanket amid the detritus of battle, Youngdeer and Holdren used it as a sled to drag Everett. A Japanese machine
gun stuttered and the Raiders hit the dirt. A Jap sniper tucked away up
in a tree now opened fire. One slug wounded Holdren. Youngdeer was
trying to help him when the sniper fired again, his bullet striking
Youngdeer in the face, just beneath the left nostril, grazing his tongue,
shattering several teeth, and exiting behind his right ear. Youngdeer

collapsed, unconscious. When he regained consciousness, he could see, but he was unable to speak and, he recalled later, he was breathing through the bullet's exit hole in the back of his neck. He also realized that he was alone except for Everett. Badly injured himself, he attempted to drag Everett, but he could not and was forced to abandon him.

"I'll send help back," he whispered, and left.

The wounded Joe Rushton, still dragging the badly injured Ken Ritter, avoided using trails, knowing the enemy would be watching them. Joe worked his way around the northern part of the lagoon, hoping to reach the midpoint of the ridge. Then came a sharp yell and three Jap soldiers charged out of the undergrowth. Joe got off a round, dropping one of his attackers. But now his BAR jammed. Reversing the Browning, Joe used it as a club and bashed the heavy butt plate into the face of a second attacker. The man fell dead, his face smashed in, but before he died, he bayoneted Joe in the leg. The third attacker, seeing his two comrades die, scuttled off into the jungle.

Lying low to avoid any other Japs in the vicinity, Joe faced a new problem. Ritter was becoming delirious.

"Momma, momma," he began calling. For some reason, possibly seeking comfort or out of fear, dying men always seem to call out for their mothers.

Joe clamped a hand over his comrade's mouth, and the twenty-one-year-old was soon gone. There, by the murky lagoon, Joe hid Ritter's body beneath a large fern. He then crawled on. Rushton would be found by other Raiders just after daybreak and carried up the hill.

Near the base of the ridge and struggling to get back were Frank "Whit" Whittlesey and Edgar Shepherd, both of Baker Company. Whittlesey's best friend since they joined the Raiders, Shepherd had been hit in both legs and in the chest, where a round had punctured a lung. Whittlesey knelt over his friend, trying to stem the bleeding and get him out.

"Leave me, Whit," Shepherd moaned. "Get the hell out of here."

"Go to hell, Shep," his friend replied as he began dragging the wounded man.

Neither man was armed with more than just a knife. Shepherd's rifle had fallen into the lagoon and Whit's had been shot away. Still, Whit refused to abandon his buddy, and they labored on together for the relative safety of the ridge. Three Japs suddenly emerged from the jungle. Acting swiftly, Whit plunged his KABAR into the first, then just as quickly jabbed it into the second man. Both fell dead, their life's blood pumping onto the jungle floor. The third Jap, however, was able to stick his bayonet into Whit's back, then flee into the underbrush. Whit slumped down beside his friend, and they lay together, softly talking.

"Well, Shep," Whit muttered. "I guess this is where we came in."

He then briefly hummed his favorite song, telling Shepherd that he was trying to make himself tired so he could go to sleep. Then he died.[5]

Miraculously, Shepherd would make it back to the ridge. Whittlesey's body would be found a day or two after the battle by one of our patrols, and he was buried there, along with one of his dog tags. The dog tag, and the brave Raider's remains, would be discovered by a farmer in 1989 and returned to his family in Massachusetts for burial.

Elsewhere during the hellish dawn, machine gunner Mielke and one of his gun crew came under fire from a Jap machine gun forcing the Raiders to take cover. As the enemy gun's bullets ripped through the foliage, Mielke and the other Raider crept forward, slowly flanking the enemy position. Leaping to their feet, they charged the Japs, driving their bayonets into the astonished crew.

They had no sooner silenced that gun than Mielke spotted another enemy machine gun nest, its crew firing their weapon in the direction of the wounded Youngdeer, who was pinned down nearby.

"There," Mielke said as he pointed out the Jap gun to the man with him.

The two took aim and fired. They missed. The Jap gunner turned his weapon in their direction and loosed two sharp bursts. Mielke and the other man ducked down behind a log that absorbed most of the punishment. Now the enemy gunner again turned his attention on

Youngdeer, seemingly determined to get the Cherokee. Mielke leaped up and opened fire, killing the entire enemy gun crew.

They carried out a wounded Raider on a poncho. Youngdeer walked back to the ridge with two or three comrades until a friend saw how badly he was hit and rustled up a stretcher. Youngdeer would eventually be taken to New Caledonia, then sail home on the hospital ship USS *Solace*. Oddly enough, Youngdeer's brother, Jesse, who was with the Paramarines, had been wounded by a bayonet during one of the hand-to-hand engagements and would also be steaming home aboard the *Solace*. Neither knew about the other until they ended up in the same hospital ward on the ship.

Bob Youngdeer would return to action and end the war in Okinawa with the 2nd Battalion, 1st Marines.

The fight was over, although wounded men walked or were carried into our lines throughout the new day. Charlie Company, along with its attached Easy Company machine gun section, had been mauled, suffering about 50 percent casualties.

Watching the bleeding men stagger to the aid station or, worse, lugged back on stretchers made using rifles as poles and ponchos or shirts as the litter bed, I realized that our undersized Dog Company had been lucky. I wondered if that luck would hold.

"I'll never get used to seeing this shit," Ray Ruble said.

"We're not supposed to get used to it, Big Stoop," I replied. "And I won't forget it. I just wanna get the damned job done so we can all go the hell home."

Not far from where I watched this bloody spectacle, Edson sat on a log, eating cold meat and potatoes.

"They were testing us," he told the men around him. "Just testing. They'll be back. Maybe not as many of them. Or maybe more. I want all positions improved, all wire lines paralleled, and a hot meal for the men. Today we dig, wire up tight, and get some sleep. We'll need it." [6]

As usual, Edson was correct.

CHAPTER SEVEN

"I'LL SHOOT ANY MAN WHO HEADS FOR THE REAR"

BLOODY RIDGE
SUNDAY–MONDAY, SEPTEMBER 13–14, 1942

As the rays of the Sunday morning sun began bathing the ridge, we Raiders were more than a little bit surprised that the Japanese had withdrawn. On Tulagi, they had remained in contact all day with sporadic sniper fire and shouts of "Marine, die," "We drink Marine blood," and "Death to Roosevelt," usually followed by our own "Tojo eats shit" or "Emperor Horehouse Heato eats shit." But I guess that had to do with the fact that on Tulagi, we'd been on the attack rather than playing defense. The ridge proved to be our first encounter with this strategy of avoiding daytime combat. However, it would prove to be their preferred method throughout their struggle to retake the 'Canal, based, as mentioned earlier, on their theory that they were superior night fighters.

For us, of course, it meant we had a chance to lay our weary bodies down for a few hours of horizontal drill, wolf down a little chow, count our dead, and send our wounded to the rear. It was so hard to look upon our friends whose struggles were over, men with whom we had trained, then sailed halfway around the world and had fought beside on Tulagi. Now they would no longer join us on liberty in New Zealand or add their fists to our brawls on New Caledonia with Evans Carlson's much-hated 2nd Raider Battalion or blend their voices with ours in camp songs like "Bless 'Em All," with such stirring lyrics as:

Then we sent for the nurses to come to Tulagi
The nurses they made it with ease,
Their arse on the table each bearing this label
"Reserved for the officers please."

(Chorus)
Bless 'em all, bless 'em all
The long and the short and the tall,
There'll be no promotion this side of the ocean
So cheer up me lads bless 'em all

Edson keenly felt our losses. He was well aware that if he had been unable to form an adequate defensive line with the number of men we had on hand yesterday, he would certainly not be able to do it today when we had even less.

"I don't believe the Nip commander will make the same mistake he made last night and get bogged down in a night attack in thick jungle," Edson told his officers as he planned today's renewal of the fight. "He'll come from that direction," he added, sweeping his hand southward along the open ridge to add emphasis to his words. "He'll come right at us across the open ground so he can bring his superior numbers to bear. I'm surprised he didn't do it yesterday."

He stared at the lush green jungle for a while.

"I just need to be certain where they are," he said.

———————

As we continued to work to strengthen our lines, Lieutenant Wheeler came around.

"Edson wants contact patrols sent out," he said. I looked at him wearily, and he smiled. "Not you, Whitey. You had your turn."

After Wheeler had collected "volunteers," including Stewart and Big Stoop, they were soon off, trudging into the jungle in the direction of the Lunga.

"Thank God for small miracles," I muttered, and went back to work.

The patrol my friends "volunteered" for was a joint foray that included two platoons of Able Company, under their CO, Captain Antonelli, and Sergeant Frank Guidone. As they probed forward near the river, it wasn't long before the patrol ran into trouble. Ahead of them, another patrol, five men led by sergeants Pete Pettus and Horse Collar Smith, had crossed the log bridge spanning the lagoon. Probing C Company's former position, they were suddenly fired on by two of our .30-cals that had fallen into Jap hands. The patrol hit the ground, then Pettus signaled for a retreat. Somehow Horse Collar missed the order, and he soon found himself alone. Hearing Japanese voices growing louder, Horse Collar slipped his bayonet onto the mount at the end of his Springfield and waited. Luckily, Pettus noticed the veteran sergeant's absence. He and another man quickly returned and found Horse Collar. At almost the same time the Japs discovered them. A smattering of gunfire erupted as Pettus, Horse Collar, and the third Marine melted back into the forest, where they soon ran into Antonelli's patrol.

"Japs up ahead," they informed Antonelli, then continued rearward.

Alerted, Antonelli prepared his company for trouble. Crouching silently amid the jungle foliage, the Raiders heard a Jap sergeant snapping orders at his men, but the enemy was not visible. Cautiously easing their way forward, the patrol came across an eleven-man machine gun squad of Raiders who had been cut off the night before. The squad had lain low to avoid detection, and were thankful for the arrival of Antonelli's patrol. The machine gunners carried with them a wounded Marine lying on a stretcher made from two rifles and a couple of ponchos. As Antonelli spoke with the Marine in charge of the squad, the man on the stretcher raised his head slightly and told Antonelli, "I'm fine, sir." He then heaved a sigh and died.

Antonelli pointed the squad in the direction of the ridge and sent them off.

Cautiously continuing ahead, Antonelli's men grew more nervous with each step. Somewhere out in front of them, the shrill sounds of Japanese officers and NCOs barking commands had ceased, and a heavy silence settled in. Every veteran knew this meant that the Japs had gotten themselves into position and were waiting.

The patrol crept a few feet farther on. A fusillade of Nambu machine gun fire ripped through the air, and the Raiders scrambled for cover. They returned fire, vigorously working the bolts of their Springfields, shooting at the noise, because there were no visible targets to be seen. Just above their heads, the foliage danced as bullets pierced the leaves and vines. The Raiders lay prone as they fired, knowing that to rise meant instant death. Antonelli had a couple of mortars with him, but he hesitated using them, because he didn't know exactly where the enemy was positioned.

One Marine pulled a grenade from his belt, yanked the pin, and tossed the pineapple, only to have the grenade come back at him, returned by unseen Japanese hands. Everyone rolled for cover as the grenade burst.

Amid this cacophony of battle sounds, Frank Guidone thought he heard someone call "Marine." Suspecting a trap, he listened closer. The voice came again, not far away. Guidone tapped a couple of his men and indicated they were to follow. The trio slithered forward and spotted a Raider lying on the ground. Antonelli, meanwhile, had pulled his men back and was readying his mortars when he was told Guidone was still out in front.

The wounded man was Charlie Everett, whom Youngdeer had been forced to abandon after being wounded himself. Everett had lain there silently all night, remaining undetected as Japs practically stepped on him. Guidone saw Everett had been hit in both legs, so he used his web belt to bind them and stop the bleeding. Then he and the others dragged Everett rearward.

Antonelli had discovered what Edson wanted to know, and it was time to get the hell out. He could tell Red Mike exactly where the Japanese main line was set up.

"Back to the ridge," Antonelli said, and the men began to pull back the way they had come, hurried along by sporadic gunfire and bullets singing through the trees. Several rounds struck Pfc. Donald J. Coffey in the back, and he was dead before he hit the jungle floor.

Arriving back on the ridge with just that one loss, Antonelli reported to Edson that the enemy had occupied a huge chunk of what yesterday had been Charlie Company's line. Edson nodded to himself grimly.

"That puts them in a perfect position to come down hard on B Company's exposed right flank," he said. "We have to tighten our lines."

The new line Edson began laying out would start with Able Company on the right along the Lunga, exactly where they had been posted the night before. To Able's left would be Dog Company of the 1st Engineer Battalion, 115 men who were discovering the hard way that a Marine is a rifleman first and an engineer second. Yesterday these men had been positioned in reserve. Baker Company would come next, partly deployed in the jungle and partly on the west slope of the ridge, their left flank remaining in the company's original position on Hill 100. This may explain why Bill Waltrip swears he never moved his machine gun during the entire battle.

The 'Chutes would remain in their same position on the eastern slope of the ridge.

Charlie Company, battered and exhausted from the previous night's exertions, was pulled back and ordered to dig in at the base of Hill 120, with Easy Company on their right and us Dog Company guys on their left. This again put me on the extreme left of our line. If the Japs forced us to be displaced, Edson's plan was for all units to fall back on Hill 120, form a defensive horseshoe around it, and fight to the end. Suddenly, Alex Stewart's analogy of two days ago, comparing our position to Custer's Last Stand, replayed in my brain.

With General Vandegrift's reluctant blessing, 2nd Battalion, 5th Marines, was at last ordered up to form a reserve line by the northern slope of the ridge, between us and Henderson Field. He would not, however, allow them to join us atop the ridge. Edson cursed at Vandegrift's apparent misreading of how dire our situation on the ridge truly was. He wanted the men of the 2/5 sent to the ridge to fill out our badly thinned ranks. Edson knew that if the ridge fell, the island could well be lost. But no amount of cajoling by Red Mike could convince Vandegrift of the precariousness of our position. His knowledge of our degree of vulnerability was an immense weight on Edson's already overloaded shoulders.

The line, such as it was, now set, we went back to strengthening our positions, re-stringing more barbed wire where it would do the most good. We also took to clipping the grass to enable our machine guns to sweep the ridge with a grazing fire of .30-caliber slugs three to four feet above the ground level. Additional ammo was carted up from the rear, as were more grenades, "pocket artillery" as we called them. Scanning the ridge from my position, it gave me grim satisfaction to note that the Japs would have to cross at least a hundred yards of open ground to get at us.

Custer be damned, I thought. He lost. Instead, I wondered if the Japs had ever heard of Pickett's Charge.

As the sun climbed higher into the cloudless sky, the ridge was again converted into a broiler oven, intensifying the stench from the dead slain the night before, whose rapidly swelling bodies, bloated by internal body gases, littered the jungle floor. With no cooling breezes to blow away the stink, men puked, adding to the aroma of war. Sweat ran from our bodies in rivulets as we labored, and some men collapsed with heatstroke.

More patrols were sent out, with the password "Lola's thighs" being the safe ticket back into our lines.

Just before noon, Jap bombers from Rabaul were back, which was hardly a surprise. What did surprise us, though, was that the Vs of bombers skimming across the sky overhead avoided our ridge, instead focusing their loads far to the east, around Tasimboko. Somehow, we later learned from native scouts, the Japanese high command did not know where Kawaguchi's men were located. For all they knew, Kawaguchi had taken our ridge the night before, and possibly the airfield as well. Instead, the Japanese commanders assumed there were Americans at Taivu Point, occupying Tasimboko after our "second invasion" on September 8. Again, as had happened that same evening when a similar error was made by the Jap Navy, the only soldiers in Tasimboko were Kawaguchi's rear guard. These unlucky bastards were trying to salvage what they could from their shattered base when their own bombers unloaded on their heads. Frantically they waved Rising Sun flags to alert the airmen of their error, only to be mowed down by strafing Zeroes. By way of proof, the natives brought us the bullet-torn flags.

We voted to give each Jap airman the Distinguished Flying Cross.

As the afternoon deepened, I took some time to once again pore over my well-worn letters from home. After carefully folding them and replacing them in my haversack, I, like many of my friends around me, mentally began preparing myself for the moment when, should it be the Lord's will, I would be separated from this life. I asked only to be able to have the same courage God had given me the night before, and to not let down my friends and to bring only honor to the Raiders.

We were all aware that this could be our finest hour. The Japanese had one objective, which was to push us off the ridge. Should that happen, for those of us who survived, there would be only the jungle and the natives, who, up to now, had been our friends. But who could say what their attitude would be should we Marines be defeated and scattered into the jungle? Would they turn on us in order to spare their own hardships? Who knew?

As for the moment at hand, every fiber in our bodies was in tune with our minds, and all thought was on what was about to happen. Words of caution and encouragement were whispered down the line: "Hold fast. Don't break."

Standing among us men in the late afternoon sunlight, Edson stepped onto a grenade box and called our attention.

"You men have done a great job so far, but I have one more thing to ask of you." He spoke out loudly. "We have to hold out just one more night. I know we've been without sleep a long time, but I expect another attack and I believe they will come through here. If we hold, I have every reason to believe that we'll be relieved in the morning."[1]

Having had his say, he stepped down from the box.

Edson's words went a long way in renewing our spirits, and I am sure every man who heard him was now mentally resolved for the task that lay ahead of us with the fall of night.

Still obviously anxious, Edson and his runner, Corporal Burak, made one last inspection of our positions, uttering the same words of encouragement all along the line. Returning to his CP at last, he scanned the jungle with his glasses one final time before the light faded. Turning to Charlie Company's commander, Captain Thomas, I heard Edson say, "There's no one between the Japs and the airfield but us, Bob. We have to hold this position."

Edson was absolutely correct about the Japanese strategy. Kawaguchi had no intention of repeating the previous night's mistake of groping blindly through the heavy forest. The ridge was the key, and it was the ridge he now planned to take, both through weight in numbers—he had at least three thousand men on hand—and his belief that his troops were more than a match for us Raiders.

We waited nervously in the deepening night, senses on full alert. Every man there felt certain that Hell was about to come charging at us from the forbidding darkness of the jungle. Wheeler came along our company front, wishing us luck and ordering us to fix bayonets. Sliding mine from my scabbard, I slid it onto its mount by the muzzle of my Springfield, making sure it was seated properly. With painstaking deliberation, I checked that the magazine cutoff switch to the left of the bolt was set to "open," then slid back the bolt. Taking a five-round stripper clip from an ammo pouch, I placed it into the open breech, shoved the rounds into the magazine with my thumb, tossed the now-empty clip aside, and slid the bolt closed. I next did an inventory of my remaining ammo clips and grenades. Most of us had just two grenades at this point. More were coming, we were told, but they had not yet arrived.

The night was eerily still. Even the jungle seemed to be silently awaiting the rising curtain. That curtain rose around 9 p.m. when the Japanese Navy returned. Seven destroyers had quietly steamed into the Sound. Now they announced that the show was about to commence as five-inch rounds began whistling in from the north to explode on our ridge. We hugged the ground as shock waves from the detonations rolled over us, sending razor-sharp "grape-nuts" whizzing by our heads like angry wasps.

The naval fire stopped just as suddenly as it had begun, and an ominous quiet again settled over the smoldering landscape. Then from out in the jungle in front of B Company, we heard the sound, faint at first, but gradually increasing in volume. It was the distinct sound of a large body of men moving through the dense underbrush, hastened on by a chorus of shrill commands. Japanese enlisted men were not trained to make decisions on their own, and so their platoon sergeants, or maybe it was their company commanders, were doing a lot of yelling and giving directions. As a result, it proved no difficulty for us to know where they were, because they made so damned much noise. As the enemy advanced through the thick growth, they drove a wave of terrified small animals ahead of them, scampering helter-skelter around and through the waiting Marines. This would have been funny had it not been so deadly serious.

The initial blow struck Baker Company's right flank near the lagoon. The I/124 Infantry, Borneo veterans led by Major Yukichi Kokusho, surged forward into a maelstrom of Marine hand grenades. Men on both sides yelled in outrage as they clashed in the dark, killing with rifle butts, bayonets, and our thin-bladed, razor-sharp Raider stilettos. Hurling all of their grenades, B Company beat back the first lunge, but a second was soon coming at them. The mad rush of screaming Japanese soldiers flowed forward like a human tidal wave, forcing Baker's right flank out of position and back toward the ridge. Like Civil War skirmishers eighty years earlier, our guys made an orderly retreat, falling back like a jackknife blade folding on its handle, firing and throwing grenades as they went, in order to slow the enemy tide.

It was a terrifying, hellish fight, with Japanese lunging up out of the dark, bayonets gleaming, to rush the Raiders.

Baker's withdrawal was not without some confusion. Two B Company squads met in the dark, each one ready to fire on the other. Luckily, someone yelled, "Where in the hell is the goddamned trail?" Knowing no Jap cursed like that, the two squads held their fire and, instead, joined forces and pulled back as one.

The displacement of Baker Company opened a gap that led straight to Henderson Field between the base of the ridge and A Company, but Kawaguchi either didn't know this or inexplicably failed to exploit it. Or perhaps, we later assumed, this initial assault was a diversion meant to draw us off the ridge and away from his main assault point.

As for Kokusho, he also failed to press his advantage and thereby possibly missed an opportunity to roll up our exposed flank. Worse, his assault now broke down totally when his men overran a cache of our supplies. Short on food for the past several days, the hungry Japanese stopped to wolf down our C-rations. I have little doubt that, being half-starved, they enjoyed them more than we did.

The next move was Edson's. Should he use his few reserves to plug this dangerous gap, or should he risk being encircled when the Japanese returned in force, which they were bound to do?

If "Eddie the Mole" was undecided, the enemy soon decided for him. Even as Baker Company's men were executing their fighting withdrawal to the ridge, Edson received a report from a B Company runner that Japanese soldiers were massing around the southern tip of the ridge, making enough racket, via their knee mortars and loud shouts, to be heard all the way to Tokyo.

Edson nodded grimly as he received the report.

"They're gonna launch an attack on our center," he said.

He turned to Burak.

"Walt! I want Charlie Company and Torgeson's Able Company to form a reserve line around the front and sides of Hill 120," he ordered, and sent Burak off to get it done.

Picking up his radio handset, Edson ordered artillery fire on the suspected Japanese assembly areas. The attackers here were men from

2nd Battalion, commanded by Major Masao Tamura. These men of the II/4 had spent much of the day assembling in the jungle in front of Hill 100 for a nighttime assault on that high ground. Because they had so noisily betrayed their presence, the gunners of the 11th Marines began airmailing 105mm shells in Tamura's direction. This was around 10 p.m., and we grimly listened to the outgoing shells hum through the night sky overhead. Tamura's response to the artillery barrage that began pummeling him was to send two companies, around three hundred men, charging up the face of Hill 100, bayonets gleaming by the light of their own flares, covered by their own mortars.

Waves of "Banzai"-shrieking Japanese soldiers led by officers waving Samurai swords swarmed up the slopes all across our front. Dug in on Hill 120, six hundred yards behind the now besieged Hill 100, we heard their shrill battle cries mingled with the deep, blended rapid-fire chatter of 7.62mm Nambus and .30-caliber Brownings. The din was punctuated by the thunderclap of exploding shells, both from our 105s and their knee mortars. It was as if we were watching the Earth yawn open, allowing Hell to rise to the surface.

On our left, intense Japanese pressure by troops of the III/124 nearly swamped the Paramarines, and B and C companies fell back in disarray on Hill 120, where the 'Chutes A Company, down to about fifty men, were positioned in reserve.

With the 'Chutes on our left flank now rocked back on their heels, Edson immediately ordered our B Company to vacate Hill 100 and displace back toward Hill 120 before they could be cut off. The company's right flank, already bent back from its original position, quickly moved up the ridge and joined with the center. The left flank, which included Bill Waltrip detached from Easy Company, remained in place.

The pressure on the 'Chutes was intensifying. My position on the left of Dog Company meant the Paramarines were to my immediate left, and I was not only a witness to the battle below and in front of me, but an unwitting participant as Jap bullets began flying in my direction. Not being able to discern friend from foe in order to shoot, I could only watch the hellish melee and listen as the roar of battle in the flame-stabbed darkness before me grew ever louder and nearer.

Frayed nerves snapped when a Japanese magnesium flare, fired from a ship out in the sound, landed near Hill 120 and started a grass fire. A few panic-striken Marines, driven to the brink of madness, yelled, "Gas!"

"Damnit," I heard Alex Stewart curse.

Since we had long ago disposed of our cumbersome gas masks, this shout sent fear through the line. A few frightened Marines, both paratroopers and Raiders, began breaking for the rear, wildly yelling, "Withdraw." It was a terrifying moment for anyone who heard it, and fear like we'd never known began churning our guts. I gripped my Springfield tighter and waited.

As if he had materialized from the battle smoke, Major Ken Bailey arrived on the scene, and using the most colorful language he could muster, he began restoring order.

"Damn you yellow sons of bitches," he yelled. "Get the hell back in line. Shoot the bastards, don't run from them!"

And.

"Don't run. Kill the little yellow bastards."

Yelling, cursing, and, when necessary, kicking ass, Bailey and a few other officers finally got the would-be fugitives back on the line.

By now the battle had drawn near enough so that I and other Dog Company guys could truly start earning our pay. Waves of Japanese, most shrieking at the tops of their lungs, washed up the slope toward us. While I worked the bolt feverishly, the Springfield bucked against my shoulder as I emptied a five-round clip, reloaded, emptied that one, then another, and another. My grenades also went soaring to explode among the attackers. We watched them fall as our fire raked their lines, but more and more just kept materializing out of the darkness, stepping over and on their fallen brethren. I'll never know for certain if I hit anybody for all my expenditure of ammo, but in that mass of screaming, sword-waving, bayonet-lunging men, I figured it was safe to assume that I had left more then one family grieving back in Japland.

Tamura's attack spent its fury. Breaking in blood, the wave receded, leaving the ground coated with the dead, theirs and ours. Like two boxers at the sound of the bell ending the first round, both sides retreated to their respective corners: ours defending Hill 120 Alamo-style, and the Japs fading back into the darkness of the jungle below. The only activity was enemy machine gun fire that continued to sweep the field. Sweat rolled down my face from under my steel helmet.

"Do you think they'll be back, Whitey?" I heard Stewart ask.

"Are you kidding?" I replied. "They won't quit until we kill 'em all, or their CO has your balls hanging from his sword."

"Ha, ha, that's funny, Whitey," Stewart shot back. "You're as funny as a rubber crutch."

"Tell ya what, Alex," I said. "If we get out of this and off this damned island, when we get liberty, the first round's on me."

"You're on, Whitey," Stewart chuckled. "I'll be mighty thirsty by then."

"You're too young to drink, feather merchant," a gruff voice said from behind me, using the Marine slang for shorter men like myself. I turned and saw our platoon sergeant, Stan Kops, who was moving along our line and had overheard me. Kops was much older than most of us. A longtime Marine, he was married with a family and did not have to be here. But he wanted action and had signed up with the Raiders.

"All right, you old bastard," I joked. "I'll buy you one, too."

Kops guffawed.

"You're on, boy," he replied. "Lock and load."

Edson used the lull to do what he could to repair our line and strengthen our positions.

It was about midnight by now, and Edson knew his left was in jeopardy after the Paramarines were forced to give ground during the preceding fight. Sending a runner to Torgeson, he ordered him to launch a counterattack to regain his lost position. The 'Chutes did, and I watched them rush forward with a roar. Bayonets at the ready, the gutsy paratroopers plowed into the Japanese line, overrunning the enemy who was, even then, preparing to renew their attack on our vulnerable flank. With jabbing bayonets and swinging rifle butts, the 'Chutes forced the Japanese back. Men died screaming in agony or outrage, spilling their life's blood on the already saturated earth.

It was horrific, but what I didn't know was that the worst was yet to come.

The night ticked away slowly as both sides took another short breather.

Down in the jungle near the Lunga, Kokusho finally got his veterans moving again. They advanced up the ridge in the dark, aimed straight for us. The sound of the approaching enemy was unmistakable, and we readied ourselves for the hammer blow. Suddenly a painful light stabbed our eyes as the ridge was bathed beneath the glare of a magnesium flare fired by the enemy. Drawing his sword, Kokusho shouted, *"Tsu-geki!"* ("Charge!") as he and his men surged forward. Backlit by additional flares, they came on like a scene out of Hollywood, shouting "Banzai!" and "Death to Marines!" as they raced up the hill through the kunai grass. We cut loose with a deadly hail of bullets and grenades that mowed down both men and the tall blades of grass. Firing into the mass of oncoming Japanese, it was impossible to miss, especially when they bunched up at our barbed wire, where they milled in confusion. Our machine guns took cruel advantage of this and sprayed into the congested knot of men who dropped into bloody heaps three and four bodies deep. Adding to this hell were high explosive shells lobbed in by the 11th Marines artillery, their blasts erupting amid the enemy throng, sending arms, legs, and heads sailing into the night sky. Yet amazingly, many of the Japanese made it through that meat grinder of steel and lead, and were suddenly among us. All along our lines, I could hear the thuds of bodies colliding, and the grunts and shouts of men in desperate hand-to-hand combat.

The thought flashed through my mind as I fired my Springfield into the charging mass, "So much yelling. So much dying."

Time stands still during such moments, so I have no idea how long this attack lasted. But the bloodied Japanese survivors at last pulled back, leaving their mangled dead, including Major Kokusho, strewn across the ridge.

Knowing our horseshoe-shaped position around this knob of a hill was in jeopardy, Edson directed the artillery to keep up a continuous barrage close along our front.

"Whitey," Alex Stewart's whispered voice came out of the dark, "are you alive?"

"Yeah, I'm fine," I replied.

"Think they've had enough?" he asked.

"They want the airfield," I said. "What do you think? Now, pipe down and stay alert."

Alex didn't have long to wait for his answer, as Tamura's veterans, outraged at their first-ever repulse, regrouped on the east slope of the ridge. Now commenced an unrelenting series of assaults, flowing up from the saddle between Hills 100 and 120 and up Hill 100's eastern slope, where Bill Waltrip was waiting with his machine gun. Firing short bursts to keep from overheating the barrel and having to replace it in the middle of an attack, Bill swiveled the gun back and forth as he hosed the attackers. Bill could never remember how many ammo cans he drained, but he kept his loader busier than a one-legged man at an ass-kicking contest, yanking open one metal ammo box after another and feeding new belts into the weapon to satisfy its insatiable appetite.

As these new assaults commenced, a Jap floatplane circling overhead dropped parachute flares that lit up the ridge while they slowly descended to the earth. Despite the eye-squinting glare, we saw a seemingly end- less line of men dashing toward us amid a chorus of the by-now familiar cries of "Banzai," "Death to America," and "We drink Marine blood!"

With barrels hot enough to blister skin, our overworked Springfields and BARs again spat death. I watched the Japs in the front rank fall as if they'd hit a trip wire. Then the next charging line was cut down, then the next and the next. But still they came on, stumbling over their own fallen, charging through small arms fire and exploding 105mm shells that tossed men and parts of men into the air. Then they were back among us again, and I again winced at the frightening sound of bodies thudding into one another, the sickening crunch of rifle butts breaking jaws or skulls, and men yelling in rage or screaming in agony as cold steel sank into flesh.

As this terrifying hand-to-hand fight swirled around me, I again became aware of the pungent scent of chrysanthemum soap we had smelled the night before. It was a smell that I would come to recognize in future battles on other islands. It remains with me to this day.

My movements now became automatic, as a mixture of my Raider training and a sheer will to survive kicked in. Somehow, in all this yelling and crash of bodies and flash of knives and bayonets, it never occurred to me to be frightened. I just did my job as I had been trained. The Springfield bucked against my shoulder as rapidly as I could work the bolt.

Bang, bang, bang, bang, bang.

I didn't count the rounds; I just knew that when the bolt refused to close, the weapon was empty. Instinctively, I removed another five-round clip from an ammo pouch, inserted the clip into the guide inside the open breech, shoved in the rounds, and rammed the bolt closed, automatically ejecting the now empty clip. Then, *bang, bang, bang, bang, bang*, and repeat.

The first wave of attackers broke against our wall of fire, and the tide of battle subsided, but only momentarily. A new charge was approaching even before the bodies of many of those shot down in the first assault stopped twitching. Again the Japanese fell in rows, and again many, too many, reached our lines. Rifle butts again cracked against heads, and bayonets again plunged into bodies. If the bayonet stuck inside a man, as they sometimes did, we were trained to free the blade by squeezing off a round into the Jap's body.

For the third or fourth time that night, the Japanese got among us and through us. From the greenish light of yet another flare, I saw a Jap rush by me. Then a second man loomed up in front, his rifle set for a bayonet thrust. Instinctively, I parried left with my Springfield, knocking his weapon aside, then lunged forward, impaling the man on my bayonet. I felt the *whoosh* of his breath on my face as he exhaled, and heard the grunt of pain, or maybe surprise, from the impact. In the light of overhead flares, I saw the stunned look on his face, eyes open wide in shock. But this was all in the blink of an eye, for I shoved the dying man backward, withdrew my bayonet as he fell, and went back to the job at hand. Still, killing a man close enough that I felt his final breath in my face was an experience that haunts me seventy years later.

Twenty yards behind me atop the hill, Colonel Edson stood erect the whole time, directing the battle. The man seemed to lead a charmed life, for while bullets pierced his clothing, not one touched flesh. Part of the reason for that, I'm sure, was thanks to Johnny Ingalls, one of C Company's BAR men. Assigned by Major Bailey to protect Edson, he lay at the colonel's feet, emptying his twenty-round clips in all directions. If one needs further proof of Edson's luck, consider this: He spent most of the fight on field telephones, keeping in contact with the artillery and Vandegrift's headquarters. At one point, he put down his phone and moved off some distance to attend to another matter. No sooner had he walked away than a Japanese mortar round dropped in right where he'd been standing.

Of Edson's conduct during this desperate fight, one Marine officer who saw him would later recall, "I can say that if there is such a thing as one man holding a battalion together, Edson did it that night. He stood just behind the front lines—stood, when most of us hugged the ground."[2]

A few men, driven to the limits of their endurance, tried to filter toward the rear. Fear is contagious in battle, spreading from man to man until whole squads, platoons, companies, and finally whole regiments are in full flight. Acting quickly, I saw Edson standing there, angry as hell and determined to nip in the bud any attempts to leave.

"Nobody moves," he loudly proclaimed, yanking his .45 automatic from his holster and waving it toward the retreating men. "I will shoot any man who heads for the rear. The only thing they have that you don't have is guts. Get back in line. You'll die in your foxholes."

Edson paced back and forth, yelling as bullets whipped around him, yet not one touched our commander.

Bailey had now joined Edson, and he was just about as lucky, but not quite. One Jap bullet clanged off Bailey's steel helmet, briefly ringing his chimes, and another nicked his cheek, drawing blood.

The results of these two men's efforts were electric. Men who had bordered on panic regained their nerve. No Raider that I have heard of fled from the ridge during the fight.

Just thirty feet beyond where Edson and Bailey were rallying the men's courage, on the reverse slope of Hill 120, our medical team was doing its damndest to keep up with the stream of wounded flowing back from the fighting. Drs. Ed McLarney and Bob Skinner, and Corpsman Karl Coleman, treated men who had been shot, stabbed, or torn by shrapnel from grenades or those damned knee mortars. They worked by flashlights the beams of which were shielded from the enemy by Raiders bravely holding up ponchos.

As the attacks continued, I realized that I had more empty pouches on my ammo bandolier than I had full ones. And my grenades were gone. I kept firing nonetheless. There was nothing else to do. And when the ammo was spent, we still had bayonets, stilettos, and our KABARs. It was a dismal thought.

These despairing thoughts vanished as Marines dragging ammunition crates began to make their way along our lines.

"Ammo," they called to us above the battle roar. "I got ammo. Grab some."

I snatched a new bandolier from one Marine and some grenades from another, and praised God for small miracles.

What I didn't know until later was that it was Major Bailey, Walt Burak, Sergeant Pete Pettus, and a few other stalwarts who had made this life-saving moment possible. Realizing our situation, they hurried rearward, down the northern slope of the ridge and back to Henderson, where they commandeered a truck. Having loaded it with all the crates of ammo and grenades they could lay hands on, they ran the deuce-and-a-half up the ridge along the footpath until Jap fire disabled the truck, then physically lugged the boxes forward. It was one of the many actions that night that would earn Bailey a well-deserved Medal of Honor.

Around this time, a Jap mortar round severed Edson's communication line with the 11th Marines.

"Burak," Edson barked, calling up his runner. "Get back to the artillery. Tell them to keep firing on my last coordinates."

Burak, a courageous man, was off as fast as his legs would carry him. Having delivered the message, Burak returned, but not without first grabbing a reel of communication wire and stringing a new line back to Edson's CP. That was one of Walt's finest traits. He was always thinking of the needs of the battalion. For his actions this night Walt would be awarded a Navy Cross.

The roar and ferocity of the battle seemed to be never-ending, and I wondered where the hell all of these Japs were coming from. Nearing the point of total exhaustion, every one of us thought the whole damned Jap Army had somehow been landed on Guadalcanal without our knowledge and was trying to sweep us from our ridge.

One Paramarine, Captain William J. McKennan, spoke for us all when he said during a postwar interview, "The Japanese attack was almost constant, like a rain that subsides for a moment and then pours the harder. . . . When one wave was mowed down—and I mean mowed down—another followed it into death."[3]

As this longest night of our lives dragged on, we found that not only did we have Japanese swarming our front and flanks like bees to a honeycomb, but they were also starting to lap around the base of the ridge. Portions of three Japanese companies, including two from Tamura's battalion and one from Watanabe's, reeling from heavy losses on the ridge, had begun to move north between our ridge and the Lunga River. Now they were making their way, unopposed, toward Henderson Field.

Our fragile position had been compromised, and our defensive line was porous. Edson knew it was time to call on the reserve.

"I've been hit hard and casualties are heavy," Edson told division

HQ on the radio. "I need more men. Also, we have Japs moving around us to our west, so unless you get ready for them, they'll come through you like shit through a tin horn."

In response to Edson's call, the 2nd Battalion of the 5th Marines began trekking, company by company, to our assistance.

As we took a short breather between attacks, a new and horrifying sound reached our ears. It was the screams of a man, a Raider, being tortured by the Japs out there in the blackness of the jungle below my fighting position. But this wasn't just any Raider. It was Sergeant Kops, who just a short time ago had been joking with me about being too young to drink. Somehow, during their assault on our position, the Japs had grabbed Kops and dragged him off. Now his wails and howls of agony split the night as the Japanese worked him over with bayonets and knives.

"Dear God, that's Sergeant Kops," Ray Ruble said somewhere in the darkness to my right.

"We gotta get him," Stewart said.

"Can't," Ruble replied.

"Big Stoop's right," I added, my teeth gritted. "That's just what the Japs want us to do. You walk out there, and you'll be next."

So we hunkered down, and were forced to listen as Kops screamed and begged someone to come and save him. Every man among us wanted to save him, but instead, we were forced to sit tight and listen to Kops die. I would hear his screams for the rest of my life, and I have never forgiven the Japanese for this senseless act of butchery.

"Bastards," I mumbled to myself as his screams pierced my brain. "Lousy Jap bastards."

I don't know how long the screams and pleading continued, but they finally ended as Stan Kops, mercifully, died.

Now I prayed for his soul. I also prayed that the Japs would come back so we could kill more of them. I hope God granted my first prayer, because he certainly granted my second, for the Japanese were soon streaming back up the slopes of the ridge, coming straight for us.

It was about 4 a.m. now, and Edson, who would also earn the Medal of Honor this night, made the desperate gamble of betting on the accurate aim of the 11th Marine artillery by directing their fire as close as he dared to our defensive ring. Soon their shells came whistling in to burst less than seventy-five yards from our front, dropping on and among the charging Japanese. The enemy tide seemed to vanish amid the yellow-orange flashes and deep, loud roar of exploding 105s. The resulting thunderclaps left many of us temporarily deafened, while concussion from the bursting shells bowled some men off their feet. In the jungle below the ridge, the pressure waves from the ceaseless chain of explosions caused the tops of palm trees to bow in humility to mankind's deadly power.

In a scene that defies description, artillery shells erupted, glowing tracers carved blazing trails through the night in both directions, and men alive one moment were dead the next, some scattered in bloody pieces amid the deadly hell of the combat. The Japanese who survived this night would forever after refer to this battle as "Artillery Hell," and for good reason. By the end of the fight, the sweating men of the 11th Marines had fired more than twenty-eight hundred shells. To Marines back on Henderson and manning other sectors of our perimeter and watching this fight from afar, the entire ridge seemed to be blazing from end to end.

Along the Lunga River, the Japanese who had been working their way around our western flank ran into a battalion of 5th Marines near the northern slope of the ridge. Now the battle raged not only in front of us, but behind us as well. Some of these Japanese managed to skirt the 5th Marine line and make straight for Fighter One, the smaller airstrip our Seabees had recently built adjacent to Henderson. Marine engineers assigned to Fighter One's security stopped this force cold, driving the Japs back with a sharp counterattack. A few Japanese stalwarts made it to Vandegrift's HQ, killing one of the general's staffers. During this melee, it was said Vandegrift himself shot one Jap down with his sidearm. This may not have been planned by the Japanese as a suicide attack, but for these men that was what it amounted to, as many were soon lying sprawled dead on the ground.

Survivors of this deepest of enemy penetrations withdrew back into the jungle and regrouped just inside the tree line. There they looked over their shoulders toward the ridge, where they expected to see their victorious comrades coming to their aid. When none arrived, they realized that the ridge had not fallen, and they sullenly made their way back to the jump-off positions south of Hill 100.

By 4:30 a.m., the Japanese attacks were rapidly losing steam, and as dawn began to streak the eastern sky, they stopped altogether, as the Japanese, battered and bloodied, withdrew into the relative safety of the rain forest. But not all the Japs pulled back. Harassing mortar rounds continued to drop among us, and snipers periodically shot and killed Marines, including our wounded and those trying to help the wounded off the ridge and back to the base hospital. In one instance, a truck loaded with injured men was raked by a Jap Nambu machine gun. The driver and three of his passengers died before Marines killed the gun crew. Teams of Marines began the bloody work of rooting out the snipers, one by one.

Shortly after dawn, Marine observers spotted about a hundred Japanese soldiers foolishly lingering in the open south of Hill 100, possibly preparing for one final, desparate charge. A radio call was sent by Major Bailey himself to the Pagoda, Henderson Field's command center. Soon three P-400s of the 67th Fighter Squadron were lifting their wheels off the runway. As they swept in at treetop level, machine gun slugs from the trio of fighters made swift, bloody work of these men, and the very few who survived filtered back into the underbrush.

As the morning sun began illuminating the ridge, its light exposed the utter horror that the night battle had left in its wake. Bodies, mostly Japanese, were sprawled across the gore-splattered ground, lying twisted in every imaginable contortion. Blood lay in pools on the ground. Just in front of me on the slope of Hill 120, there were at least two hundred enemy dead. Many seemed to have been hit repeatedly by the intense gunfire, while others had been torn apart by the devastating work done by the artillerymen. Where the shellfire was heaviest, severed limbs and bloody guts littered the ground as if dumped from an airplane. There were headless bodies, body-less heads, and limbless torsos. By our feeble barbed wire entanglements, dead enemy soldiers were piled up, while others, unable to fall, hung snagged in death from the ridge's small, spindly trees like ghastly Halloween figures. Edgar Allan Poe could have set the scene around us.

"I'd never seen so many dead men in so small an area," Bill Waltrip would recall.

Our own dead were around us as well, including a young Raider I had befriended when we got to the West Coast en route to the war. He had been a replacement who had joined us just before we shipped out, and I recall him telling me his father was a minister. His boyish face remains in my mind to this day, but his name has been lost by the passing of years.

Gunnery Sergeant Gerald Stackpole was also among the dead, drilled through the chest by a Jap bullet. An old-timer, with sixteen years in the Corps, it was Gunny Stackpole who taught us rubber boat handling back at Quantico, thereby earning the lovingly bestowed title of "Admiral of the Condom Fleet."

A couple of men in our unit, I don't recall who, found Stanley Kops out in the jungle where the Japs had tortured him. One of the men told me Kops died a hard death. I did not ask for details.

One who has never stood in the middle of a battlefield can never grasp what it is like. Hollywood can never produce this effect: the smells, the sickening odor of spent powder, and the sight of smashed and broken bodies. Our ridge had become a charnel house permeated by the stench of death, which worsened as the mercilessly hot sun slid higher into the sky.

During this frantic, two-day fight, we Raiders suffered 135 casualties, while the 'Chutes lost 128 men. Of this number, a total of 59 of our fellows were dead or missing in action, 34 Raiders, the rest Paramarines. The overall loss was about one-quarter of Edson's command.

Although I had no inclination to count them, those whose thankless job was to bury the dead Japs said there were about seven hundred bodies. Tamura's battalion, I think the most heavily engaged, had lost three-quarters of its men. But for the survivors, their trip to hell did not end when the shooting stopped.

That afternoon of September 14, Kawaguchi admitted that his attack had failed and ordered a retreat of all his remaining forces. Since we had destroyed his supply base six days earlier at Tasimboko, Kawaguchi was now forced to take his men westward, beyond the Matanikau River and over miles of forbidding terrain consisting of deep gorges. They climbed steep, slippery-sloped ridges and hacked through dense jungle, in order to reach their comrades at Point Cruz.

Under such conditions, fatigued and haunted by starvation, it did not take long before men began lightening their burdens, by tossing away first their heavy weapons and finally their rifles, packs, spare clothes, and equipment. Without food or medicine, and weighed down with the wounded and those now growing sick from tropical ailments, this march devolved into a nightmarish journey that led Japanese survivors to refer to Guadalcanal as "the Green Death." All along the path, weapons and gear lay abandoned to eventually rust in the harsh climate. Men too badly wounded to keep up, or too sick or too starved to continue, were left where they dropped. If they were able to commit suicide, they did. If not, they simply died, their rotting corpses marking Kawaguchi's retreat route. The laborious six-mile trek would take these miserable wretches five days, and almost every soldier able to walk helped to carry the wounded.

The men of the Kuma Battalion suffered the worst hardships. Trying to follow Kawaguchi's main body, they became disoriented and wandered in the jungle for three weeks before the starved, skeletal survivors stumbled into Point Cruz. Many had been subsisting on roots and tree bark. They drank river water, which left them doubled over with severe and even debilitating stomach cramps. When they finally joined their comrades, they begged morsels of food from men who were almost as starved as they.

Adding insult to injury, our Marine fighters continued to dog the Japanese along the way, and enemy columns foolish enough to leave a visible path or to venture out into some of Guadalcanal's open expanses were bombed or strafed.

When Kawaguchi's emaciated columns finally reached Point Cruz and linked up with other units, the tattered survivors, especially the few left from the Ichiki detachment, spread rumors that we Marines are all blood-thirsty criminals recruited from jails and mental asylums. They told stories of how we severed the arms and legs from Japanese corpses and ran over them with steamrollers. This would have made us proud had we known.

Kawaguchi's report stated that, of the 6,700 men he started the campaign with, he had lost 41 officers and 1,092 enlisted men killed or wounded.

The Japanese high command on Bougainville and back in Tokyo was stunned by Kawaguchi's defeat. The possibility of losing had never entered their minds. But now confronted with the reality, they stiffened their resolve to eliminate the American threat, dispatching elements of the Sendai Division, victors in Hong Kong and Sumatra. Soon these battle-hardened veterans would be sailing along The Slot on barges and destroyers.

As their reward for so hard-fought a battle and for so much suffering, Kawaguchi's shattered Bloody Ridge survivors were kept isolated from these incoming reinforcements so as not to deflate morale. [4]

Just as Edson had told us before the second night's action, we Raiders and the 'Chutes were relieved the morning of September 14.

When the order came to pack up, I remember leaving my fighting position. My legs felt like lead weights. I stumbled about as if in a daze, numbed, looking into the faces of other stunned men whom I knew well but now did not recognize. Like me, they seemed like dulled, almost lifeless forms, moving about this infernal landscape. Suddenly, caught up in the grip of emotion, I lost control, fell to my knees, and openly wept. For whatever reason, fatigue most likely, the thought came to me that we had lost and that we were now retreating. I recalled how Edson had given us instructions that if we should lose the battle and be overrun, we should head for the hills and either kill ourselves or try to link up with the natives and fight as guerillas. But we were to never get captured. So, in my heavily fatigued mind, I now had the impression that we were heading for the hills. Thankfully, those thoughts did not last long. Other Raiders grabbed me and hugged me, and I realized that they, too, had tears running down their faces. It was at that moment that I knew, by some miracle, we had won.

This is the true image of victory following a desperate battle.

———————

As men of the 5th Marines trudged up the hill to relieve us, they gazed at us Raiders as we shuffled down, trance-like, hollow-eyed, feverish, dehydrated. Even Edson looked terribly weary now that the intense strain of the past two nights was behind him. Many of the 5th Marines saluted us or called out, "Well done" or "Good job, Marine."

Passing through the line of the 11th Marines, where the artillerymen were swabbing out the barrels of their pieces following the preceding night's work, it was our turn to show gratitude. We warmly shook their hands and hugged them. They'd saved our asses, and we all knew it.

By late morning, we were back in the familiar confines of our coconut grove. It had been just four days since we had left here to take up position on what was now being called Edson's Ridge, but it seemed more like four years. Many of us, tired beyond all endurance, collapsed. Clean clothes to replace our torn and blood-streaked fatigues, a refreshing bath in the Lunga to wash away the stink of sweat and death, and a hot meal to satisfy our grumbling bellies would all have to wait.

We slept.

CHAPTER EIGHT

"THIS PLACE IS LOUSY WITH NIPS"

"FIRST" MATANIKAU
SUNDAY, SEPTEMBER 27, 1942

If anyone had asked us Raiders what we really needed after two gut-wrenching and terrifying nights of face-to-face combat on Bloody Ridge, many of us would have had the same response: Bring in the ships and get us off this God-cursed island. What we needed was a few weeks of total rest and recuperation, far away from flying bullets, singing shrapnel, and the smell of that damned chrysanthemum soap. We needed time to heal our wounds, mend our jangled nerves, renew our spirits, and shake the high fevers and bone-rattling chills of the malaria that was running rampant among far too many Marines, me included.

That was what we needed. What we got was two days in our familiar coconut grove; two days to lounge in the sun, bathe in the cool, soothing waters of the Lunga, and try to prepare ourselves for whatever Edson had in store for us next.

But even that time was far from fun and games. Every day we heard the shout of "condition red" as the V formations of Jap bombers creased the blue skies overhead. Every day we Marines ran for the meager protection of our foxholes or coconut log–reinforced bomb shelters, and prayed for God's mercy and forgiveness as the rattle and whine of descending bombs grew louder and louder. Every night the Japanese Navy sat offshore and lobbed every caliber of shell at us, the larger ones especially sounding like approaching locomotives. And after each shellacking, we took a tally of the dead and wounded.

Given all the "relaxation" we were enjoying, we might as well have remained on the front lines.

And if the Japs failed to arrive, it was only because rain was falling in torrents, forcing them to remain in their dry barracks at Rabaul, while we were left to hunker down in flooded foxholes, soggy, wet, and miserable. And when the blazing sun returned, so did the Japs, who had as many as two hundred aircraft, including one hundred Zeroes, ready to throw at us. In response, our poor Cactus Air Force, on a good day, of which there were few, could round up twenty-nine Wildcats, six P-400s, sixteen dive-bombers, and three torpedo planes.

These were not good times for the Marines on Guadalcanal. Besides malaria, men suffered from dysentery, gastroenteritis, fungal infections, and a wide array of ailments carried by mosquitoes and the blood-sucking flies that swarmed everywhere. The number of men hospitalized from illness in the division in September was 1,724, and it would climb to 2,360 by October, more than 10 percent of our force.

In addition to illness, we had to contend with large spiders and centipedes six to eight inches in length, rats the size of cats that seemed to be everywhere, and the endless parade of land crabs.

But chow continued to be our biggest health concern. The amount of food supplies our ships could off-load between the time they scurried into Iron Bottom Sound during daylight hours and when they guiltily fled with the setting sun, was insufficient to properly feed the entire garrison. We mainly subsisted on Jap rice, sometimes supplemented with raisins or made into a slimy rice-gruel. We ate only twice a day, leaving many of us malnourished, which added to our exhaustion, as well as our bone and joint pain. And of course, we had to fight off the clouds of flies that hovered around our plates, swiping the insects away with one hand and hurriedly gulping down the food and as few flies as possible with the other.

To help control the symptoms of malaria, during each meal corpsmen stood in chow lines handing out Atabrine tablets. If you didn't take the pill, you didn't eat. Weighing the thought of possible sterility caused by Atabrine (the rumor was not true) against the rice gruel sometimes proved a difficult choice.

Our supply of American cigarettes was also scraping bottom, and many of us began puffing on Jap scrags we'd picked up at Tasimboko or scavenged off corpses we'd looted on Bloody Ridge.

"Seconds on that snipe," a man would call out, requesting the final few puffs on a butt some other Marine was smoking.

What we didn't know, but would later learn, was that this shortage was caused in large part by an air of defeatism that swept through our top-ranking commanders, starting with Vice Admiral Robert L. Ghormley. The South Pacific area commander, along with much of his staff, was not convinced we Marines could maintain our hold on Guadalcanal. Therefore he was reluctant to commit more than the bare necessities in the way of supplies, even though loaded transports bobbed at anchor at New Caledonia and other harbors.

Through all of this, morale among the Raiders plunged unlike anything I had seen before, even though men in other Marine units continued to admire our fighting spirit and courage in defending the ridge and the airfield.

Amid these miserable conditions, we did have some reason for hope. Scuttlebutt making the rounds said that the Paramarines would soon be taken off the 'Canal. Between Gavutu-Tanambogo and Edson's Ridge, they had suffered 55 percent casualties. We considered their impending departure to be good news because we figured we'd be next. The Raiders had suffered losses very similar to the paratroopers, although our percentage rate, 33 percent, was less because our initial numbers had been twice as great.

During our two-day respite, I hiked to the Marine cemetery, located north of the airfield, near the beach. Walking slowly among the rows of graves, most covered with palm fronds and marked by makeshift crosses and headstones of scrap wood, I saw the handwritten names of men I knew and had fought beside. I paused by the marker that denoted the resting place of Stan Kops. The brutal manner of his death at the hands of those animals came back to me, and my mind replayed his screams. To this day, I have never totally forgiven the Japanese for the things they did during the war.

Yet I could not help but think of the Japanese we had slain. They were gathered up and trucked off the ridge to level ground by the 2/5, which had initially relieved us on the ridge. Then a bulldozer was brought in, a trench gouged into the earth, and the torn bodies were tossed in by hand or shoved in with the dozer blade. It was callous and impersonal. But at the time, no one gave a damn. They were the enemy. We killed them because they were trying to kill us. It was that simple and that cold. Yet I knew that the families of those soldiers would most likely never know what had happened to their loved ones. I thought about the letters from my parents safely tucked away in my pack. If anything happened to me, I hoped someone would cover me properly and tell my family where I fell.

Surrounded by these ghosts who kept poking at my soul, I trudged back to camp.

On September 16, the Raiders resumed light patrol duties, mainly probing south along the Lunga. We knew the Japs had withdrawn after the ridge, but we were not sure where they had gone or how far they had fallen back. Except for the persistent snipers, none of our patrols made any major contact, and the only notable incident was, as mentioned earlier, when a patrol led by Captain John Sweeney found and buried the body of "Whit" Whittlesey.

September 17 was a big day. Transport ships dropped anchor off Lunga Point, and landing boats were soon ferrying much-needed supplies to the beach. We stood in awe as we watched shore parties unload what, to us raggedy-assed Marines, seemed like the wealth of the world, right on our doorstep. There were more than 4,000 drums of aviation fuel to feed our air support; 137 vehicles, including trucks, jeeps, and light M3 Stuart tanks or, as we deemed them, "Galvanized Geldings"; rolls of critically needed barbed wire; untold crates of ammo, including 10,000 hand grenades; and 1,000 tons of rations. These latter were largely K-rations, a distinct step up from the C-rations we'd brought with us to the 'Canal. Packed in light brown cartons coated in wax as weatherproofing, they generally contained a tin of meat; jam or canned cheese; crackers; a chocolate bar, "pogey" bait in Marine lingo; cigarettes and matches; powdered lemonade or orange drink mix, although this latter had a nasty acidic taste that left a burning sensation in the mouth and throat; a small packet of toilet paper, which was very popular; coffee; sugar; and chewing gum.

Among the supplies were boxes of condoms, and each of us was issued three packets; not for the usual purpose, but to enable us to store cigarettes, matches, letters, and other valuables in something that was waterproof.

But perhaps just as important as the supplies, the transports also carried fresh troops of the 7th Marines, who were now sloshing ashore through the gentle surf. It was not without some degree of amusement that we watched these men trudge onto the beach in their clean uniforms, with faces not yet sallow from poor nutrition or yellow from the effects of Atabrine, and eyes that were not sunken and bloodshot from strain and fatigue. In return, this boisterous gaggle of new cannon fodder gaped fishlike at us tattered veterans in our rotting uniforms. It made for one helluva contrast.

After the 7th Marines finished off-loading, we remained on the beach, watching the Paramarines prepare to depart. As they passed us, looking every bit as gaunt as we did, we shook their hands, slapped their backs, and said, "Good job, Marine" and "Semper Fi, Mac." We were grateful to them for the way they had held our flank on the ridge, taking their losses but remaining solid. We were happy for them. But we were just as sad for us, and we prayed we'd be catching the next ships steaming away from Guadalcanal.

The outgoing ships also carried 162 of our more seriously wounded men, mostly guys hit on the ridge.

Edson was fully aware of our feelings of envy and disappointment as we watched the Paramarines steam toward the horizon, and he called a general meeting in our camp that evening. Standing amid us as we sat cross-legged on the sand, he said there were no plans to relieve us.

"We are here for as long as it takes," he told us. "In fact, if I had my way, I'd take this battalion straight to Bougainville, and we'd be celebrating Thanksgiving dinner there. We are embarked on a long and bloody road that will eventually lead to Tokyo, so you can pretty much forget about going home until it's all over. You are an elite fighting force of highly trained, tough-as-nails bastards who have earned the respect of our enemies as well as our fellow Marines, and we need you here."[1]

Some of the men appreciated Edson's hard, fighting words, while others grew morose over the bleak prospects of the fighting going on and on until God knows when, and began referring to Edson as Mad Merritt the Morgue Master.

As for the incoming 7th Marines, they quickly learned the hard way about life at the front. Fatigued after their long sea voyage, many chose not to dig in for the night, despite our words of caution, but went to sleep on the sand. As expected, the Japanese Navy paid us a visit after dark, blanketing the Marine perimeter with high explosives. Three men of the 7th Marines were killed and two wounded before they'd ever seen a Jap soldier.

———————

The days of relative inactivity since we left the ridge played on the minds of Edson and his executive officer, Sam Griffith. They did not want us losing our sharp edge, which, although somewhat blunted by poor diet, illness, and the harsh violence we had experienced on the ridge, was still razor-like.

On September 19, orders arrived for a patrol in force along the Lunga to again look for any signs of an enemy buildup to our south. Two battalions would be involved, us and the newly arrived 1/7, led by Colonel Lewis B. "Chesty" Puller. Having saddled up our gear, we struck out through the grassy plain and into the jungle. As we crossed Henderson Field, men watching us whispered, "There go the Raiders." War correspondent John Hersey was there, and later wrote that we struck him as "a gang of bush-fighting specialists."[2] I don't recall that we felt special. Our numbers were down by half from casualties and sickness, but we were determined and self-confident, and more than a little proud of the admiring looks the other Marines shot our way.

Our column snaked south along the Lunga, the 1/7 patrolling the west bank, we Raiders the eastern shore. Our route skirted the base of Bloody Ridge, across the same ground where Charlie Company had been overrun just five days earlier. For the men of C Company, this part of our trek was especially sobering, as memories of that terrible night, fresh scars on the brain, came flooding back.

We found plenty of signs of that hard fight in the way of discarded equipment, shattered weapons, trees pockmarked by bullets, and underbrush stained black with dried blood. Farther along, we began finding the decaying remains of dead Japanese who had been wounded in the fight. Some had staggered this far before dying from their injuries, while others, simply too weak to keep up, had plopped down here to await death, alone and probably afraid, thinking, no doubt, of home. War is horrible regardless of what uniform one wears.

We found no signs of any large buildup, but we knew that Japanese were still close, because we began attracting sniper fire. One of the bastards almost punched my ticket as I felt a bullet buzz past my ear, even before I heard the crack of the rifle. Diving for the ground, I hugged the jungle floor as the Arisaka snapped again and again. With each bark, I felt a plucking sensation as rounds penetrated the small LMO (light marching order) pack strapped to my back. Desperately, I rolled hard and fast to my right. The bullets stopped coming at me, so either I had rolled out of his sight or one of the Raiders who was returning fire had hit him. I didn't know which, nor did I care. All that concerned me was that the fellow never touched my flesh.

Edson was not taking any chances on this patrol. Artillery fire delivered by the 11th Marines was called in whenever we encountered even the slightest resistance. We simply crouched low and let the men working the smoke wagons pulverize enemy positions.

Our patrol was not fired on again until our return trip. Passing the foot of Bloody Ridge, now on our right, bullets once more came humming our way, accompanied by the sound of rifle fire. Only the rifles sending rounds our way were not Arisakas, but Springfields held by the jumpy men of the 2/7 and 3/7, recently posted atop the ridge. We hit the ground and some of our fellas shot back. Edson, who characteristically remained standing, scanned the ridge with his binoculars.

"Cease fire," he yelled. "Cease fire, damnit. They're our guys."

"We know," came an angry reply.

The shooting on both sides was halted before anyone was injured, and we continued on into camp. However, the friendly firefight by the ridge had alarmed the airmen on Henderson, who feared the Japs were returning to attack the field. When they saw us crossing the plain from the direction of the ridge, they heaved a collective sigh of relief and gratefully handed us cigarettes and pogey bait.

We found and killed nineteen Japanese during this patrol. We also captured a Jap howitzer that had been partially disassembled for transport then abandoned by men too weary to drag it away. Three of our number had been wounded.

On September 21, the Raiders received more shocking news. Edson was being promoted to full colonel and given command of the 2/5. Sam Griffith would take over the reins of the Raider battalion. Some men were happy to be rid of Edson, whom they wrongly felt was somewhat cavalier with the lives of his men. Others were sad to see him go, for they knew he was a terrific combat leader. I tended toward the latter, although I knew Sam Griffith was also able, having been groomed by Edson for the job. Most of us who knew Griffith were confident he'd do well.

When Edson moved up in command, he took a few men with him, most notably Lew Walt, who would serve as his operations officer but would eventually command the 3/5, and Walter Burak, his runner. Edson also wanted to take along Ken Bailey, but he knew Griffith would raise holy hell about it, so he left Bailey with the Raiders. Not unexpectedly, Griffith made Bailey his executive officer.

Edson did not bother with any type of farewell speech to the men; that wasn't his style. He simply informed us in a matter-of-fact manner of the changes by releasing a Battalion Order, in which he expressed his pleasure in leading such an "admirable body of men."[3] It was typical of Edson's reserved personality.

One of Griffith's first moves was to reorganize the Raiders and tighten up the unit, which was riddled with holes from our losses. The change that most affected me was the elimination of Dog Company. Lieutenant Wheeler, our company CO, was promoted to captain and placed in command of Baker Company, displacing John Sweeney, who had less seniority. With Lew Walt's departure, A Company was permanently placed under Captain Antonelli; C Company remained under Captain Robert Thomas. The men of Dog Company were dispersed among the remaining companies.

I wound up in Easy Company, and assigned to a machine gun squad that included Bill Waltrip. At first I wasn't happy about being separated from Big Stoop, Alex Stewart, Mac MacNeilly, and the others, but with the Raiders so depleted from losses, I was still able to see them regularly. But now I had a new squad to get used to, a seven-man machine gun squad into which I was now being thrown.

I had met Bill Waltrip before, just as I had met and gotten to know many of the Raiders, but we had not yet become the tight friends we would be years later. Bill, who insisted on calling me "son," which he does to this day, hailed from Illinois and served as the machine gunner. His assistant gunner was an Iowa boy named William L. Brown. Like Waltrip, (John) J. T. Allen was a product of Abraham Lincoln's adopted home state, hailing from Mount Vernon, Illinois; Boyer White was from Arlington, Texas; and Charlie Carrigan lived in Los Angeles. The nearest to my home state of Pennsylvania was Hank Green, who was from Canton, Ohio.

Our section leader was Corporal Daniel Carroll, but he was soon transferred to B Company, and I never got to know him very well.

Carroll would survive the war only to die during the landings at Inchon in Korea in 1950.

All this time, about five miles to our west, the Japanese were building up their forces, still intent on wiping out our foothold on the island. But Kawaguchi had his work cut out for him as he tried to establish a solid front consisting of his own weak, sick, and emaciated veterans fortified by healthy, fresh incoming troops who were arriving via the Tokyo Express.

We knew about these incoming fresh troops, of course, thanks to our Henderson Field flyboys and the British coast watchers manning lonely outposts on islands bordering The Slot.

One Jap infantry unit, the III/4, the Aoba Regiment, had landed at Kamimbo Bay on the far western point of Guadalcanal on September 11 and moved to join Colonel Akinosuke Oka's troops of the II/124 near the Matanikau. There the two units were supposed to attack eastward in support of Kawaguchi's assaults on Bloody Ridge. But even as their comrades of the II/4 were falling before our guns on the ridge on September 14, the III/4 failed to get into position in time to take part in the battle.

After Bloody Ridge, the Tokyo Express kicked into high gear. Using fast destroyers, the enemy delivered 280 infantrymen of the I/4, along with supplies and ammo, between September 14 and 24. In addition, the Jap high command turned to the Dutch East Indies, transferring the 2nd and 38th Infantry divisions, more than seventeen thousand men, to Rabaul in preparation for possible deployment to Guadalcanal.

Still reeling from his defeat at the Ridge, Kawaguchi knew the only way the Japanese would retake the 'Canal was to capture Henderson Field. To that end, he dug in along the Matanikau River, bringing up several newly arrived Type 96 150mm field pieces from Kokumbono. This put Henderson Field within Japanese artillery range.

General Vandegrift and his staff were aware of this enemy presence breathing down our necks just a few miles beyond our western perimeter. So Vandegrift decided that the only way to keep the Japs off-balance and maintain the initiative we had gained in such victories as Alligator Creek and Bloody Ridge was for us to strike them first. To accomplish this, Vandegrift would use a two-pronged advance up the Matanikau Valley using the 1/7 under Puller and us Raiders.

Four or five miles west of the Lunga, the Matanikau River was deeper and more turbulent than its eastern neighbor. The waterway cut a swath between sheer coral ridges, the slopes of which were blanketed with gently waving fields of tall grass, before reaching the more level coastal plain. About two thousand yards upstream from the beach sat the One Log Bridge, which spanned this largely unfordable waterway. Since it had been placed by Japanese engineers, we dubbed this span the "Jap Bridge" or "Nippon Bridge." The best place to cross this river on foot was at its mouth, which, like the Lunga's, the Tenaru's, and all the others, featured a large sandbar where the river's waters blended with Iron Bottom Sound.

Vandegrift's plan, approved by Edson, who would be in joint command of this operation, was for Puller's Marines to push west from our perimeter, then cross the Matanikau at the One Log Bridge. They then would "mop up" any Japanese they found, clearing the way for us Raiders, who would advance west another six thousand yards, or, as we put it, "deep into Indian country," to set up an advance base at Kokumbona. The goal was to prevent Jap heavy artillery from getting within range of Henderson Field.

But now it was our turn to make a critical error. Just as the Japanese misjudged the number of Marines that had landed on the 'Canal, now we underestimated their numbers. Vandegrift guessed there were about four hundred Japanese clustered around and beyond the Matanikau. We discovered the hard way that there were closer to two thousand.

That's because, convinced that the American high command was going to make a major landing around the Matanikau River, Kawagu-chi had ordered Colonel Akinosuke Oka to dig in there with his 124th Infantry Regiment, nineteen hundred men. Oka did his work well,

sending one unit, the Maizuru Battalion, across the Matanikau to defend both the eastern bank of the river and the base of Mount Austen.
The rest of his men he deployed on the river's western shore. Also unknown to us was the presence of a large enemy force at Kokumbona,
putting as many as four thousand battle-tested Japanese veterans within
easy marching distance of our advancing forces.

We, on the other hand, had 930 men under Puller and a meager 200
or so Raiders. As Sam Griffith would later put it, this was a major intelligence snafu (situation normal all fucked up).

Puller's 1/7 stepped off first. Marching westward on September 23, they
quickly clashed with two Japanese patrols that were sent to scout our perimeter. Brushing them aside, the Marines pushed on. By nightfall, they
had made camp near Mount Austen, ready to climb the hill the next day.

They did, and at around 5 p.m., as they cautiously picked their way
through a field of kunai grass ten feet in height, often making it impossible to see the man next to them, they blundered into a Japanese bivouac. After the brief, violent firefight that followed, all sixteen of
the enemy lay dead. But the gunfire had alerted men of the Maizuru
Battalion, which Oka had placed there to defend the area. These battle-
hardened veterans launched screaming attacks against the Marines,
who reacted with a blaze of rifle and machine gun fire that mowed
down attackers and kunai grass alike. Oka ordered his men to slowly
pull back to the west side of the Matanikau. They did as ordered, leaving thirty of their comrades lying dead amid the bullet-clipped grass.
Puller had lost thirteen killed and twenty-five wounded, and he radioed to Vandegrift for help. In response, Vandegrift dispatched the
2/5, under Lieutenant Colonel David McDougal, to reinforce Puller.

McDougal's men linked up with Puller's 1/7 early on September 25.
Puller sent his casualties to the rear, along with three of his companies,
most of whom served as stretcher bearers. He then pushed on with his
assignment with what remained of C Company and the men of the 2/5.
Reaching the bank of the Matanikau the next day, they attempted to
force a crossing at the One Log Bridge. Japanese resistance across the

river, however, proved formidable, so Puller changed direction north toward the beach, hoping to cross the river at the sandbar. But Oka's men staunchly defended the river's mouth, and this attempt also failed.

As Puller's crossing the Matanikau was being thwarted, upstream at the One Log Bridge, more than one hundred heavily armed Japanese re-crossed to the eastern shore and began setting up a defensive position along the river.

That evening, Puller and Edson devised a new plan. This called for the Raiders, whom Vandegrift had begun calling his "fire brigade," to step off next morning and make our way upriver to cross at the One Log Bridge, which, so far as Puller knew, was now almost undefended. Once across, we were to push back downriver and attack the Japanese at the sandbar on their flank. As we assailed the enemy, the 2/5 was to charge across the sandbar while Puller's three companies who had served as stretcher bearers on September 25 boarded Higgins boats and were landed behind the Jap lines near Point Cruz, with the objective of cutting off any Jap retreat.

At least, that was the idea.

It would all kick off the next day, September 27.

We Raiders were given the orders to break camp on September 26, so we packed up and began the westward hike. As we formed, I walked past an E Company buddy named Eugene Diamond, who was a cutup. He was still squatting in his foxhole.

"What the hell is with you?" I inquired.

"I can't get out of my hole," he replied.

"Like hell you can't," I told him. "Get your ass moving."

"Nah," he answered. "I'll see you at the Golden Gate, Whitey."

"You son of a bitch," I said. "You're gonna die right here on this damned island just like me. So come on."

I moved, and Diamond soon caught up.

As we approached the Matanikau, we heard the rattle of gunfire from up ahead, a sure indication that Puller and his men had made contact. Nearing the east bank of the river, we dug in just as a heavy rain began to fall. We spent a gloomy, miserable night listening to the heavy drops drumming incessantly on our steel helmets and the rubber ponchos we had laid out in an attempt to keep our gear from becoming totally saturated.

At 7 a.m., abandoning our swamp-like foxholes, we trudged south along the river, emitting clouds of evaporation as the rays of the morning sun warmed our wet uniforms. This was slow going through heavy vegetation and we made about five hundred yards an hour. We knew the Japanese across the river could see us. Every so often, they'd send a mortar round our way, which generally either crashed into empty jungle beyond us or splashed into the river on our right, sending up a geyser of brown water.

My machine gun section had been assigned to 3rd platoon of A Company. The platoon leader was Lieutenant Richard "Red" Sullivan, who had landed on Tulagi as a sergeant but earned himself a battlefield promotion. We were point platoon for this march, meaning we were at the head of the column as it snaked along the riverbank. Advancing with us was Major Ken Bailey, our battalion XO. I was glad to have Bailey with us. He was as popular as he was courageous, and something of a good luck charm. Bailey had been wounded on Tulagi, and we had missed him. He returned in time to join us atop the ridge, where he had served magificently, standing up amid the hail of flying lead to make damned sure none of our guys bolted to the rear. A Congressional Medal of Honor was in his future for his actions in that fight.

I happened to be walking beside him, and he glanced over at me and smiled.

"Ready to kill some Japs today, Whitey?" he asked.

"Yes, sir," I replied with youthful bravdo. "We'll send them to their ancestors."

Bailey chuckled.

"How is your wife doing, sir?" I inquired. "Have you heard from her lately?"

I remembered how he had gotten married just before we shipped out, and how he had so proudly passed around her photo to make the rest of us jealous.

"She's doing just fine, Whitey, thanks for asking," he replied with a grin. "Just like you and me, she's eager for this damned war to end."

He moved on to chat up the next man. He was like that. Officer or enlisted man, you just liked the guy.

It was around noon when we reached a spot about two hundred yards downstream of the One Log Bridge, where a small tributary fed into the Matanikau. As our column wound at a snail's pace along the river's eastern bank, the sharp rattle of a Japanese Nambu machine gun sent us sprawling as bullets swept by overhead.

"Stay low," Bailey told us.

He crept forward a short distance, accompanied by his runner and a radio operator. Along with Red Sullivan, they formed a small circle along the trail, just by where the bank sloped down to the water, and began to discuss the situation in hushed tones. Bailey raised his head in an attempt to spot the Jap emplacement. The Nambu sang again. Bailey grunted slightly, then dropped to one knee, holding his head in his hands. The machine gun continued firing.

"Get down, sir," Sullivan yelled to Bailey.

When Bailey did not respond, Red grabbed an ankle and yanked him to the ground. But it was too late. One of the sharp-eyed enemy's slugs had struck Bailey squarely between the eyes. That quickly, he was dead, just three weeks short of his 32nd birthday.

Red Sullivan, kneeling over Bailey, needed but one glance to know that the popular officer was beyond mortal help.

"Oh, damn," Sullivan moaned, speaking for all of us as he sank back on his haunches.

Disbelief was our first reaction, then tears began glistening in the eyes of some of the toughest men in the United States Marine Corps as word spread back the column that Bailey had been hit. To a man, we felt his loss deeply.

As for me, I just stared at his lifeless body. I recalled having spoken to him so briefly just a short time ago, and the hope that was in his voice of a rapid end to the war and a return to Elizabeth, his young bride. Now his war was over. Then I thought of her, and wondered what she was doing at this very moment, unaware of the grief heading her way via Western Union.

But maybe this wasn't Ken Bailey lying on the ground before me in a lifeless sprawl. It didn't look like him. I found that in death, most men didn't change appearance. Facial recognition of the dead is generally easy. But Bailey did not look like himself. He'd been hit hard and his face was mishapen, his skin so dark. Yet, deny it as I might, I knew better.

As is the case in combat, we were forced to postpone our mourning as more Japanese machine guns opened fire, and we realized they had this area covered by deadly, interlocking fields of fire. Rounds from sniper rifles began nipping at the foliage above our heads, and a few mortar rounds began dropping in, most falling short, killing nothing but fish in the Matanikau. Our guys began firing back. Waltrip set up his machine gun and sent bursts across the swirling river, shooting not so much at men, but at sounds and movement in the underbrush across the water. We of the squad added our rifle fire to the cacophony of battle.

Griffith soon arrived, the news of Bailey's death having reached his ears. As he took one look at his dead XO, a dark anger crossed his face. Enemy fire was coming from everywhere, including in front of us, where the Japs held the ground between a ridge to our left and the river to our right.

"God damnit," he raged. "This place is lousy with Nips."

Under heavy fire, Griffith assigned Able and Baker companies to hold our positions, while he took C Company out to see if there was some way to outflank the Japs. As they departed, Bailey's body was carefully placed on an outstretched poncho by Corporal Tom Driscoll and Sergeant Horse Collar Smith. With profound sadness and great care, the two NCOs began lugging their mournful load to the rear. Bailey was a solidly built man, and quite a load for Driscoll and Smith.

The poncho kept slipping from their grip, and they frequently tripped on tree roots, but they were determined to bring Bailey out.

As that small, sorrowful procession stumbled rearward, Charlie Company followed Griffith forward. Griffith's idea was to scale the steep, slippery slope of the ridge on our left in an attempt to get around the Japs. Again, the going was painfully slow as the men were forced to walk in a single line. As the column neared the top of the ridge, the Japanese spotted them. Machine gun and mortar rounds rained down on the Raiders. Griffith went down as a bullet ripped into his shoulder.

"Keep going" was the order shouted to the men, possibly by Griffith. Dutifully, they tried to push along the ridge, only to be stopped by some of the heaviest fire they'd experienced since Bloody Ridge. Grudgingly, C Company was forced to concede that they were stymied. Griffith, his painful wound temporarily dressed but still throbbing, led his men back down the slope. At the base of the ridge, A and B companies rejoined the column, and we started a slow withdrawal back toward the beach. We'd not only been stopped, but, for the first time, we had been turned back. We could not believe it and our anger became mixed with humiliation.

But things were about to get worse, although not for us. Griffith sent back a radio message, telling Edson that there was no way we could force a crossing of the river at the bridge. However, the radio transmission got garbled thanks to a Jap air raid on Henderson Field, and Edson thought Griffith had told him the Raiders were across the river. Orders went out to the 2/5 to attack over the sand spit and for the 1/7 to land their Higgins boat force west of Point Cruz.

The 2/5 surged ahead and ran into a wall of fire from the Japs west of the Matanikau, where the enemy had been reinforced the night before by the 124th Infantry Regiment. The Marine attack was stopped cold, and McDougal's battered survivors fell back.

Puller's men walked into a near disaster. His three companies, under the command of Major Otho L. Rogers, stormed ashore from nine landing boats. What they were unaware of until it was too late was that the landing zone was directly in front of a Japanese bivouac area. The wary enemy watched them land, and then allowed the Marines to push inland about six hundred yards before storming down on them from three sides. Frantically digging in on a rise that would become known as Hill 84, the Marines fought savagely as enemy bullets and mortar shells tore into their ranks. Rogers, giving commands to his men, died when an exploding mortar round severed his body in half.

Captain Charles Kelley, a company CO, assumed command of the force, which now found itself totally surrounded by Oka's men. The besieged Marines had taken no radios with them, so there was no way to signal for assistance. Desperate, they stripped white T-shirts from their bodies and used them to spell the word HELP in a clearing on the ground. An SBD Dauntless dive-bomber assigned to provide air support spotted the plea and radioed back to Henderson.

By now, Edson had learned that Griffith had not been able to cross the Matanikau.

"Damnit." He fumed and turned to Vandegrift. "They can't seem to cross the river. We've got to call them off."

Puller, thinking of his men now cut off from the beach, was with Edson and Vandegrift at HQ when the situation became clear. When he asked about how best to withdraw the men on Hill 84, Puller was dismayed when he realized that Edson was balking at risking more Marines on a rescue mission.

An outraged Puller, thinking his men were to be abandoned to their fate, stormed out of the HQ, headed for the fighting.

Outside, the feisty Marine leader managed to get a lift from the Navy, boarding the destroyer USS *Monssen*, one of the ships assigned to support the operation. He had the *Monssen* take him to a position just off the mouth of the Matanikau, then secured ten of the landing boats that had taken the Marines ashore and headed for the beach. There, using signal flags, he made contact with Kelley. Now it was the Navy's turn to shine. With Puller playing the role of artillery spotter, the *Monssen*'s five-inch guns began pulverizing the Japanese positions that blocked Kelley's escape route. For half an hour, the *Monssen* blasted the area, and the jungle exploded with fire and smoke, mingled with the screams of Japanese caught in the dead-on-target shelling. The plan worked. Kelley and his bloodied survivors were able to punch through the devastated Japanese lines and struggle back to the beach. Oka's men made one more attempt to prevent their escape and laid down a heavy fire on the beach. The *Monssen*, along with the Coast Guard men manning the machine guns on the Higgins boats, returned a concentrated covering fire.

During this withdrawal Coast Guard Signalman First Class Douglas A. Munro was killed. The twenty-two-year-old Munro was in charge of the Coast Guard's end of the rescue mission and was covering the last of the Marines being evacuated. Grievously wounded, the young man's dying words were "Did they get off?" He would receive the Congressional Medal of Honor posthumously, making him the only member of the Coast Guard to be so honored.

As we Raiders plodded back toward Henderson Field and our bivouac area, every one of us knew the operation we'd just experienced had been a defeat. We'd failed in our mission, and it stung us deeply. We'd lost twelve men wounded, including Griffith. One of the wounded men, Pfc. Julian Dobson, an eighteen-year-old kid with C Company, would later die in the field hospital. Perhaps worst of all, we lost Ken Bailey forever. All that, and we had gained nothing in return.

Griffith, before he was evacuated to a hospital, not to return for several months, called the First Matanikau "ill-conceived" and "ill-conducted," and said it was "the only really inept operation that the Marines conducted on Guadalcanal."[4]

He was correct. While we only knew the portion of the action we had experienced, in point of fact the entire thing was a tactical and strategic train wreck. The idea was for the Marines to "mop up" the remaining Japanese on Guadalcanal once and for all. Instead, the Japanese took that mop and beat us about the head with it, inflicting over two hundred casualties on us, including more than sixty dead. When the Japanese reoccupied Hill 84, they counted thirty-two Marine bodies.

As we dragged our sorry asses away from the river, the Japanese were elated. Turning back our offensive energized their headquarters back in Rabaul into renewed efforts to retake the island. This had been the first bit of good news to reach their ears since we first stormed ashore on August 7. After our invasion, except for Savo Island, it had been one defeat after another for them. Now they felt the initiative had turned in their favor.

For the Americans, it didn't take long for the finger-pointing to begin among our commanders for what was considered an embarrassing defeat. Puller, possibly with some justification, blamed Edson. To a much lesser extent, he also blamed Griffith and, by extension, the Raiders, for our failure to complete our end of the assignment by crossing the One Log Bridge. He complained that he had led a patrol across the very same ground we followed just a day earlier with minimal effort. What Puller did not take into account was that between the time he had led his men along this trail and the time we marched in, an entire company of heavily armed Japanese had taken up position squarely in our path. Puller and the 1/7 had missed them literally by minutes. The next day, we ran squarely into them.

But blame for the Matanikau setback continued. Griffith blamed his former chief, Edson, as well as Vandegrift's assistant operations officer, Lieutenant Colonel Merrill B. Twining, who had jury-rigged the operation without adequate information. Twining, in turn, blamed Puller and Edson.

For Edson, "First" Matanikau would be the only defeat of his career. For the Marines on Guadalcanal, it would be our only defeat as well. (Historically, this was actually the second Matanikau battle, the first being fought by the 1/5 on August 19. Since the Raiders were still on Tulagi at that time, we dubbed the September 27 action as "First" Matanikau.)

What we did not know, as we dropped our packs and settled wearily back in our familiar coconut grove "home," was that within nine days, we'd be back on the bloody banks of the Matanikau.

CHAPTER NINE

BACK TO THE MATANIKAU

"SECOND" MATANIKAU
WEDNESDAY–FRIDAY, OCTOBER 7–9, 1942

With Colonel Griffith headed toward a field hospital to be treated for the wound he received on the ridge above the Matanikau on September 27, Captain Ira "Jake" Irwin took over as our commanding officer. At age thirty-three, Irwin was a pudgy, jovial sort of guy. He was a very caring and competent officer, but unlike Edson and Griffith, he was not overly warlike when it came to combat. As his executive officer, Irwin tapped Charlie Company's commander, Captain Bob Thomas, who would be replaced as C Company's CO by Lieutenant John "Black Jack" Salmon. One other change was to replace A Company's commanding officer, Captain Antonelli, who was suffering a relapse of his malaria, with Captain Robert Neuffer.

For us Raiders, we stayed in our coconut grove home, which over the many weeks of our stay had become dotted with lean-tos and small shacks, built by Raiders using scrap pieces of corrugated iron, Jap rice bags, old supply crates, palm fronds knocked down by incessant bombings and shellings, and similar "building material." The place had taken on the appearance of photographs I'd often seen during the Depression of a Hooverville, the ramshackle villages erected by displaced, out-of-work families and named for President Herbert Hoover.

Our routine also included keeping a wary eye out for enemy bombers by day and ships by night. In other words, things were back to what passed for normal on Guadalcanal. But even normal can be dangerous, as I soon found out.

A day or so after our return from the Matanikau, Japanese Bettys were overhead in their all too familiar V formation, bomb bay doors open. The frequency of these raids, plus the fact that most were headed for Henderson Field, left many Raiders with a blasé attitude toward this daily annoyance. Men bathing in the Lunga didn't even come out of the water to take shelter. Not one to tempt fate, when the Japs were overhead, I ran for my foxhole, dove in, and hunkered down.

On this particular day, as I cowered there, I heard the swishing sound of a descending bomb, louder than I had ever heard it before. With a wrenching in my gut, I realized this one was coming close. Silently I prayed for my soul, while digging down into my foxhole as deep as I could go, as the noise grew louder and louder. The blast, when it came, jarred the earth worse than anything I had ever experienced. I felt myself being lifted up as if plucked by the fingers of God, and I was tossed several feet into the air, tumbling over and over, until I was slammed, none too gently, back onto the ground. I lay there, momentarily stunned as Alex Stewart and Big Stoop Ruble rushed to my side.

"Whitey! Whitey!" Big Stoop said urgently, checking me for wounds. "Are you all right?"

I was, and with their help, I rose unsteadily to my feet and shook myself off. Looking at my friends, I saw their mouths opening, but their words were garbled and sounded as if they were calling to me from a great distance. A corpsman arrived, called I assume by one of my buddies, and checked me out. No shrapnel had touched me, so I was not leaking blood. The only injury seemed to be to my hearing. Over the next few days, my hearing was still a problem, and there was talk of sending me to a rear area hospital, possibly as far as Pearl Harbor, but I insisted that I wanted to stay with the company. Over the next few days, the problem slowly subsided and my hearing returned.

My ears weren't my only ailment. Like so many others, I suffered a renewed bout of malaria, undergoing alternating moments of sweating through high fever followed by the uncontrollable shakes of bone-numbing chills. Luckily, I was able to work through it, with the help of our corpsmen, and again avoided a trip back to the hospital.

The blazing heat of Guadalcanal, combined with the frequent rainfall, caused our uniforms to chafe our skin, especially in the armpits and crotch. This led to skin lesions or "jungle rot." Our boondockers seemed to be constantly wet, leading to blisters on our feet that had to be lanced by the blister mechanics.

On September 30, a Wednesday, we looked up to see a B-17 bomber buzzing in the sky overhead, making preparations to land. We did not see too many of these large, four-engine Flying Fortresses on the 'Canal, so Mac, Big Stoop, and I hustled over to Henderson to take a gander, arriving just as the B-17's wheels touched the runway. When the plane rolled to a halt, and the hatch between the right waist gun and the tail popped open, we saw that the bomber was carrying a special cargo. A ladder was pushed up to the side of the airplane, and out stepped Admiral Chester A. Nimitz, the commander in chief, Pacific Command (CINCPAC) himself.

Vandegrift was there to meet Nimitz as he debarked, and the two men shook hands. It was interesting to watch, until I saw who next emerged from the plane. It was Lieutenant Colonel Evans Carlson, commander of our sworn enemy, the 2nd Raider Battalion, the man who had so insulted Edson when he denounced the latter's training program by rejecting many of the men Edson had been forced to send him when the 2nd Raiders were forming. Edson, in fact, was standing near Vandegrift as Carlson climbed from the B-17, and I could feel his temper rise even from a distance. The two men barely acknowledged each other.

General Merritt Austin Edson.

Merritt Edson, center, explains the Battle of Bloody Ridge to Marine Corps Commandant General Thomas Holcomb, at left. General Alexander Vandegrift looks on at right.

All photos courtesy of the U.S. Marine Corps unless otherwise indicated.

Marlin "Whitey" Groft, 1942.

Marlin "Whitey" Groft's machine gun squad on Guadalcanal.
Kneeling from left: Charles Carrigan, Henry R. "Hank" Green,
Boyer C. White, John "J.T." Allen, and Whitey Groft. Bill Waltrip
lies beyond the gun, William L. Brown, by his side.

Marine Raiders practice landing in rubber boats on New Caledonia.

Easy Company at Camp Bailey, New Caledonia. Marlin "Whitey" Groft kneels in front row with Clarence Terrell's arm around his neck. Lee Minier kneels at far right, Bill Waltrip stands fourth from left.

Marines advance through Naha on Okinawa.

The Bloody Ridge battlefield after the fight.

Aftermath of two days' fighting on Bloody Ridge, September 13, 1942.

Pvt. Kenneth E. Bowers on leave in Nazareth, Pennsylvania.
Courtesy of Holly Bowers Toth

Pvt. Kenneth Bowers's body being re-interred near Nazareth, Pennsylvania, in 1947.
Courtesy of Holly Bowers Toth

Marlin Groft at the Edson's Ridge Memorial on Guadalcanal, August 2002.
Eric Groft

Holly Bowers, left, shares family photos with
Marlin and Vivian Groft, March 23, 2014.
Larry Alexander

Marlin Groft and Holly Bowers, March 23, 2014.
Marlin holds a photo of Kenneth Bowers.
Larry Alexander

Carlson, I learned, was along because, like Edson, he was to receive a Navy Cross at an awards ceremony that was planned for October 1, here on the 'Canal. Carlson's medal was for his August 17–18 raid on Makin, when his Raiders knocked out a Japanese installation in order to gain intelligence on the enemy-held Gilbert Islands. The only good thing about this whole affair was that after the ceremony Nimitz would be leaving and taking Carlson along with him.

(Carlson's raid was made into a movie, *Gung Ho!*, which depicted the Makin raid as a stunning success, when, in fact, it was badly bungled and nearly cost Carlson the bulk of his troops. Other than killing most of the Japanese garrison, it did not achieve any of its goals, and in fact, at one point, a dejected Carlson considered surrendering his force to the enemy. Saddest of all, historians have speculated that the raid may have alerted the Japanese to the threat against the Gilbert Islands, causing them to more heavily fortify places such as Tarawa. The only goal the raid, and the movie, truly achieved was to boost home front morale and recruitment.)

Nimitz and Carlson came perilously close to not arriving on the 'Canal at all. The B-17 had gotten lost in a driving rainstorm. By the time the plane did arrive at Henderson, it was nearly out of gas.

During CINCPAC's stay, Edson, along with Vandegrift, gave Nimitz a tour of Bloody Ridge. For more than an hour, they walked the length of the ridge, which still showed its battle scars. Edson was the perfect guide, pointing out to Nimitz where our positions had been and the direction of the attacks made by the enemy. Nimitz also visited the battlefield at Alligator Creek, walked around portions of the Marine perimeter, and dropped by at the base hospital.

Later, the battalion formed up as Nimitz presented Navy Crosses for our action on Tulagi to Edson and Pfc. Wilfred Hunt, whom I still think got the decoration I was nominated for when we attacked a machine gun emplacement on Tulagi. Hunt stabbed the gunner to death when he charged the gun, but not before I blew the man's hand off as he was trying to load a new banana clip into the receiver atop his

Nambu. That's what allowed Hunt to get to the Jap. Other deserving Raiders were also decorated during this ceremony throughout which, I noted, Edson snubbed Carlson.

For Nimitz, this trip nearly became a disaster, both coming and going. In addition to getting lost on the way to Guadalcanal and landing with almost no gas, heading back the plane almost crashed on takeoff when the aircraft failed to get enough lift as it raced along the runway. Finally the pilot slammed on the brakes, causing the 'Fort to slide sideways. Nimitz was riding in the nose and damned near came to grief as the plane slid toward a grove of trees. It stopped just short of colliding with the tree line, which might well have crushed Nimitz inside the plane's Plexiglas nose. The second attempt to take off went much better, and the big war bird parted company with the Earth, banked right, and soared off.

One positive result that came from Nimitz's visit was that, within two weeks, he had relieved Ghormley of command and replaced him with the feisty, aggressive Admiral William B. "Bull" Halsey.

———————

It was early October and we'd been almost two months in action, living under conditions that were, at best, primitive. Disease, casualties, poor food, and eight weeks of unrelenting tension caused by combat, long patrols, and Jap naval shells and aerial bombs were rapidly eroding both our health and our effectiveness. Our skin was yellow from the Atabrine used to control our malaria, our eyes stared from sunken sockets, and we had all lost weight. In short, we looked and felt pretty damned pathetic. But the fight for Guadalcanal was not finished with us yet.

Vandegrift had learned that Japanese forces were massing west of the Matanikau with the goal of launching a new offensive against Henderson Field. In response, he and his staff contrived a new plan to secure the river and the ground around it, much like our failed attempt on September 27, only this time with a larger force. The 5th Marines would push toward the river's mouth, while the 3rd Battalion of the 2nd Marines and the 1st and 2nd battalions of the 7th Marines crossed upstream at the One Log Bridge. Once over the river, this force would move west, then wheel right to hit the Japs on their exposed right flank and drive them into the sea. We Raiders would act as reserve for the 5th Marines, so we felt pretty confident that this show could succeed without our help. In fact, we did not want to get into this fight, because we knew we'd soon be leaving this damned island, to be replaced by a U.S. Army unit, and no one wanted to get killed now.

As the orders came that we were soon moving out, recently promoted Corporal Joe Connolly told several of us that he had dreamt we were being pulled off the island by Higgins boats, where new troop transports would be waiting for us to board.

"There'll be clean beds, hot showers, movies, and steak and ice cream for us all," Connolly said and beamed.

At age thirty-three, he was an old man in the eyes of eighteen-year-olds like myself. He had a reputation among the Raiders of being a top-notch bullshitter, but everyone loved his crap so no one called him on it.

On the morning of Wednesday, October 7, the 5th Marines, in full combat array, headed west, tramping along the coast road in preparation of jumping off against the Japs the next day.

The new Japanese commander on the island, Lieutenant General Masao Maruyama—Kawaguchi had been recalled to Rabaul to explain his failure—got the jump on us. He, too, planned to launch an assault, albeit a limited one, on October 8. In preparation for that, on October 6 he moved a company of about two hundred men of the 3rd Company, 1st Battalion, 4th Infantry Regiment under a lieutenant named Ito, across the Matanikau to the eastern shore. Digging in feverishly, they established a fortified semicircle four hundred yards wide and five hundred yards deep. Within that circle they set up a dozen machine guns with interlocking fields of fire, emplaced in well-camouflaged foxholes, backed by pre-sighted mortars, and all connected by a trench system. Maruyama's intent was to secure the sandbar area at the mouth of the river in order to bring up his four 150mm guns and pound Henderson Field. Possession of the sandbar would also allow him to easily move tanks across the river when he launched his big drive on Henderson, set for October 17. So confident was Maruyama of success that he had already selected the site along the Matanikau where he would accept Vandegrift's surrender. [1]

So it was that as the 5th Marines advanced to their assigned jump-off position, they ran smack into this unexpected Jap strongpoint. The 2/5 managed to reach its assigned spot a little farther upriver, but the 3rd Battalion was stymied despite our shelling the Japs for half a day with 75mm guns mounted on half-tracks. With the attack stalemated even before it officially began, Edson called up his beloved Raiders.

By now there were only about two hundred of us left who were fit for duty. Approximately half of these men were in Lieutenant Bob Neuffer's A Company, while the rest of us were split among Company C, under Lieutenant Blackjack Salmon, and B Company, commanded by my old Dog Company CO, Ed Wheeler, who had just received his captain's bars.

Edson now needed one company of Raiders to support his assault, so I guess it made sense to detach Neuffer's men. I watched the boys of Able Company pack up, and we joked with them, figuring, like they were, that they were being sent up to perform patrol duties.

One of the men marching forward with A Company was Pfc. Donald Steinaker, a mortarman from New York who a day or two earlier had been informed by the Red Cross that his wife, Hazel, had given birth to their first child back in Syracuse. Proud as a strutting peacock, Don told every Raider who cared to listen, and many of those who didn't, about his new status as a father. He was still flapping his gums about it when he headed off to the Matanikau, lugging a mortar base plate. The rest of us Raiders were ordered to move closer to the line and serve as A Company's reserve.

In a way, weary as we were, we took some pride in the fact that we Raiders were being called on to pull the 5th Marines' chestnuts out of the fire. The word had gone around that a Marine who had been captured by the Japs but managed to escape had heard them mention that there was a reward being offered for any man who would kill or capture one of the Americans with "rags" on their helmets. The Japs, of course, were referring to our habit of draping our helmets in burlap.

So with our hopes of being evacuated in the near future riding high, it might have been a bad omen when, as A Company trekked forward along the coastal road, the skies opened up and a torrential rain fell. Sloshing through the muck, the company passed a battery of 75mm pack howitzers, the crews of which were shoving rounds into the smoking breeches as rapidly as possible. The mounds of empty brass casings, some still hot to the touch and sizzling as the cold rain struck them, showed how long they had been at their work. Closer to the river, sniper fire cracked ominously.

As Able Company hiked through this position, they passed the foxhole of a grizzled veteran mortarman, Leland "Lou" Sanford Diamond, a dead-eye shot who could drop an 81mm mortar round into an enemy's back pocket. At Guadalcanal, it was rumored but never confirmed that he dropped a round down the smokestack of a Jap cruiser that was shelling our perimeter. A veteran of the 6th Marines' legendary fight at Belleau Wood during the First World War, the colorful Diamond, now fifty-two years old, was affectionately known as "Mr. Leatherneck." Amazingly to us young guys, he held a Yangtze Service Medal, which he had earned while stationed in China in the late 1920s. Diamond was taken off the line after Guadalcanal, kicking and screaming some of us heard, and would retire from the Corps in November 1945 as a master gunnery sergeant.

As A Company moved past him en route to the Matanikau, Diamond called out, "Damn! Here come the Raiders. No wonder it's raining. We'll get no sleep tonight." [2]

"Go to hell, old man," the Raiders laughingly called back.

The rain was still pouring down in bucket loads when A Company reached the river, and Neuffer was directed to fortify the sandbar area.

His orders were to guard against an attempted crossing, which might include Jap tanks, the small, fifteen-ton Type 97 medium tank, which packed a 57mm gun. For that eventuality, Neuffer would be supported by two 37mm anti-tank guns, which were wheeled into place. Our comrades in Europe would find these weapons almost useless against German armor, but they served us quite well against the more lightly armored "Fujiyama Flivvers." Neuffer also had use of a disabled half-track with a 75mm howitzer that was still operational.

In expectation of an attack from across the river, Neuffer laid out his defenses accordingly, creating a horseshoe-shaped line, with one end anchored on the shore and the other on the river, the line between curving eastward. He placed his 3rd platoon, under Sergeant Joe Buntin, closest at the beach to guard the sandbar that made a natural attack route for enemy tanks. Along the river, he placed 1st platoon under Gunny Cliff McGlocklin. On the extreme left of the line was 2nd platoon under Red Sullivan, who had led the patrol I was on a few weeks earlier when Ken Bailey got killed. Red was upset because his left flank was wide open, inviting an attack. Neuffer understood and agreed. His sole reserve was nine mortarmen under Sergeant Woody Thompson, whose 60mm tubes were useless due to the thick jungle canopy overhead. So Neuffer ordered Thompson and his men, all armed with carbines and pistols, to hold down the company's left. Regardless of that, the line was vulnerable and all knew it. The 3/5 was out there somewhere and were supposed to tie in with A Company. They were also supposed to handle the small Jap pocket on the east side of the river that lay to Neuffer's left rear. Unfortunately, as A Company was about to discover, they did neither.

The heavy rain that began on Wednesday continued on Thursday, forcing a twenty-four-hour postponement of Vandegrift's planned attack. All day, we Marines, and I guess the Japanese as well, hunched down in muddy holes and endured the shitty weather as best we could. At the Matanikau, Sergeant Frank Guidone moved along the A Company line. He dropped into the soggy foxhole next to Joe Connolly and struck up a conversation with his friend. Guidone found Connolly, usually a cutup sort of guy, unusually morose.

"Are you OK, Joe?" Guidone asked.

"Sure," he replied. Then said, "Take care, Frank."

Throughout the day, rain or no rain, our artillery and mortars pounded the Japanese pocket east of the river. With the shells bursting to their rear, the Raiders strengthened their positions by the river, stringing double strands of barbed wire along the bank and placing machine guns in the best positions to sweep the charging enemy ranks. Lew Walt, now with the 5th Marines since Edson had taken over command of that regiment, dropped by to visit. He passed among the men, shaking hands, greeting old friends, and telling all he was proud to have them back at his side.

"I feel good having you fellas here," he said. "I know what you boys can do."

Around twilight, Jap mortar fire burst among the Raiders. Red Sullivan was struck twice but refused orders from Neuffer to leave and get to the rear.

Around 6:30 p.m., the Raiders noticed an unusual fog rising up to their rear. Too late, they realized it was not fog, but Japanese smoke canisters. The enemy in the pocket had endured all the punishment they could stand, and had decided to fight their way back across the river. Neuffer's boys suddenly were confronted with 150 Japs screaming out of the jungle to their rear, plunging through the gap where A Company's line ended and the 3/5 was supposed to be dug in but wasn't.

What followed next was sheer hell as the Japs swarmed in on the Raiders. Connolly fell even before he could bring his weapon to bear, struck down by a sword or knife. Red Sullivan swiftly emptied two clips from his Reising gun before he was hit in the shoulder, his third wound in less than an hour. Losing his weapon, he dove from his foxhole and into a nearby hole occupied by Sergeant Donald Wolf and a corporal. Three Japs were hot on Red's tail, but Wolf and the other man cut loose with their rifles and shot them all dead. The corporal was killed as Wolf and Sullivan hurriedly left the foxhole and made for the Raider line. A Jap officer waving a sword loomed ahead of Red, who bowled him over and kept going. Red scooted rearward until he came to a tangle of vines. He plunged in among them, taking cover as he gathered his wits and caught his breath. Wolf was nowhere to be seen. After a time, bleeding from his three wounds, Sullivan crawled toward Raider lines, where he called out, "Coming in," before reaching relative safety.

Meanwhile, Andy Anderscavage saw three Japanese racing toward him. Raising his BAR, he squeezed the trigger, only to hear the frightening *clunk* of a misfire. With no hesitation, Anderscavage hurled the fifteen-pound weapon sideways at the charging enemy, knocking two of them down on their asses. The third man, bayonet thrust out ahead, came on. Anderscavage neatly sidestepped the man, snatching the Arisaka rifle from his grip as he went by. Reversing the weapon, he used the man's own bayonet to kill him. Then he turned to the other two, who were still scrabbling on the ground trying to regain their feet, and drove the bayonet into them as well. [3]

On the left of the Raider perimeter, Pfc. Sammy Mitchell suddenly found himself all alone, surrounded by dead comrades. Frightened and desperate, Sammy raced toward the Raiders' main position yelling, "Gangway, gangway. This is Sammy Mitchell coming through!" [4]

This attack into their rear had been the last thing Able Company had expected, and all along the line, the machine gunners were forced to quickly reverse the direction of their weapons. Some hesitated about opening fire, knowing their comrades were out there being swamped by the Jap tide. Finally, they had to relent, and the .30-calibers began their deadly chatter.

Neuffer, at his command post, was inundated with terrified men flowing back from where their foxholes were being overrun. He stopped their rearward movement and quickly formed them into a new line. He sent the wounded farther to his rear, after first making sure each in-jured man capable of holding a rifle was armed, in case the Japs punched through A Company's defenses and reached them.

The Japs kept rolling up A Company's line on their way to the sandbar, which they hoped to cross in order to reach safety. Whenever the Japs came across a wounded Raider, they would hack him to death, the man's screams of agony ringing through the night above the gun-fire. Everywhere, men were engaged in the bitterest of hand-to-hand fighting with bloodied knives and bayonets. Raiders put to use the training that had been drilled into us at Quantico on the proper way to kill a man with a knife, which called for either stabbing him under the rib cage or slashing his throat, cutting and ripping out his windpipe.

Neuffer got on his radio to Edson.

"The Japs are hitting us from the rear!" he shouted. "We're being overrun."

"Neuffer, you hold that position," Edson commanded. "I'm sending you help."

The Japanese attack finally broke through to the sandbar, and now it was their turn to be surprised. They had not figured on the double strands of barbed wire, and they began bunching up, many becoming entangled in the razor-sharp wire.

Their dark silhouettes plainly visible against the light sand of the beach, the Japanese now came under a galling fire as Raider machine guns and small arms began sweeping the struggling mass. Scythed down like sheaves of grain, they fell in gory heaps.

Then, as suddenly as it began, the fight was over. It had lasted less than forty-five terrifying minutes. Lew Walt, dispatched by Edson to secure the line, arrived to find dead Raiders and dead Japanese lying side by side, some with ghastly wounds. Daylight revealed a nightmar-ish scene of death and blood. Frank Guidone and Cliff McGlocklin walked the position, finding many dead friends, including Joe Con-nolly, sprawled on the ground where they had fallen. At the sandbar, Japanese bodies lay in heaps around and on the barbed wire.

When the count was taken, twelve Raiders had been killed and twenty-two wounded. Of the nine mortarmen Woody Thompson had led to the company's left flank, only two survived, John Carson and a badly wounded George Simmons. The others, including Thompson and new dad Don Steinacker, all lay dead in the mud. Eleven Raiders would get the Navy Cross for their actions that night, seven of which would be awarded posthumously. Among them would be Connolly, Steinacker, Wolf, and Thompson.

Some Japs, to be sure, made it back across the river, but, by our count, fifty-nine did not. Their bodies lay among our dead, although by far the largest number of enemy killed lay in a tangle by the barbed wire, the sand absorbing their blood.

A search of the enemy's personal effects left us with a disconcerted feeling. These were not the battered, sick, and hungry men we had faced on Bloody Ridge. Their backpacks bulged with fresh food, including rice, meat, and fish. They were well uniformed and well equipped.

What the hell was going on? we asked ourselves. And how many of these fresh troops were out there?

As A Company tended to its wounded and dead, the rest of Vandegrift's attack proceeded. The three battalions to our south successfully crossed the One Log Bridge, moved west, and then swung north to assault the Jap flank. Here Chesty Puller's men scored a spectacular victory when they came across the 3rd Battalion of the Japanese Sendai Division gathered in a woody, steep-sided ravine. Puller called in concentrated artillery fire that blanketed the ravine. Then he added his own mortars, blasting men and trees alike. Under this intense pounding, the trapped Japs tried to flee for safety by scaling the slopes of the ravine. There they ran right into the muzzles of Puller's rifles and machine guns. It was like shooting fish in a barrel as the Japanese fell by the score before the Marines' blazing guns. When the bloodbath ended, the seven-hundred-man Jap battalion had been nearly wiped out.

As the Marine advance proceeded, Vandegrift arrived at the Matanikau and walked along A Company's line. Seeing the masses of dead Japanese by the river mouth, he turned to Edson, who had come up earlier, and asked who was responsible for that carnage.

"My Raiders," Edson replied proudly.

Vandegrift answered, "They're my Raiders, now." [5]

But regardless of whose Raiders we were, this fight at what we called "the Second Matanikau" left many of us uneasy, and some downright angry. Why in the hell had A Company been put in such a vulnerable position, their flank in the air and rear unprotected? Wasn't there some fresher, better-equipped, and larger unit that could have been used to plug that end of the line more effectively? Edson knew that many of us were sick and weary. "What the hell had he been thinking?" men wondered, and some said it out loud. And who was it who failed to tie in Neuffer's left flank with the 5th Marines' right? Both Edson and Walt were excellent tacticians, but one of them had screwed up. The scuttlebutt was that Edson, unhappy with the performance of the 5th Marines, was using us to show off what a "fighting unit" could accomplish. Whatever the reason, it had cost us dearly.

The very next day we suffered our last, and possibly our most grievous, loss. On Saturday, October 9, Edson called his runner, Walt Burak, to his HQ and gave him orders to carry forward to one of the 5th Marine companies. Burak was aware that the area was alive with snipers, but as usual, he never flinched from doing whatever Edson needed done. As he cautiously made his way along the Matanikau River bank, a burst of fire from a Nambu machine gun struck down the twenty-two-year-old Greensburg, Pennsylvania, man. Burak never knew what hit him. When he received the news, the tough Red Mike Edson wept, as did more than a few of us Raiders. (Four years later, Edson was in Burak's hometown, where he eulogized Walt in a Veterans Day speech. He said Burak was "faithful to the end to me, to you, and to the country." He also told Burak's father, "Walter was like a son to me.") [6]

Walter Burak was posthumously awarded a Navy Cross for his actions on Bloody Ridge.

———————

The Matanikau offensive ended on October 9, and by October 10 we were back in our coconut grove, wishing to hell we'd never left. There were fewer of us now than there had been three days earlier, and with illnesses still running rampant, we were getting fewer every day. Wracked by disease, physical fatigue, and mental strain, the battalion was shot, and not a man among us doubted it. We were barely a shadow of what we had been when we stormed ashore on Tulagi what seemed a lifetime ago but what had actually been just sixty-five days.

Then, on Tuesday, October 13, there was a great stir on the island. Just the night before, our Navy had engaged the Japs in what would be called the Battle of Cape Esperance. We had heard the distant rumbling of naval guns in the night off to our west, but were unaware of the outcome, and after Savo, we refused to speculate. But the fight had been an American victory. We had lost a destroyer and 163 men, but a Jap cruiser and three destroyers had been sunk with the loss of more than 400 sailors. Better yet, the Tokyo Express, lifeline for the enemy on the 'Canal, had been turned back.

With the victory on the 13th, two transports, the *McCawley* and the *Zeilin*, both named for former Marine Corps commandants, dropped anchor off Lunga Point and began unloading. We Raiders flocked to the beach to watch, and what a treasure trove our eyes beheld. The bounty included twenty half-ton and seventeen one-and-a-half-ton trucks, forty-one jeeps, sixteen British-made armored Universal Carriers, also known as Bren Gun Carriers, twelve 37mm guns, seventy days of rations, and countless crates of ammo and other supplies. Also being unloaded were skids of white wooden crosses for the ever-expanding cemetery, an unpleasant reminder that the battle for this island was yet to be won.

The ships also brought along 210 new ground personnel for the airfield and 2,852 soldiers of the U.S. Army's 164th Infantry Regiment of the

Americal Division. Their arrival was of special significance to us; they were our replacements. We had known since October 11 that we would soon be shipping out, and here was the living proof. These fresh-faced "Doggies" were also a ready market for trade, for they brought along something many of us were starving for: Hershey bars. Swiftly, trading opened up between the Army guys and us Marines, with thirty-six Hershey bars buying a Samurai sword, and twelve bars of "pogey bait" purchasing a Jap rising sun flag (some of these were handmade by Marines as the supply of authentic ones ran low).[7]

We'd begun packing our gear on October 12, so when the orders came the next day to board ship, we were ready and eager. Lining up for the Higgins boats that would ferry us out to the waiting ship, we probably made for a sorry sight. Only 19 officers and 426 enlisted men would be boarding the transports, and many of those men would have to be lifted on board by stretcher or in some other way assisted to the decks by stronger arms. At least 260 of us had active cases of malaria.

Edson came to the beach to say his good-byes. Walking among the line of waiting men, he told us how proud he was to have been a part of such a fine bunch of fighting men—the best he had ever known, he said. But even as Edson spoke, the first Jap artillery shells from Maruyama's 150mm "Pistol Petes," positioned some ten thousand yards to our west, began falling on Henderson Field and the surrounding perimeter. A few exploded on the beach and splashed in the water, sending up geysers of spray laced with dead fish, whose slick, wet bodies glittered like shards of silver in the sunlight. But it wasn't the bursting of those seventy-nine-pound shells that worried us. It was a message from coast watchers on station between Guadalcanal and Bougainville, warning that a major Japanese task force, including the thirty-one-thousand-ton battleships *Haruna* and *Kongo*, was steaming down The Slot toward the island.

Orders came to speed up the loading, and by dusk, the winches were cranking up the anchors and the boilers began making steam. So eager was the Navy to get going that a number of Higgins boats were left behind. We were soon under way, and I stood by the rail of the *Zeilin*, watching Guadalcanal growing ever more distant as the ship churned to the southeast, bound for New Caledonia. I thought about the men we had left behind, buried in the soil of Guadalcanal and Tulagi. I thought about Kenny Bowers, Stan Kops, Joe Connolly, and the rest. Ninety-four of the men we'd trained with and who had become like family to us, and who had sailed to these islands with us on August 7, would not be returning. Another two hundred of our comrades were wounded, some never to rejoin our ranks, and countless others were sick, myself included. On the positive side of the butcher's ledger, we were credited with killing more than eleven hundred of the enemy.

Nightfall found us well away from Lunga Point, but not so far that we could not see the spectacular light show taking place that night. Shortly after midnight, the Jap task force arrived off Lunga Point, and the fleet, including the battlewagons, each carrying eight fourteen-inch guns, "walked" their monstrous rounds the length of the airfield. These shells heavily damaged the airstrip, pulverizing airplanes and exploding ammo, fuel, and supply dumps, including one that left scorched hunks of Spam scattered far and wide. The battleships' fourteen-hundred-pound rounds splintered thick, log bomb proofs, killing six pilots and forty-one men, including some of the brand-new Army Dog Faces. Even Vandegrift was knocked to the ground by the incredible concussion.

Of ninety planes at Henderson Field that night, daylight found only thirty-five fighters and six dive-bombers still operational.

During the ninety-minute bombardment, called by some survivors "the Night of the Battleships," *Kongo* and *Haruna* dropped ten thousand shells on the airfield and surrounding perimeter. The shelling was unlike anything experienced during the campaign.

From our vantage point, many miles distant, we could see the flashes of light in the sky, but the rumble of the guns and the drumming of the explosions did not reach our ears. But what we saw was enough for us to know that none of us wished he was back on the 'Canal. It was a terrifying experience, and we'd missed it by just a few hours.

But we weren't out of the woods yet. With the coming of daylight, danger returned, this time with the threat of enemy submarines. Swabbies cast eager eyes over the surrounding waters of the Coral Sea, and at around noon came the alert that a sub had been spotted.

"All crewmen, man your battle stations," the loudspeaker blared. "Marines, clear the decks."

To a man, we hated going below, especially with submarines prowling the sea. We knew that if even one torpedo struck our ship, there was every chance that we'd be trapped inside, and that these steel hulls would become our coffins. Every one of us much preferred his chances in a foxhole.

Outside, the destroyers danced around us protectively, and soon came the dull pounding of depth charges, some so close that it seemed as if the steel plates of our transport were bowing inward against the shock waves. This went on for I don't know how long, before the all clear was sounded and we could go back topside. We were later told one submarine was seen breaching, and still later informed that we had sunk two subs. However, postwar records do not show any Japanese submarines lost in the Coral Sea on that day.

It's about a thousand miles from Guadalcanal to New Caledonia in the New Hebrides, and once the threat of submarines was over, we could relax. The first order of business once we boarded the ship was showers and new clothes; these latter we peeled off gratefully because most of us had been wearing the same shirt and rotting dungarees for ten weeks. Hot food came next, and plenty of it. We were permitted to pile as much chow as we could hold on our mess plates, and the ship's soda fountain with ice cream and cold Coca-Cola never closed. Scraggly beards were scraped off, and for the entire trip, our time was our own. There was no training schedule, no periods of calisthenics, and no drills of any sort. And although we were sleeping in cots stacked three and four high in the steamy troop holds, following ten weeks of living in foxholes, they felt like feather beds in some posh Honolulu hotel.

It was a bright, sunny Saturday, four days after leaving the 'Canal, when our ship steamed through one of the channels in the 995-mile-long barrier reef, second largest in the world, that protects New Caledonia. The lush, green, cigar-shaped island was a welcome sight as we glided across the Earth's largest lagoon, bound for Nouméa and the deep-water anchorage at Moselle Bay. On our right was the whale-shaped Nou Island, once site of the island's penal colony, and where Pan American Airways had established a station for its California-to-New Zealand clippers back in '39. With the war, the Navy had taken over the seaplane base.

As our ship drew closer, we Raiders lined the rails to gaze at the beautiful island in anticipation of living in a Jap-free environment. Every man smiled at the thought of obtaining liberty so we could prowl the streets of Nouméa. We had been here before, of course, prior to leaving for Tulagi, so we were familiar with much of what we saw. But as we sailed near enough to see some detail on shore, something new came into view: a large house, pink in color, set on the slope of a hill and surrounded by a white picket fence.

"What in the hell is that?" Mac asked, awestruck.

"Beats the shit outta me," I replied. "Looks like something Shirley Temple might live in."

As the coastline got close enough that we could discern more detail, we made another discovery.

"That's not a picket fence," Ray Ruble said. "That's a line of swabbies. That's a cathouse."

We all got a good chuckle out of the discovery and looked at each other.

Damn, but it was good to get back to civilization.

CHAPTER TEN

REST AND REFIT

NEW CALEDONIA AND NEW ZEALAND
OCTOBER 1942–JUNE 1943

Setting foot on shore at Nouméa was the best medicine we weary Raiders could have asked for, injecting sparks of life into our near-dead eyes and our dulled spirits. I'm sure as we filed ashore, we made one helluva sight with our emaciated bodies, our gaunt faces, and our skin turned pumpkin-like in color from the Atabrine tablets we gobbled down to fight off the symptoms of malaria.

Approaching the line of waiting trucks, I noted wryly that they were far fewer in number than those required to carry us to the transports back in July. Reaching the trucks, we struggled aboard, some men, weakened by illness, having to be helped. The Detroit engines turned over and roared as the trucks jolted and rumbled the twenty-five miles to Camp St. Louis. Arriving, we hopped down from the truck beds and were shown to our assigned billets, pyramidal sixteen-by-sixteen-by-twelve olive drab canvas squad tents. It felt wonderful to be back in something resembling civilization and off the firing line, but the number of empty cots told more than words of our sacrifices during ten weeks in the lion's den that was Guadalcanal.

Initially, Major Irwin, who commanded the Raiders in Griffith's absence, demanded little of us. Our main job was to rebuild our strength, physically, psychologically, and emotionally, so that we would be ready for whatever the Corps had in store for us next time. And every one of us knew there would be a next time.

Liberty was granted, and men flocked into Nouméa, where many of us busted loose, moving from bar to bar, and, inevitably, to places like the pink house on the hill, all designed to separate us from our pay. I plead guilty to some of this as well, for during the thirty weeks we were there on New Cal, as we called it, I got into more than a few brawls and did plenty of three-day stints in the brig, subsisting on "piss and punk," meaning bread and water.

Shortly after we arrived on New Cal, we were recruited for a work detail at the harbor. Civilian dockworkers had launched a strike against a British merchant ship lying at the quay and refused to unload her holds, which bulged with flour and cans of meat and fruit. The dockworkers' problem was that the British vessel consisted of all white officers who oversaw a crew of Indian laborers, whom they habitually mistreated, lording their superiority over the workers as only the Brits can. The Navy command decided this interruption in the flow of supplies was intolerable, and we were put to work replacing the striking stevedores. Still, we felt sorry for these poor Indian bastards and slipped them cans of food. This was more than a little ironic considering how blacks were routinely mistreated back in the States. It was the least we could do, and the Indian laborers were grateful, actually bowing to us and trying to kiss our hands. Since we Raiders were not into hand-kissing, we drew the line at bowing.

In November, around the time I turned nineteen, we got word that we'd be shipped to New Zealand for the Christmas and New Year's holidays. At first we thought this was bullshit spewed out by guys flapping their gums over things they knew nothing about, but then we got the official word.

Our transportation would be one of the ships that had brought us out of Guadalcanal, the attack transport USS *McCawley*. The "*Wacky*

Mac" was the flagship of Admiral Richmond Kelly Turner, commander of the Amphibious Forces in the South Pacific and had been named for General Charles G. McCawley, the Marine Corps's eighth commandant. It was scheduled for an overhaul in Wellington and would earn five battle stars during the war.

The *Wacky Mac* hoisted anchor at Nouméa on Tuesday, November 24. As we cleared the harbor and headed for the open sea, Admiral Turner, having second thoughts about unleashing us on the unsuspecting New Zealanders, issued a plea for us to be on our best behavior.

"I remember what grand fighters all of you are," his proclamation read. "I also realize that I will be held responsible for all your misdeeds and explain them to my boss. I hope all of you have a grand time, but please remember to maintain the grand name you have established."

We thought it all "grand," but few took it to heart.

We made the trip in the *Wacky Mac* unescorted, which spoke volumes to us on how secure Allied Command felt when it came to vulnerable, lumbering ships traversing these waters.

Wellington, with its lush, green hillsides, was a beautiful sight to behold, and we Marines eagerly lined the ship's rails to watch "Welly" draw closer and closer. To our port side, the snowcapped peaks of the Kaikoura Mountain Range seemed to scrape the sky. We approached through Cook Strait, which connects Wellington Harbor to the sea. The strait creates a natural funnel that allows the strong westerly winds so prevalent in these latitudes, the "Roaring Forties" they're called, to blow in on the city, which is why natives call it "Windy Wellington."

Gliding across Wellington Harbor, we turned in to its smaller offshoot, Lambton Harbor, which approaches the city.

It is difficult to describe our feelings of excitement as we looked forward to this trip. Since August, all we had seemed to be living with was sand, natives, dungarees that never really dried and soon rotted, little food, and too many Japs.

Upon landing, we Raiders were divided into groups and instructed as to what we could and could not do during our shore leave. We were permitted to live in the city wherever we could find lodging, we were told, but we had to check in every two days at designated stations. If we chose, we could also live on board the ship.

"To hell with that," I told Dick MacNeilly. "I have four hundred dollars in my pocket, and I plan to see this city."

Mac heartily agreed, so with five months of back pay to blow, we made our way into the city and checked in at the swankest hotel we could find, the Royal Oak. We knew this was going to be costly. But we also knew that, sooner or later, we'd be heading back into combat, so running out of money or, as we said, "getting beached" was the least of our concerns.

The Royal Oak proved to be a wonderful choice for accommodations. The folks were so friendly. In fact, every New Zealander we met seemed to love us, and some even joked about becoming America's forty-ninth state. Their love for us was reciprocated. We roamed the city, dining at its better restaurants, dancing the night away at the Majestic Cabana or at the Allied Services Club on Manners Street, and getting drunk in one of Welly's many pubs. This latter often led to trouble, sometimes with New Zealand soldiers angry that we were dating the local girls, other times with American soldiers and sailors who, for whatever reason, pissed us off. One such incident swelled into a massive street brawl between us and the Kiwis, dubbed "the Battle of Wellington," which spilled out from barrooms and into the streets and involved hundreds of men, mostly intoxicated. A lot of us got into this fist-swinging donnybrook and didn't even know why. The fight was going on, and we just wanted to be part of it. We vented a great deal of pent-up steam through our fists.

A few Raiders who could carry a melody—Lee Minier, Rufus Rogers, Bill Vollack, George Ward, Joseph "Red" Kennedy, Tom "Jinx" Powers, Ed Dunn, and Eugene "Rebel" Fullerton—formed "the Singing Eight Balls." Blending their voices together, they entertained us in bars and in camp with bawdy songs.

While I was staying at the Royal Oak, I stopped by a pub near my hotel and bumped into a New Zealand soldier named Arthur Priestly. When I say bumped into, I mean it almost literally. Priestly had been wounded fighting the Germans in North Africa and his eyesight was seriously impaired. He could see well enough to get around, but he was no longer fit for active duty. Slightly older than me, he was outgoing and friendly, and we really hit it off. This proved to be a wonderful friendship because he helped me, a nineteen-year-old kid from America, navigate through a foreign culture and not feel lost. Art played the role of tour guide, and we'd go sightseeing, both around Wellington and out into the country, traveling by rail through some of the most beautiful countryside I had ever seen. He also took me to social events and parties hosted by his friends, where I had the opportunity to meet girls my age. I danced and partied the night away and had a great time. On occasion, Art served as my moral compass, possibly keeping me out of trouble. Once, when I became too fond of a woman I had met at a party, he pulled me aside and warned me that she was not the kind of woman with whom a vulnerable young soldier should get entangled. I was left with the impression that she was what we called "khaki wacky," eager to hook an American serviceman and earn herself a ticket to the States.

Not all of our time in New Zealand was spent drinking, fighting, and prowling the streets on "skirt patrol" with our buddies. We also had some work to do. As part of our "fare" for being given transport on the *Wacky Mac* was a promise to help scrape and repaint her hull while she was in dry dock for overhaul. It was a hot, backbreaking job. Bitching and moaning as only veteran Marines can, we'd scrape and chip off the old paint and barnacles, then slather on primer and new paint. After work, I'd head back to the Royal Oak for dinner. Often Art met me there, and we'd sit and yak over a couple of beers.

"You know," he told me one evening. "Every day you Yanks are here is one day closer you are to being sent back into battle."

I nodded thoughtfully.

"Where do you think they'll send you, Marlin?" he inquired. He never called me Whitey.

"Damned if I know," I told him. "Wherever it is, you can bet it'll be some stinking, rotten jungle overflowing with rain, mud, and inhabited by a shitload of Japs."

Luckily, at that moment, I didn't know how right I was.

"What will you do when you get back to the United States?" he asked me.

"Get drunk for a week," I said. Then laughed. "I don't know. Honestly. The war is nowhere near over, so I don't think that far ahead. I like the Corps. Maybe I'll re-up. They clothe you, feed you three squares a day, unless you're on Guadalcanal, so it's generally a pretty good life."

Art was quiet for a while. Then he said, "We lost a lot of good mates fighting the Boche in Tunisia, and I saw a lot of my cobbers die. After that, I promised myself I'd never again form a friendship with a fellow in a uniform. But I've found that I am very fond of you. We share a lot of interests and I enjoy your refreshing look at life. I shall miss you when you leave."

I leaned toward him, put a hand on his shoulder, and said, "You've become a good friend to me. We'll keep in touch."

The job on the *Wacky Mac*'s hull took the better part of two weeks, but at last it was finished, and the ship looked as good, if not better, than she had that day in 1928 when she first rolled down the slipway at Furness Shipbuilding Company in Haverton Hill-on-Tees, England. But our time in New Zealand was finished as well. Christmas was over, and I had spent a great New Year's Eve celebrating with Art, Mac, Big Stoop, Alex Stewart, and my other friends. It was early January now, and we were ordered to pack up. Fun and games were over. It was back to work.

Art came to see me off before we departed that Sunday morning, January 10, 1943. I knew he was worried about where I was going and what might lie ahead for my friends and me, and there were tears in his eyes as we shook hands and then embraced in a bear hug.

"Be careful," he said.

"Don't worry," I replied. "I plan to."

I then climbed the gangplank with the rest of the Marines. Stepping onto the deck, I turned and waved. Oddly, we never thought to exchange addresses, and I never saw him again. Years later, I made inquiry in Wellington about Art's whereabouts, and was informed that he had passed away. Why we never exchanged contact information despite our pledge to stay in touch, I will never know. To this day, I still pause and reflect on this man who gave me such comfort and joy in that terrible and distant war.

Our return trip to New Cal was as uneventful as our earlier voyage, and we soon found ourselves back in the familiar environs of Camp St. Louis. Only it was Camp St. Louis no longer. On January 14, just after we debarked from New Zealand, Sam Griffith had returned from the hospital, recovered from his First Matanikau wound, to resume command of the Raiders.

One of the first things Griffith did once back was to rename our base of operations Camp Bailey, in honor of Major Ken Bailey, now lying under the sand on Guadalcanal. This change was fully agreeable to us. We could not think of a better way to honor the man.

Griffith's changes did not end there. He tapped Major Charles L. Banks to be his executive officer. At age twenty-eight, Banks, who hailed from New Jersey, was a Virginia Military Institute graduate and son-in-law to Major General E. P. Moses, commander of the Parris Island training camp.

Griffith reshuffled Raider leadership. Captain John Sweeney was named S2 intelligence officer. Tom Mullahey, now wearing captain's bars, was given A Company, Wheeler retained command of B Company, "Black Jack" Salmon was left in command of C Company, and newly promoted Captain Clay Boyd took over a reinstated D Company. Easy Company, our weapons unit, was eliminated, and that company's machine guns and mortars were distributed among the remaining companies.

Each company was broken down into three-man fire groups. Griffith borrowed the idea from Colonel Carlson, but adapted it to our needs. Each squad had a fire group, which included a BAR man, an assistant BAR man armed with an M1 carbine, and a fire team leader. Most of us gave up our beloved Springfields in lieu of the more modern M1 Garand, although each squad kept one Springfield for use as a sniper rifle. Also, the M1 grenade launcher malfunctioned when attached to the Garand. We replaced our burlap helmet coverings with camouflage "cammie" coverings. They were hot and took forever to dry when wet, but at least they did not itch like the burlap.

Griffith also formed a demolition platoon and gave command to Angus Goss, just back from his Tulagi wounding and now a gunny sergeant. (He had vehemently refused to accept a battlefield commission to lieutenant, as had Gunny Tony Cafarella.)

Goss drilled his squad on Bangalore torpedoes while shamelessly regaling them with tales of his exploits on Tulagi. Gruff and courageous as he was, though, Goss seemed to live under an unlucky star. He had been wounded on Tulagi and returned, only to accidentally shoot himself in the leg while cleaning his .45 pistol. Then, when his demo squad trainees blew up a practice bunker, Goss was conked on the head by a chunk of debris because his guys packed too much TNT into the charge. Goss's helmet saved his ass, but he suffered headaches for quite a while.

Griffith had nominated Goss for the Congressional Medal of Honor, but Nimitz and Vandegrift both reduced it to the Navy Cross. The Brits also put Goss in for the Conspicuous Gallantry Medal. He would not live to receive either.[1]

Some men were gone for good from the Raiders. Horse Collar Smith had been reassigned after a crippling knee injury. Gone also were Pete Pettus, Jake Irwin, Tiger Erskine, Joe Buntin (who so tenaciously held the Raiders' right flank at Second Matanikau), and Cliff McGlocklin. Captain Antonelli was promoted to major and sent stateside to train

Raider recruits at Camp Pendleton. Doc Robert W. Skinner, who loved to play with our heads whenever we bitched about our ailments by deadpanning, "Yeah. I had that," returned to Lancaster County. I would miss him because Doc Skinner and I often swapped hometown stories.

Skinner was replaced by two new doctors, James F. Regan and Stuart C. Knox, who would crack us up when he told us how, when he informed his wife of his reassignment to the South Pacific, she asked him what he'd done wrong to deserve that. [2]

There were other replacements as well. Two or three times a week, trucks rolled into Camp Bailey with prospective Raider candidates. They were screened by Griffith and Banks. Some stayed, but many left on the same trucks.

I missed some of this activity, for soon after we arrived back in New Caledonia, my malaria flared up. We had been on a work detail on one of the transports sitting in the harbor, and we were being shuttled back and forth from shore to the ship on a workboat. Our shift was over and the boat was chugging back for the shore when my head started reeling and I felt as if my body was being incinerated. Then the chills overtook me, and even though it was a hot day with the mercury hovering in the nineties, I started shaking like a leaf in a high wind. I thought I was going to shake my teeth right out of my head. When the boat docked, I got off and stumbled my way to the seawall that ran along the beach. I found a piece of an old tarp, lay down, and covered myself, trying desperately to keep warm. Other Raiders rushed to my assistance, but I knew nothing of that. My next memory was three days later, when I awoke in a bed at the MOB (Main Operating Base) hospital in Nouméa, looking up into the worried face of my squad leader.

"How are you feeling, son?" Bill Waltrip asked.

From about that moment on, Bill and I formed a bond closer than the one between me and my own brothers, the kind of friendship that only comes about through sharing experiences such as camp life, raucous liberties, and life-and-death moments in battle. My malaria symptoms soon receded and I was ready to resume my duties.

Now the preparations for another show began in earnest. The training was hard, a grueling regimen of physical conditioning that included long, hot hikes, tactical field problems, and beach landings in rubber boats. Day and night seemed to blend into one. We would "celebrate" each weekend with a twenty-five-mile hike. We would be off at the crack of dawn with "the old man" setting a brutal pace that left a number of men panting by the wayside. We traveled with light marching orders, meaning we carried only a knapsack, a change of underwear, one day's rations, and a full canteen of water. We also lugged along our designated weapons, which in my case was a .30-cal machine gun.

Our machine gun squad had been attached to B Company, which suited me just fine. Baker's CO was Ed Wheeler, who had been my platoon leader and, later, company CO on the 'Canal and with whom I had a great relationship, both during the war and in the years afterward. Marching along with my new squad, I was amid the group of men with whom I would form a bond that remains to this day.

The training was rugged and remorseless, and a number of men could not take it and requested transfers. One of these was Mike Rihaly, my friend since joining the Raiders and our Dog Company BAR man who had frozen up on Tulagi, forcing me to take his weapon for the rest of the battle. Mike had tears in his eyes as he shook my hand before he left camp. We wished each other luck. I would not see him again until a Raider reunion forty years later.

On March 24, the battalion was formed up for an awards ceremony, during which Colonel Griffith was given the Navy Cross for First Matanikau. On this same day, back in Washington, D.C., at the White House, President Franklin Roosevelt was handing the Medal of Honor to Elizabeth Bailey.

Then it was back to forced marches with full gear, night operations, time spent on the firing range, and rubber boat and landing craft drills.

We had no idea what we were gearing up for, but if the training was any indication, it was going to be a bitch.

The high command had a pretty good idea of where we were going next.

In December, while we were drinking and brawling in Wellington, HQ had learned that the Japanese were constructing an airfield at Munda, on the southeast coast of New Georgia, and another near the mouth of the Vila River on Kolombangara. These two airfields presented the Americans with the dual threat of endangering our bases on Guadalcanal and cutting off any attempts we might make to seize Bougainville. Targeting New Georgia and Kolombangara, Headquarters began marshaling its forces, including us Raiders. Only now there were more of us to marshal. The Marine Corps, which had been reluctant to embrace the entire concept of Raider battalions, and still wasn't totally sold on the idea, had approved the organization of two more battalions, mostly at FDR's prodding.

Back in September, a new Raider Battalion, the 3rd Raiders, had been formed under the command of Lieutenant Colonel Harry Bluett Liversedge, and on October 23, the 4th Raiders were formed under Lieutenant Colonel James Roosevelt, the president's son.

By early June we men of the 1st Raiders had reached the end of our reconditioning period, and word came down that we would soon be boarding a troop ship bound for Guadalcanal. This came as a real surprise to us since the 'Canal had long since been secured and was now, we thought, something of a backwater to the war. The other scuttlebutt to reach our ears was that the ship taking us there would be the *Wacky Mac*, which we had scraped and painted back in Wellington. This was great news, since we had become pretty chummy with the members of her crew and felt secure on the old girl. That rumor proved not to be true. When we packed into trucks and arrived at the harbor at Nouméa, the ship waiting for us was the 9,500-ton USS *President Hayes*. We hoisted anchor on Monday morning, June 7, and watched New Caledonia fade over the eastern horizon. During the voyage, we were required to stand ship's watch, and my assigned post was a twin .50-caliber machine gun mount on the *Hayes*'s fantail.

It was boring as hell, standing there scanning the skies and watching mile after endless mile of ocean recede behind us as our transport's frothy wake creased the blue Pacific. Occasionally a fellow Raider passed by and chatted, or I exchanged words with a swabbie doing deck duty, but for the most part, I was strictly on watch.

Two days out from Guadalcanal, a thrill ran through the ship. Radar on one of our escort vessels had picked up Jap planes heading our way. Hot damn, I thought. Here was my chance to take one of those meatballs out of the sky. But even as I fingered the twin 50s, my joy was short-lived, as the sailors sprang to their battle stations and the regular gun crew arrived.

"All Marines, go below," bellowed the ship's PA system, and it was with a mix of anger and disappointment that I trudged back to rejoin my machine gun squad in our troop hold belowdecks. There my emotions about being denied the opportunity to take on a Jap plane were replaced by nervous jitters. We could hear the deck machine guns chattering and the deep, rhythmic *pom pom pom* of the 40mm Bofors antiaircraft batteries. The *Hayes* reverberated as Jap bombs detonated in the water. Enemy machine gun slugs pinged off the steel hull as if someone was throwing ball bearings against her sides.

"Give me a foxhole in the dirt any day," Waltrip said, as he sat on his bunk, eyes cast upward as if he were trying to watch the battle through the steel decking.

The ship shook again with another near miss.

"Shit," Boyer White cursed. "Did someone paint a damned bull's-eye on our deck?"

"I'll give those swabbies one thing," I said, with a new appreciation of the sailor's plight. "They might sleep in a dry rack each night and get three squares a day, but after this trip there's no way in hell I'd trade places with them. I can hike a damned sight further than I can swim."

Our little flotilla survived the attack and pressed on.

———————

It felt odd to watch Guadalcanal come back into view. The lush, peaceful-looking green of her mountains belied the hell we had experienced there ten months earlier. Rounding the easternmost tip of the island, we glided into Iron Bottom Sound and cruised along, the 'Canal's coastline passing by our port rail. Having dropped anchor off the all-too-familiar Lunga Point, we were ferried ashore in Higgins boats, to be deposited three miles west of Henderson Field at Tetere, one of Kawaguchi's staging areas for his assaults on Bloody Ridge, the "left hook" that failed to materialize.

Now we began hearing scuttlebutt that New Georgia was our next target. We had suspected this since May, so it came as no big surprise. This was going to be a joint Army/Navy operation, involving both Marines and Army personnel, and would be a test of the new command structure that had been set up recently.

Back in March, our 1st Raider Battalion had been combined with the untested 4th Raiders, now under the command of Lieutenant Colonel Michael Currin after Colonel Roosevelt became ill from jungle ailments. Together we became the 1st Marine Raider Regiment and were placed under the overall command of Colonel Liversedge. Not long afterward, two units from the Army's 37th Division were also attached to us, the 3rd Battalion, 145th Regiment, and the 3rd Battalion, 148th Regiment, both green to battle.

Liversedge, at age forty-eight, was a twenty-six-year veteran Marine officer someone had dubbed "Harry the Horse." He was very athletic, having won a bronze medal for shot put in the 1920 Olympics. He had served in Haiti, France, and China, and onboard the battleship USS *California* back when he was a seagoing bellhop, our term for a Marine assigned to ship duty. However, he had no combat experience. In Haiti he had been an aide-de-camp, and he arrived in France in 1918 just after the Armistice.

As we passed the hours and days on the 'Canal awaiting orders, we had a great deal of free time. This was in quite sharp contrast to the last time we were here, when we had been constantly on watch for a possible Jap attack on our position.

One warm June day, a group of the new guys were chatting with me about what it was like when we were here the previous summer. Some of them had hiked up to Bloody Ridge and looked around, although I would not revisit that place for another fifty-nine years. During our discussion, the topic of Tasimboko came up, and the guys expressed an interest in seeing the place. I had heard that a group of men from the weapons platoon were going to take Higgins boats to Tasimboko to see if our Boys .50-caliber guns were capable of penetrating the three-sixteenth inches of armor that the Japs were using on the transport barges that traversed Kula Gulf between New Georgia and Kolombangara. A similar Type A Jap vessel, *Barge 609*, was beached at Tasimboko, and the weapons platoon fellows were going to test the Boys rifle on it. I managed to finagle a ride for myself and my interested bevy of new Raiders.

Stepping back on shore at Tasimboko and seeing the charred and shattered village, littered with the scattered debris left behind when we ravaged the place last summer, had a surreal quality. *Barge 609* lay exactly where we had been told it would be, on the sand by the high tide line, like a beached porpoise. Twin-keeled, with a steel hull and eight-foot-wide wooden ramp, the forty-seven-foot vessel had a sixty-horsepower diesel engine that could push it through the water at almost eight knots. This particular barge had been used to ferry Kawaguchi's men to Guadalcanal from the Shortland Island.

While the weapons guys went about setting up their gun for their practice shots, I gave the new fellows the ten-cent tour, pointing out where we had come ashore and the direction of our approach. We walked about what remained of the village, and they stared in wonder at the ruins of the Jap supply base that we had totally destroyed during what would be our one and only raid of the type for which we had been recruited and trained.

As we were poking about the rubble and the surrounding bush, one of the men called out, "Oh my God. Over here! Quick!"

I ran over to his side and stared down in the direction of his pointing finger. There, amid the underbrush, were the skeletal remains of a Marine, killed nine months ago and somehow missed when we withdrew. Something glittered in the sunlight beneath the man's rotting shirt. It was his dog tag. I did not touch the body, but we left him where he had lain since September 8, the day his life ended. When we arrived back at our bivouac, I reported our find to Colonel Griffith. A recovery team was dispatched to Tasimboko, and the poor soul was collected and buried in the Marine cemetery with our other fallen. His dog tag identified him as Pfc. Seraphine B. "Buddy" Smith of Baker Company. In discovering Smith's body, I felt satisfaction that at last his family, who most certainly had gotten a "missing in action" telegram, would have closure, although the sight of the decomposed corpse did unnerve the new guys. (After the war, Smith, as well as the rest of our dead on Guadalcanal, would be brought home. Smith lies in the National Memorial Cemetery of the Pacific at the Punchbowl in Hawaii.)

As our time on the 'Canal grew shorter, the Japs may have suspected something was up, and they launched heavy air raids on Henderson Field and our ships lying at anchor offshore. Luckily, the superb coast watcher system gave us plenty of warning as the Japs winged in from Rabaul. All morning we watched as our bombers, nice, fat juicy targets for Japanese planes, took off for safer locations, rather than be caught on the ground and destroyed. Then the Japs arrived, flocks of them, buzzing high overhead, including Betty bombers, Nakajima "Kate" torpedo planes, and Aichi "Val" dive-bombers, all being shepherded by a swarm of the nimble Zero fighters.

Our stubby little Wildcats and twin-tailed P-38 Lightnings, newly arrived since we were last here, were all over the Japs, diving, firing, and swooping back up into the sky to make another pass. The sky became a mass of twisting aircraft. I watched one Kate make a torpedo run on a transport. Suddenly a Wildcat was on its tail, and the sound of the fighter's six wing-mounted machine guns rattled loudly. Jap planes did not possess self-sealing gas tanks—the Kate exploded in a fireball and cartwheeled into Iron Bottom Sound.

More planes fell in flames or trailing smoke. Bombs crashed into the sea and the airfield. Then the Japs were heading home. They had lost thirty-nine planes to our six. All of our pilots survived. The airfield was severely holed by bomb craters, but I did not hear of any ships being lost or seriously damaged.

This air battle, the first I had seen from beginning to end and the first combat I had witnessed since last October, provided a diversion for me after I'd suffered an excruciating experience the day before. I had developed a toothache that was driving me crazy. My mouth was throbbing when I went to look for the base dentist. Unfortunately, with our departure imminent, most of his equipment, including Novocain, had been packed away on a transport ship, and all he had was his pliers. So I ended up sitting on a K-ration box on the beach as the doc, apologizing the whole time, yanked my tooth.

While we were still on New Caledonia, our company CO, Captain Ed Wheeler, had seemed to disappear and later, just as suddenly, reappear. Now, as we prepared to board ships for our next fight, we learned the reason for his absence.

While we were watching air battles and getting teeth pulled, other events were transpiring. Wanting to know what we might be getting into on New Georgia, Colonel Liversedge had sent out two long-range patrols. For the one, he selected Wheeler. Ed was twenty-six at

the time, a native of Port Chester, New York, who had left law school
to join the Marines in 1941.

To hear Ed relate the mission years later, Griffith directed him to
select two men to accompany him on a 350-mile journey by native
canoes from Segi Point on New Georgia's eastern tip to Kula Gulf on
the island's western side. There they were to check on the progress of
the Japanese air base on Kolombangara, as well as Jap barge traffic
crossing the gulf. For the rest of his team, Wheeler tapped 2nd Lieutenant Phil Oldham, who had been a corporal but was given a battlefield promotion after the Matanikau fight, and Sergeant George B.
Lewis. He needed men who were strong swimmers and good at map
and compass reading.

The three climbed into a PBY Catalina flying boat on March 22,
which carried them to Segi Point, where it made a graceful landing on
the waters offshore. There the three were met by a native canoe. On
board was Lieutenant Donald Kennedy of the Royal Navy, a coast
watcher whose base was in the mountains overlooking Segi Point. Kennedy got the three Raiders onto the canoe with about a dozen strong
native oarsmen, and they were soon off. Traveling only in the darkness,
they covered about fifty miles per night, crossing Blanche Channel,
rounding Rendova, passing near Munda Point and through the Diamond Narrows, sandwiched—one stretch is just 224 feet wide—between
Wanawana and Arundal islands. They rowed across Blackett Strait,
where Lieutenant John F. Kennedy's PT-109 would be rammed and sunk
by a Jap destroyer nineteen weeks later. Landing on the southern coast
of Kolombangara, they made a patrol on foot, picking their way through
the harsh landscape to investigate the Japanese airstrip. Finding it, they
quickly discovered that the Japs had stopped work on the airstrip at the
mouth of the Vila River because the ground was too soft for a runway.
Reboarding the canoes, the team circled Kolombangara, noting that the
island had no suitable invasion beaches. Entering Kula Gulf between
Kolombangara and New Georgia, the canoe dodged Jap barge convoys

passing back and forth across the gulf near Bairoko Harbor. They estimated that the enemy had several thousand men on New Georgia. Then they made their way back to Segi Point.

Because of the information Wheeler brought back, Kolombangara was scratched off the list as a possible invasion site.

Another patrol was later led by Captain Clay Boyd, and it mapped out much of the island. A second patrol led by Boyd set up a base in the area of Rice Anchorage on Kula Gulf, near the Jap bases at Enogai and Bairoko Harbor where, it turned out, we would be landing very soon. These patrols were done in conjunction with coast watchers Kennedy, Flight Lieutenant J. A. Corrigan, and Corrigan's natives, who were referred to as "Corry's Boys." It was Corrigan who warned the Navy that the Japs had several 140mm shore guns at Enogai, a fact the Navy planners chose to ignore.

Boyd's patrol, along with the natives, also took the time to cut trails through the thick jungles using machetes and bolos. These would prove invaluable to us once we got ashore, but because of the increasingly swampy ground between the Giza Giza and Tamakau rivers, the work was slowed and the natives and Boyd's patrol did not have enough time to do the entire route to Enogai.

These trails loomed large in Liversedge's plan for our landing, and their absence would have a telling effect on the colonel's ambitious timetable.

———————

Early on the morning of the Fourth of July, we Raiders hiked to the beach at Tetere to be loaded onto the waiting APDs anchored offshore. Loaded down under full packs, we clambered aboard Higgins boats for the ride, eager faces peering over the gunwales as we stared at the cruisers and destroyers that would serve as our escorts. I scanned the ships to see if the *Wacky Mac* was present, that friendly ship we had grown to love when she carried us to New Zealand, but she was not there.

Arriving at our transport, we hastily climbed the cargo nets and were herded to the troop holds below. Having stowed my gear, I went back topside and watched Guadalcanal fade into the distance as our convoy rounded Cape Esperance and entered the waters of The Slot. As I stood on deck, watching the Pacific close over the ship's wake, erasing any sign that we had passed that way, I asked a swabbie where the *Wacky Mac* was.

"She's gone," he told me. "She was sunk during landing operations at Rendova a few days ago. I don't know the details."

My heart sank. The *Wacky Mac* was lost. I thought about the men who manned her and wondered what had happened. When we learned the details of her sinking, which we soon would, it spawned within us a lasting animosity—not at the Japanese, but at the United States Navy.

What had happened, we were told, was that Jap planes had attacked our ships while we were landing forces on Rendova, an island immediately south of New Georgia. Five Jap torpedo planes made for *Wacky Mac*, whose guns brought down four of them. But the fifth managed to drive its torpedo into the ship, killing fifteen sailors and knocking out all of her power. Admiral Turner transferred his flag to a destroyer, and the crew was also taken off the ship, and a salvage party went on board to stabilize the vessel. More Jap dive-bombers swooped in and strafed the *Wacky Mac*, but did no serious damage, and the swabbies manning her guns dropped three more of the enemy. Her end came that night, sometime after 10 p.m., when she was attacked and struck by torpedoes from surface craft. But the surface craft were not Japanese. They were American PT boats whose skippers mistook the *McCawley* for an enemy transport. She went down in thirty seconds to her watery grave, 340 fathoms below.

We loved her and never forgave the crazy PT boat crews.

At the briefing held the day after we left the 'Canal, the battle plan was laid out for us. Our landing zone was on a prominence of land that juts out from the island's southwest coast and is called the Dragons Peninsula. Our invasion group, the Northern Landing Force, comprised of the 1st Raiders and our two attached Army regiments, 3/145 and 3/148, would go ashore on rubber boats at Rice Anchorage, then make a wide, looping eight-mile march through the jungle and around Enogai Inlet to strike the Jap base at Enogai, on the coast along Kula Gulf. After neutralizing that place, we would turn and attack the larger enemy base at Bairoko and seize the harbor. Our mission was to cut off the Jap supply line between Bairoko and the airfield at Munda, which would also be under attack by Army units landing east of the airfield.

"Speed is of the essence," we were told. "We have to accomplish the march from the landing zone to Enogai in three days, so we will be traveling light. You'll carry three days of rations and only what you need in the way of personal gear. We will have no artillery support going with us, and just what ammo, medical, and other supplies you can carry on your person. HQ thinks that will be sufficient as resistance is expected to be light and we should catch the Japs off guard."

The plan was called Operation Toenails, although, in retrospect, Operation Harebrained might have been a more appropriate name. Having launched the mission with insufficient data on the Japanese troop strength and defenses, and with no heed paid to the type of terrain we'd have to cross, neither we, nor, more importantly, the men who were sending us there, had any idea what was awaiting us.

CHAPTER ELEVEN

THE DRAGONS PENINSULA

ENOGAI, NEW GEORGIA
SUNDAY–SATURDAY, JULY 4–10, 1943

The Northern Landing Force consisted of three APDs escorted by nine destroyers and three cruisers. Most of the landing force, mainly the Army's 3/145 and 3/148, were on board the APDs, the USS *Schley*, *Kilty*, and *Crosby*. We Raiders rode on the destroyer USS *McCalla*, a new ship commissioned just fourteen months ago. *McCalla* had been sailing in company with the USS *McCawley* during her final moments five days earlier, and had splashed at least one of *Wacky Mac*'s attackers. When *McCawley* went down, *McCalla* plucked ninety-eight of her crew members from the waters off Rendova.

Our invasion force had left Guadalcanal behind and now knifed its way up The Slot at a lusty twenty-three knots. Our destination was the island of New Georgia, about halfway up the Solomon chain, with the 'Canal 180 miles to the southeast and Jap-held Bougainville just 110 miles to the northwest. I sat pensively in the hold belowdecks with the rest of my platoon, feeling the ship gently rock as her twin screws pushed her through the water, and thinking about the operation to come. Outside, driving rain lashed the steel hull.

This rain would be the first of the serious impediments to Colonel

Liversedge's delicate timetable. The patrols he had dispatched under Ed Wheeler and Clay Boyd were done in relatively dry weather between March and June. Now a period of heavy rain, carried by the southeast trade winds, had set in, with drenching downpours that would turn streams into raging rivers, and bogs into nearly impenetrable swamps. And this was still "the dry season."

New Georgia, codenamed "Celery," is the largest island in the eleven main islands of the New Georgia group, and the sixth largest overall in the Solomons. Forty-five miles long, New Georgia consists of two landmasses connected by a six-mile-wide isthmus. The western mass, the one we were concerned with, is thirty-five miles wide from Munda Point in the south to Visuvisu Point in the north, along the waters of The Slot. It proved to be an inhospitable land consisting largely of a helter-skelter, patchwork landscape of razor-backed ridges, dense jungle, thick, twisting underbrush, rivers, and reeking, stagnant swamps. This factor of terrain is one of the reasons Corry's Boys so willingly helped the Allies. The people of this region mostly inhabited the coastline, moving by canoes, with just a few narrow footpaths and crude roads leading to inland locations. The Japanese presence forced them to move deeper into the jungle with all the hardships that entailed.

For the most part, the jungle runs right up to the point where the land meets the ocean, so outside of Bairoko Harbor and Enogai Inlet, both Jap-occupied, there were damned few places to put troops on shore. One place was Zanana Beach on the southern coast of New Georgia, six miles northeast of Munda. Originally, it was Liversedge's intent to land us there and have us move overland to cut the road between the Jap airfield at Munda and their supply base at Bairoko. However, thanks to Clay Boyd's efforts, and the native scouts', it was discovered that the whole terrain was crisscrossed with coral ridges two hundred to three hundred feet high, separated by deep ravines. The rest was all a chaotic mix of streams, tangled jungle, bottomless swamps, and rocky outcroppings. There was a single, winding footpath, but that would assist us little.

For that reason, our task force was swinging around the northern part of the island to come in on the Kula Gulf side, between New Georgia and Kolombangara. On that side of the island—the Dragons Peninsula it is called—there were three suitable landing places: the aforementioned Enogai Inlet and Bairoko Harbor, and Rice Anchorage, a jungle-lined, deepwater inlet located about four miles north of Enogai.

The Japanese had first arrived on New Georgia the previous October, mainly to find a good location for an airfield to support their efforts to defeat us on Guadalcanal. Consisting of two infantry companies and two anti-aircraft batteries, they constructed a seven-hundred-foot runway at Munda. No planes were based at Munda. It was used mainly as a refueling stop for bombers and fighters en route to hit us on Tulagi or the 'Canal. In the early part of 1943 the garrison was heavily reinforced by the 8th Combined Special Naval Landing Force under Rear Admiral Minoru Ota. This organization was made up of men from the Kure 6th and Yokosuka 7th Special Naval Landing Forces, a total of about four thousand men. The 7th SNLF was soon dispatched to Kolombangara while the 6th SNLF, led by Commander Saburo Okumura, scattered its units between Munda and Bairoko, with about one thousand men defending Bairoko and Enogai. Munda was also soon reinforced by the 229th Regiment of the 38th Division, plus some artillery sections. To add muscle to their defense, the Japanese possessed four 90mm mortars, thirteen Type 93 13.2mm machine guns, and plenty of heavy and light Nambu machine guns. They also had four 140mm fieldpieces, which our Navy knew about but, almost unbelievably, dismissed.

Shortly after midnight on the Fourth of July, our convoy rounded the northwest tip of New Georgia and entered Kula Gulf. Liversedge's plan was to land Colonel Griffith and us Raiders, along with the Army's

3/148, commanded by Lieutenant Colonel Delbert "Dutch" Schultz, and the 3/145, led by Lieutenant Colonel George Freer, at Enogai Inlet. Initially we'd all move together, winding our way southeast to the tip of Enogai Inlet. Then the 3/148 would keep advancing to block the road between Bairoko and Munda, and the 1/145 would go into reserve to secure our rear. The Raiders would continue around the watery finger of the inlet and seize Enogai itself. Then we'd attack south, taking and holding Bairoko Harbor.

"Landing force to your debarkation stations," a voice blared over the *McCalla*'s PA system, and we hoisted our packs on our backs and made the climb from our hold to the main deck. Stepping from the dry bowels of the destroyer to the rain-whipped world outside was a discouraging start to this mission. We moved to our debarkation spot on the ship's port side and waited.

By 1:30 a.m. our ships were off Rice Anchorage. Higgins boats were lowered into the water, not to land us, since there was no landing beach. Rather, they would tow us in rubber boats, allowing us to finally put to the test some of the knowledge hammered into us by Gunny Stackpole, Edson's Admiral of the Condom Fleet, whose body lay under a white cross on Guadalcanal. At the signal, we piled into the rubber boats, which were held tightly against the sides of the destroyer by sailors clutching ropes. Once we were all aboard, we paddled across the choppy water to assigned Higgins boats, where a towrope was attached to our craft, which bobbed on the waves like a fishing cork. That done, the Higgins boats headed for shore, churning through the roiling surf ahead of us. It was a wet ride, both from the rain and from the spray of the Higgins boat's wake.

The night was blacker than Satan's heart as we headed for the unseen coastline cloaked as it was by darkness. Then, suddenly, the night was alight, as Japanese shore batteries, discovering our ships, opened fire from both Enogai and Vila across the gulf on Kolombangara. Our fleet, cruisers and destroyers returned fire. The night air was torn as invisible shells streaked back and forth overhead. Blazing muzzle flashes lit the ships with each volley. Before too long, flares dropped by a Jap float plane droning unseen above us burst, illuminating, not just the surface ships, but our landing force as well, leaving us naked and exposed, bobbing on the water surface like so many apples in a dunk tank. Tracers began carving fiery arcs through the sky from onshore gun positions. We put our heads down and prayed. God listened. We were sitting ducks, but the Japs overshot.

Their 140mm guns, which the Navy had paid little heed to, scored several hits on ships, and a long-lance torpedo launched from a Japanese destroyer, eleven nautical miles out, found the year-old Fletcher Class destroyer USS *Strong*, and, in the words of one witness, opened up the ship "like a punctured beer can."[1] She went down in thirty minutes, carrying forty-six dead crew members with her.

The way into Rice Anchorage was marked by blinking lights on canoes tied fast to either side of the seventy-five-yard-wide entrance. They'd been placed there by Captain Boyd and his men prior to our landing. After entering the anchorage, an inlet fed by the Pundakona River, the Higgins boats cast us loose, and we began paddling to designated landing areas about six hundred yards up the black river. As the racket of naval guns and shore batteries roared behind us, we rowed like hell for the jungle-choked shore. Rain thrummed hard on our helmets and whipped into our faces, further obscuring our vision on this blackest of nights.

"God bless Admiral Turner," a Marine behind me snarled sarcastically, speaking for all of us.

The night landing was an idea decreed by Turner, who mistakenly envisioned himself as some sort of land tactician as well. His meddling in this operation would plague the Marines throughout.

Now came a harsh growling sound as our rubber boat grated against the submerged mangrove roots.

"Out," a voice said, and we went over the side into slimy water that was anywhere from waist deep to as much as seven or eight feet. The only good thing was that we couldn't get any wetter than we already were. As we struggled in the water, men already on shore helped us safely to what passed for land on this rotten island. Even though we had just arrived, the stench of jungle decay was already assaulting our nostrils. Our landing area was nothing more than a tangle of twisted vines and mangrove roots, sprawled snakelike across a soggy landscape of mud, ankle deep and higher, churned up by the rain and hundreds of Marine boondockers. Rainwater cascaded down from the trees above us like waterfalls, forming streams that flowed freely everywhere.

Raiders Clay Boyd and Frank Guidone, along with coast watcher Donald Kennedy and a number of Corry's Boys, were there to meet us, scouring the coastline with flashlights to guide in the boats, which had become widely scattered in the rainy darkness. Things on land were chaotic as men struggled in the near zero visibility to locate their squads and platoons. We were then directed toward a clearing the natives had carved and told to wait. So we would not get lost, the natives brought us a jungle fungus with phosphorescent qualities and helped us smear the residue on each other's back so we could follow the man ahead by the dim glow of the fungus.

After we arrived at the assembly point, there wasn't much to do until everyone was present. I had not gotten much sleep on the voyage from Guadalcanal and was dead tired. I now located a mass of tree roots that was not covered by mud or water, and settled down on them. I stretched out on the roots, making myself as comfortable as I could, considering there was a small stream flowing over my legs. Yet, despite my miserable surroundings, I soon nodded off.

As I snoozed, the landing continued until around dawn, when Admiral Turner, worried about the new day exposing his fleet to more accurate Japanese shore battery fire, ordered the Navy to skedaddle. That was promptly done despite the fact that seventy-two men and 2 percent of our supplies remained on board. Two percent wasn't bad considering the way the Navy had left us practically naked at Guadalcanal after Savo Island, but it would prove bad enough since the ships carried away with them some rations, ammo, and, worst of all, as events would prove, our only long-range radio, leaving us with TBXs of questionable value in the jungle. The Navy was fortunate in one regard: Ten minutes after they departed, Jap planes appeared over the now-empty gulf.

Aside from that, and despite the coal-black night and driving rain, the landing went surprisingly well, although some two hundred men landed on the wrong side of the anchorage. It would take them several days to catch up to us. Overall, some two thousand men were landed, with our only casualty being one Raider who drowned, possibly after leaving his rubber boat to wade ashore.

At around 6 a.m. our cross-country march commenced as the Raiders and our attached Army troops began filing into the jungle. I was still asleep on my tree-root bed when I felt someone kick my feet. I opened my eyes and looked up. Gazing down at me was a tall man in an Australian bush hat, a .45 dangling from a belt on one hip and a machete on the other.

"Better get a move on, lad," Flight Lieutenant Corry said. "Your mates are moving out."

I scrambled to my feet.

"I never seem to have trouble sleeping," I explained.

"I can see that," he said and smiled. "Off you go, then."

We felt pretty miserable as we left the staging area by the anchorage and began to slog south, and that feeling would only worsen as the days wore on. We moved en masse, Marines and Army together, using two trails cut for us by Corry's Boys prior to our arrival. Even though crudely chopped through the jungle, these proved to be a godsend, as the rain hammered us relentlessly. Still, even with the trails, our advance was slow, mainly due to the deep, sticky mud that tried to suck our boondockers off of our feet.

The terrain was the worst I had ever experienced. Trees ten stories high towered above us, their leafy canopies blocking the sunlight, had there been any sun. Gnarled roots large enough to conceal enemy pillboxes sprawled across the ground like the tentacles of some giant octopus, and heavy vines clutched at us and lashed our faces. We slopped through the mud. Men lost their footing and fell, rose, slipped, and fell again, and rose again, caked in dark, smelly muck and cursing a blue streak at everybody from Admiral Turner on down. We waded waist-deep through stagnant swamps, surrounded by small geysers of water as if from bullets, but in fact caused by the pelting raindrops. And all around us, inescapable, was the stench of dead and decaying foliage.

"Damnit, Son," Bill Waltrip puffed at me as we trekked along, the .30-cal across his shoulders. "I've been in outhouses in August that smelled like perfume compared to this damned place."

"I'll say this," I replied. "We have nothing like this back in Lancaster County. If there really is a Satan, this has gotta be his garden."

A heavy vine slapped hard across my body, and I checked to make sure it had not dislodged the condom that I had placed over the muzzle to keep the rain and mud out of my Garand.

"I still say that's a damned waste of a good rubber," mused J. T. Allen, who was walking behind me.

"We got no other use for 'em," Boyer White injected.

We lapsed back into silence. We were too damned tired for conversation. The fierce humidity, intensified by our rubber ponchos, made it seem as if we were walking through a Turkish sauna. The resultant sweat soaked our clothes beneath the ponchos, making us as wet as the rain would have without the rubber cloaks.

As darkness fell on that first night, we continued on, each man following the dull glow emitted by the man ahead. Finally we stopped, exhausted, and settled down. But where? There was no dry place to lie down, so men did what I had done earlier, selecting the least wet and muddy place they could find, usually amid the sprawling tree roots. As we hunkered down and devoured our meager rations, another thought occurred to us. Even though our objective was just four crow-flight miles from Rice Anchorage, we had to cover an eight-mile route, around Enogai Inlet, to get there. HQ wanted us to do it in three days, so we had been issued just three days' worth of rations. But even a private like me now realized that there was no way in hell we were going to get there in three days. The absence of the long-range radio that never got landed now became painfully evident as Colonel Liversedge, using just our TBX, found himself unable to report about our snaillike progress and, worse, was unable to request an airdrop with additional rations and ammo. We were totally on our own.

On that dismal thought, we went to sleep.

P rogress the second day wasn't any better than on the first, especially when we had to scale the island's many hills and ridges. It was bad enough climbing one side of the muddy slope, but it was quite another to descend the rain-slicked reverse side without losing one's footing in the muck and tumbling down, bowling over other Raiders like tenpins. We'd continue the march well into the night, guided by the phosphorescent glow on the backpack of the man in front of us. When we halted for the night, we again underwent the ritual of trying to wedge ourselves into the tree roots, ankles often remaining awash in pooled rainwater. There, mostly out of sheer exhaustion, we fell asleep, despite the harsh sounds of unseen birds and animals that cawed and growled somewhere off in the inky black forest.

Our movement was hampered even more on the third day when the scout's trail ended at the Giza Giza River, which was waist deep and had to be forded carefully to avoid being carried away by the strong current. Still dripping wet from that crossing, we soon reached the bank of a second waterway, the Tamakau River. These two rain-swollen rivers join their waters just before they merge with Enogai Inlet. The Tamakau, its swiftly moving, muddy brown water as much as nine feet deep, held us up the longest. Luckily Corry's Boys had earlier located a downed tree that stretched across to the opposite shore. Working feverishly, they rigged rope handholds, and one by one, in a slow, deliberate procession, we began the perilous crossing. The tree trunk was wet from rain and dangerously slick with moss, forcing total concentration on each footstep. Still, as many as eleven men lost their footing and plunged into the frothy water. They would no doubt have drowned had several of our strongest swimmers not gone in after them, fighting the deadly current to pull each unfortunate man to safety. Amazingly, no one was swept away to a watery grave.

The crossing was a god-awful slow process, and we thanked our lucky stars that the Japs seemed unaware of our presence. Had they hit us as we straddled the river, half on one side and half on the other, we'd have been sitting ducks.

The Tamakau was not our only impediment. The land around the juncture of the inlet and the river was one vast rain-swelled swamp. With weapons held high, we sloshed through knee-deep, and even waist-deep, pools of stagnant water. By this time our feet, trapped inside socks and boots that had been saturated for four days, were turning purple. When we finally cleared the swamp and reached relatively solid ground, the narrow foot trail split off. The Army took one path, en route to their assigned positions, as we Raiders swung around the inlet's tip and struck out for Enogai and the Jap base.

Having rounded Enogai Inlet on July 7, we had officially entered the Dragons Peninsula. As we picked our way toward Enogai, it did not take long for us to make contact with the enemy.

Amazingly, it seemed the Japanese garrison was still unaware that we had come ashore at Rice Anchorage and were advancing on their rear. That may be why one of our advance patrols, coming across a two-man enemy outpost, was able to close in on it and silence the guards using knives. With that post eliminated, we slowly, cautiously continued forward. Shortly after crossing a small stream near a small village called Marenusa, a patrol of men led by Angus Goss ran into an enemy force that had been headed for the village of Triri, on the southern shore of Enogai Inlet. Gunfire now erupted, echoing through the stillness of the jungle. Two of the Japanese fell dead, but their numbers proved too much for Goss's small group.

"Fall back," Goss ordered, and he and his men began a fighting withdrawal, back across the stream they had just forded. Once across, they took cover and made a stand, pouring fire at the pursuing Japs.

Clay Boyd, who had resumed command of Dog Company after we landed on Monday, now pushed his men toward the hot firefight up ahead. Approaching the skirmish, he swung D Company to the right, through the underbrush, and launched a sudden attack on the Japanese flank. The enemy was horrified to find a company of Raiders come down on them seemingly from out of nowhere, hollering at the top of their lungs, with weapons blazing. Goss now ordered his men forward, and as the Raiders crashed through the jungle, the enemy fled in chaos. Ten of their men lay dead on the jungle floor, and one more was wounded and dying. Three Raiders had been killed and four wounded in the fight.

As we would later learn, the Japs were caught totally off guard by our sudden emergence from the jungle. The enemy commander thought the terrain between Rice Anchorage and Enogai, with its interminable swamps, was impassable. Had we attacked in strength after the fight at Triri, we might have swept the Japanese out of Enogai in a single surge. However, no such strike with pile-driver force was possible, as our column was strung out for more than a mile and a half, bogged down by swamp and jungle.

Rifling through the pockets and knapsacks of the slain Japs for important papers, Boyd made a disturbing discovery. Locating Griffith, who had now come up, he called him over.

"Colonel, take a look at this," he said, indicating the dead Jap at his feet. "Look at his uniform insignia."

Griffith did, noting that the man wore anchors on his clothes, and not chrysanthemums.

"They're not regular Army," Griffith noted. "They're Special Naval Landing Force."

We'd been led to believe the defenders here were all Imperial Army troops. Now we knew differently. We had fought men like these all too often. In fact, except for Tasimboko, every one of our battles seemed to pit us against the elite men of the SNLF, including the 3rd Kure SNLF at Tulagi. Better trained and tougher than regular Imperial troops, the *Kaigun Tokubetsu Rikusentai*, or Special Naval Landing Force, was sometimes mistakenly referred to as Japanese Marines. They were specially trained and even less prone to surrender than regular Army troops. Raised and trained at various Japanese naval bases, for which they were named, these dead men at our feet were from the 6th Kure SNLF. Every one of us who heard this news now realized that with SNLF men waiting for us, the fight had just gotten a helluva lot more difficult.

Even as this revelation was being mulled over by our commanders, I watched as a detail of Raiders buried the three of our men who had died. A large grave was dug by the base of a massive banyan tree, and the three bodies carefully laid inside, each man covered by a rubber poncho. Digging was no problem since the rain of the past few days had turned the earth into a gooey sponge. Then the grave was reverently shoveled closed. Two men had made crude crosses by securing six small logs and tying pairs of them together with communication wire. As I watched the crosses being placed in the ground, a shiver ran down my spine. Getting killed on Guadalcanal was one thing, but I sure as hell didn't want to wait for kingdom come lying in this stinking, rotten place.

Our dead now buried and our wounded being carried by native scouts, we prepared to move on. All hope of surprising the enemy was now gone. They'd be ready for us. We weren't afraid to take on the Japs, but one concern I heard Griffith and Boyd share was that we had fired off a lot of ammunition in the skirmish just ended, and we had no way to resupply.

———

Even as we prepared to attack Enogai, the Jap high command, reacting to our presence, dispatched the 13th Infantry Regiment across Kula Gulf to Bairoko, then sent them down the Bairoko/Munda Trail to strengthen the guard at that vital airfield. Between July 9, when the movement began, and July 12, they would ship men to Munda in batches, which is precisely what Lieutenant Colonel Schultz's roadblock on the vital trail was supposed to prevent. But the 3/148 was having a tough go of things. First off, there was not just one trail, but several paths running parallel to one another. Colonel Schultz dug his men in at the junction of what appeared to be the best-traveled main path and a native trail. The Japanese struck the Army with repeated attacks, boxing Schultz in while they cut a new trail around the roadblock.

Meanwhile, our attack on Enogai would not be launched until to-morrow. Griffith deemed the hour too late, so we were ordered to dig in. All night long, we hunkered down along our line as Japs shouted insults about Eleanor Roosevelt, and we'd yell back the by now familiar "Tojo eats shit" and something insinuating that the emperor has sex with barnyard animals. And so it went. At least the rain had ended.

Dawn arrived and Griffith dispatched two ambush patrols. The one from Dog Company, under Lieutenant Joe Broderick, a Nicaragua veteran experienced in jungle warfare, had barely started out when they ran headfirst into a Jap patrol coming the other way. Rifle fire crackled at the firing spread along our line like a burning fuse. Our machine gun squad laid down covering fire as Bill Waltrip shifted his .30-cal to a better firing position. J. T. Allen, serving as his loader, tore open an ammo can and threw in a new belt as Bill cocked the bolt and cut loose. There is just nothing more reassuring in the midst of a hot firefight with the enemy than a Browning machine gun chattering away, spitting hot, spent brass casings from its breech.

As our fight here roared on and on, Griffith ordered up Captain Tom Mullahey.

"Tom," he said sharply. "Take A Company and outflank the Nips."

Mullahey did as ordered and moved out quickly, a couple of Corry's Boys in the lead. However, as mentioned earlier, these natives were coastal dwellers and did not make the jungles their homes, and while

Corry's Boys were extremely capable scouts, this time they lost the trail, and Able Company wandered aimlessly deep into thigh-high swamps. Finally, Mullahey was forced to retrace his footsteps and return.

The fighting raged on. Two companies of Army troops from the 3/145 were ordered up from the reserve. Green, but eager to prove their mettle, they fought with determination, but the battle-tested veteran Japanese began forcing the Dogfaces to give ground.

Our drive on Enogai bogged down by heavy and determined Jap fire, Griffith turned to Lieutenant Robert C. Kennedy, my platoon leader who had joined the Raiders in New Caledonia, and ordered him to attempt another flanking attack.

"What you have to do," he told Kennedy, "is make your way northwest until you hear that firing over your left shoulder. Then do a ninety-degree flank march until the firing is to your left rear, then wheel again to the left. That should put you in the enemy's rear. Then give 'em hell."

Kennedy, whom we nicknamed "Plowjock," did just that. We moved through the thick underbrush, our column turning when Kennedy heard gunfire over his left shoulder. Griffith's idea worked to perfection. We found ourselves behind the Jap defensive line, and Kennedy ordered us forward. We came screaming out of the woods like banshees, weapons blazing. The Japanese were caught completely flat-footed as we bore down on them yelling "get 'em" and "kill the bastards." The Japs broke and ran in the face of our charge, leaving twenty of their number sprawled across the jungle floor. We'd broken their forward defensive line, but Enogai remained untaken.

––––––––––––

Early the following morning, Corrigan sent his boys back into the jungle to find the trail they'd lost the previous day, the elusive path that would get us around the Jap main line and into Enogai. Luck was with us. This time they picked it up, and by 7:30 a.m., we Raiders had been roused to our feet, and with Charlie Company at point, we were heading back into battle. A mere 750 yards from Enogai harbor, all hell broke loose up front. C Company had blundered into a prepared killing field of Jap Nambu machine gun nests aided by snipers cleverly concealed in the surrounding trees. C Company's lead platoon took heavy losses.

We were ordered to deploy in a line of battle, and began swiftly returning fire. Rifles, BARs, machine guns—we poured it all at the enemy. Waltrip's machine gun raked the jungle ahead of us, sweeping back and forth. With C Company in the center, Able Company fanned out to the left and Baker to the right. Able Company also ran into withering Japanese machine gun and sniper fire as both companies now found themselves pinned down.

We in Baker Company were luckier. Ed Wheeler had stumbled across an opening in the Jap line, and he signaled us forward. But with the rest of the battalion unable to move, we did not push ahead too far, for fear of being cut off.

By now, dusk was quickly enveloping us, and both sides quit the heavy firefight.

Our losses today had been substantial, including Lieutenant Phil Oldham, who had accompanied Wheeler on his canoe patrol a few months earlier. Wheeler took the loss of his friend with quiet courage, much as I had responded on Tulagi as I knelt beside Ken Bowers's body. War affords little time for mourning.

An unfortunate accident occurred that night. Griffith had set up his HQ by a large banyan tree that had sustained battle damage. Under this tree, two radiomen, Sergeant Joseph Szakovics and a pfc. named Henry Seymer, were working the cumbersome TBX radio, clicking off Morse code messages requesting a food drop by air. Our chow by now was pretty much limited to water from our canteens, crackers if we had any, and jungle leaves. Suddenly there sounded a tremendous snap and a gigantic branch fell from the damaged tree, landing on the two radiomen. Szakovics died instantly. Seymer was pinned under the heavy limb, and Griffith cradled the man as others worked to free him. He was quickly carried to our hospital, a cleared area behind a fallen tree.

There Doc Knox and a corpsman amputated Seymer's shattered arm. After the surgery, groggy as he was from the morphine, Seymer insisted on returning to his duties and actually continued sending out the message for food, using his other hand. If the Japanese high commander had seen that type of devotion out of us Americans, I think he might have thrown in the towel and surrendered, knowing he could not defeat that caliber of men.

In fact, at that moment, the only thing that could have defeated us was hunger. I had never been so famished in my life, and I am certain I speak for every man who was there that day. Griffith knew our pain and tried to bolster our will.

"Remember, boys," he told us as he walked the line. "Enogai is just ahead, and the Japs have food there. We just need to go and get it."

We had heard that same message before from Edson when we were on Guadalcanal, abandoned by the Navy and left with little food. It worked then, and we knew it would work here on this hellhole island.

The next morning, starting at 7 a.m., we undertook the task of going after that food with determination. The battalion swept forward in a line abreast, in the same order we had ended the previous day's fight in, with A Company on the left, C in the center, and B on the right. Dog Company under Clay Boyd was held in reserve, but facing away from Enogai in case any Jap reinforcements arrived in our rear.

With loud volleys of gunfire and equally loud, albeit weak from hunger and exhaustion, war whoops, we surged ahead and quickly isolated the enemy garrison at Enogai from their brethren at Bairoko. Finally free of the wretched swamps, we kept rushing forward, under a protecting umbrella of 60mm mortar fire. Our mortarmen, finally unhindered by the thick jungle canopy, dropped a heavy barrage on the Japs, while clearing a path for our final drive ahead. We rushed the enemy, passing smoldering gun positions and their dead inhabitants, blasted to eternity by the mortarmen overjoyed to finally be able to use those stovepipes they had lugged across eight miles of the worst terrain God ever put on one lousy little island.

Still, Enogai's final fall was not a piece of cake. The *Rikusentai* put up a fierce fight worthy of their name, and the machine guns and snipers that plagued A and C companies continued taking a toll. However, our Baker Company line extended beyond the Jap defensive position, and we now took advantage of this gap. At Wheeler's order, we surged forward, bayonets fixed, firing our rifles from the hip and screaming like the souls of hell. The Japs, startled from their cover like a flock of quails, were impossible to miss, and they fell before our blazing muzzles. We raced through the village, with its mortar-blasted huts, not stopping until we arrived on the shore where the Enogai Inlet flowed into Kula Gulf, a trail of dead men marking the path of our attack. Survivors of the Jap garrison fled toward Bairoko, only to be mowed down by a machine gun section set up earlier in that direction and manned by Gunny Joe Cafarella's weapons platoon from A Company.

With victory just one last push away, Griffith now called up a platoon from his reserve, led by Lieutenant Tom Pollard. Three squads, one led by Wilfred Hunt, my assistant squad leader on Tulagi, charged forward, bayonets fixed and shouting like demons. They burst through to the shore of Kula Gulf, then turned and launched a rear attack on a network of Jap machine guns that were still hammering away at C Company.

Baker Company now ran into some stiff resistance by one holdout band of Japs who desired to die for their emperor. One of our squad leaders, Bennie Bunn, led his men into an attack, only to fall with a wound that would cost him his life. Vince Cassidy, promoted to corporal after Tulagi, took over, leading the squad in a determined push that wiped out the final three machine gun nests. This action pretty much ended all Jap resistance in our front.

By 3 p.m. on July 10, Griffith had declared Enogai secured, but it was far from Jap-free. Another stubborn, no-surrender group was entrenched out in front of A Company, and when Boyd led his Dog Company boys against them to take out this final viper's nest, he lost twenty men, mostly wounded. The Japanese remained in place. It was not until the next morning that D Company, a gleam of vengeance in their eyes, overran the enemy and wiped them out.

When the shooting stopped, we counted the dead. No less than 350 Jap bodies lay ripening in the tropical heat, black clouds of flies feasting on the blood and gore. We buried 47 Raiders in all, for a total loss of 51 counting the 4 men missing. In addition, our corpsmen and doctors worked on 74 men touched by lead and steel but still alive in our field hospital, or walking around with an arm or shoulder in bandages.

On the plus side of the bloody ledger, our conquest of Enogai netted us a much-needed supply of Japanese field rations, including tinned meat and fish, canned vegetables, and dried plums. Even better, we liberated several cases of sake.

With Enogai's harbor now in our hands, it wasn't long before landing boats were coming in from the gulf with supplies, mainly food and ammo. A trio of graceful PBY Catalina flying boats touched down, gliding across the surface of the water in order to fly our wounded back to the main hospitals on Guadalcanal and Tulagi. Among the men flown out was Captain Boyd, who was suffering from a serious bout of malaria. He was a good man and an excellent officer and we hated losing him. We hoped he'd return. In his absence, another fine officer, 1st Lieutenant Frank Kemp, took over D Company.

As we settled into our new surroundings that evening, word came down that Griffith had renamed Enogai Camp Cain, after a twenty-two-year-old NCO named William Cain, a new guy but one who had shown lots of promise. Cain had died in the assault on Enogai, leaving a young wife, Mary, back in San Diego, who did not yet know she was a widow.

As we pondered the recently ended fight, our thoughts turned to the coming one. Two miles to the west-southwest lay Bairoko, with its excellent harbor, and until it fell, the Japs would continue to supply the airstrip at Munda. We'd be attacking Bairoko all too soon, we knew, and we wondered how many more widows would be left back home before we were finished.

CHAPTER TWELVE

"YOU ARE COVERING OUR WITHDRAWAL"

DEBACLE AT BAIROKO
TUESDAY, JULY 20, 1943

Following the harder than expected fight to seize Enogai, we Raiders were exhausted, hungry, and in need of more ammo. Yet, as things shook out, we would have been far better off to keep going, follow the retreating Japanese clear into Bairoko, and take the damned harbor in one violent swoop.

We didn't do that. In fact, we wasted ten days at Enogai before assaulting Bairoko; ten days that saw us reinforced, but also saw the Japs bring in more troops from Kolombangara, fortifying Bairoko far beyond anything we had been led to expect.

Captain Wheeler had B Company dig in, and we erected shelter halves and pup tents in a vain effort to stay dry during the all-too-frequent periods of rain. I had never experienced rain like what fell on us here in New Georgia. Saying it came down in buckets doesn't even come close to describing it. The constant deluges and the resultant mud meant we were never totally dry. It grew maddening, and some men actually cracked under the strain. Worse, any open wound could become infected and, combined with our lousy diet, could lead to tropical ulcers or, as we called it, "jungle rot." These open, oozing sores ate into the skin, muscle, and even the bone, which, in some cases, could mean having an arm or leg amputated. I had developed a mild case of jungle rot around my lower legs and feet, and was trying my damnedest to keep that area dry. Antibiotics in conjunction with nutritious food were the best means of combating the disease. Unfortunately, we had neither on New Georgia.

As far as I am concerned, and I am sure I speak for any man who was there, the Japs were welcome to keep this damned, stinking, rotten island.

The village of Bairoko lies on the opposite side of the Dragons Peninsula, a scant two miles west-southwest of Enogai. It boasts a fine, deepwater anchorage with piers and beaches, all on the Enogai side of the inlet, capable of handling barges and landing craft traffic from Kula Gulf. The Japs felt Bairoko was vital to the defense of their airfield at Munda, and our HQ felt it was just as vital as a means of isolating and destroying that same airfield.

Bairoko, we knew, would be a tough nut to crack, starting with just getting there in the first place. Even though it was only two miles from where we now were, the ground between was largely jungle-choked. Only two trails led toward our destination. One was the Triri/Bairoko Trail, which was basically a narrow, native path that connected Triri on the coast of Enogai Inlet to the Bairoko/Munda Trail south of the harbor. The other, better used trail more or less hugged the coast of Leland Lagoon, which cut inland from the gulf, then swung west, pointing toward Bairoko like a watery finger. Between the two trails was tangled jungle and vile swampland, which we all knew meant there would be no opportunity for fancy maneuvering. When we attacked Bairoko, it would be a desperate, head-on frontal assault.

Colonel Liversedge knew it, too. He was also aware that he had zero chance of catching the Japanese by surprise. When we attacked, we'd be facing tough SNLF veterans, well entrenched, well armed, and well prepared to die where they stood. Worse, they grew stronger and more determined every day we delayed.

He needed help, so he ordered Captain William Stevenson to hop a ride back to Guadalcanal on board a Catalina flying boat, to consult with Admiral Turner. After hearing Stevenson out, Turner agreed and ordered the 4th Raiders, also fighting on New Georgia, in the area of Segi Harbor, well to our east, to go to our assistance. He also asked the Army for additional units to lend a hand. Stevenson managed to secure a new, high-powered radio in hopes of easing our communications problems. On the negative side of the ledger, he refused to provide the requested naval support, claiming that Kula Gulf was too much of a contested battle zone and he did not wish to risk his ships in order to provide the Raiders with naval gunfire for the coming assault.

As agreed, the 4th Raiders, commanded by Lieutenant Colonel Michael Currin, were soon ordered to embark for Enogai, but help from the Army would not happen. Turmoil at the top of the Army command had led to a change in leadership, and the new commander's focus was on Munda. He did not wish to throw more men into a campaign on the Dragons Peninsula. On top of that, four days after Stevenson spoke with Turner, Admiral Nimitz plucked the admiral out of his job and put him into a new command position for the upcoming Central Pacific drive. Turner was replaced by Rear Admiral Thomas Wilkinson, who, to our misfortune, was also fixated on Munda.

Meanwhile, we waited for something—anything—to happen, as we contemplated our plight. As Raider Frank Guidone later calculated, we were getting paid $36 a month to be shot at, and since our "workday" was twenty-four-hours long, seven days a week, our pay rate boiled down to less than a nickel an hour. And for that twentieth of a dollar, we lived in crappy conditions. We had no dry beds, were always out in the rain and mud, wore wet clothes that stank to high heaven, ate little food, and lived with the constant threat of a Japanese counterattack. It made one stop and wonder.

The time we spent waiting gave me the chance to hang out with my old Dog Company buddies, Ray Ruble, Alex Stewart, and "Mac"

MacNeilly. I liked the men in my machine gun squad, especially Wild Bill Waltrip, but the old crew were the guys with whom I felt most at home. We had shipped over together, fought on Tulagi and at Tasimboko together, and endured the hellish fighting on Bloody Ridge together. We also shared fun memories. On one occasion, my former squad leader, Corporal Spike Edwards, strode past our bivouac. Back on the 'Canal, Spike had somehow managed to procure a major's uniform and brazenly walked into the Officers' Club to quench his thirst.

"Hey, Corporal," I called. "If you meet Al K. Hall anywhere, you bring him around. We wanna renew his acquaintance."

"You won't find him anywhere around here, Whitey," Spike fired back with a grin. "We got no OC."

We all guffawed. Spike was a fireball, and we all wondered what sort of blackmail he had on the brass that he managed to keep his stripes.

The days between our securing Enogai and the attack at Bairoko weren't all just sitting on our asses, thinking of booze and women— neither of which we had enjoyed since leaving New Caledonia—and being miserable. There were always patrols, during which we earned that five-cents-per-hour wage. All of us ran patrols during this time, and being in a machine gun squad did not exempt me. Selected for a recon foray toward Bairoko, about a dozen of us entered the jungle, cautiously probing for the Jap lines. The jungle was incredibly thick, with just a narrow trail cutting through the tangle. In the lead was Lieutenant "Plowjocks" Kennedy, our platoon leader, who had led us forward when we broke the Jap line at Enogai. Fairly new to combat, Kennedy was somewhat clumsy and inexperienced, a trait that would now cost him dearly. With visibility ahead limited to just a few feet due to the foliage, a veteran officer would have known enough to stay off the trail and not walk at point. Kennedy either did not know those details or ignored them. Not only did he foolishly walk at point while sticking to the path, but he carried his map case on his shoulder and binoculars around his neck. He may as well have carried a sign saying "I'm an officer, shoot me first." I heard one of the NCOs urge caution and respectfully advise him to step off the trail, but Kennedy followed neither piece of advice. What came next was no surprise.

A Jap patrol approaching from the opposite direction suddenly appeared ahead of us, and both sides opened fire. Kennedy had been walking with his hands down, his carbine held low. Several Jap rounds stitched through both of his arms. He grunted in shock and pain and dropped. The sudden exchange of gunfire was both thrilling and frightening as bullets buzzed past our ears, thudding into trees, snipping off thick vines, and shredding foliage. I saw two or three Japs appear to fall to our return fire, but in the dense underbrush, it was hard to be sure. I emptied one eight-round clip from my Garand, fed in another, and emptied that one. As the spent clip was ejected from my weapon with a metallic ping, the shooting died away. The sudden silence was eerie. The breech of my rifle yawned empty, a thin wisp of smoke curling from it, so I inserted a new clip and peered ahead into the jungle. The Japs had vanished as if they had never been there at all, leaving only a thin cloud of gun smoke hanging nearly immobile in the humid air. Now a new sound came to my ears, the whimpering of the injured officer lying on the forest floor near me. Our sergeant was kneeling by Lieutenant Kennedy and said to me, "Whitey. Your first aid kit. Give me some morphine."

I fished open the small first aid kit attached to my web belt and drew out one of the small tubes. One for pain, it was said, and two for eternity. I handed it to the sergeant, who removed the clear plastic covering. He gripped the wire loop at the tip and pushed it in, piercing the metal seal on the tube. Then he tossed the wire loop and jammed the exposed needle into the lieutenant's shoulder, adjacent to the nasty-looking bloody wound. Squeezing the tube, he fed the half grain of blessed pain relief into the injured man.

"Rig up a stretcher," the sergeant commanded.

Quickly, using two rifles and a couple of ponchos, the stretcher was thrown together and the lieutenant gently lifted onto it.

"Grab an end," I heard someone say.

I didn't know if he was talking to me or not, but I bent down and grasped one end of the stretcher, and we lugged Kennedy back to Enogai, the only man on our patrol who was hit in the exchange.

———————————

Around July 17, the 4th Raiders began landing at Enogai from Higgins boats. As I watched them come ashore, I wondered how much help they'd be. They had been fighting on the other end of New Georgia since June 27, and they looked almost as weary and worn out as we did.

Colonel Liversedge's idea was to launch a double envelopment attack, with the Raiders, both us and Lieutenant Colonel Currin's men, moving directly at the harbor along the main Enogai/Bairoko Trail, while Lieutenant Colonel Schultz and his 3/148 advanced to our left along the Triri/Bairoko Trail. While we Raiders launched a frontal assault, it was hoped that the Army's sudden appearance on the Jap right flank would come as a rude surprise and jar them out of their works and into the open where we could deal with them. The 3/145 was to be held in reserve at Triri. Our much depleted A and C companies would remain at Enogai to guard our base camp.

To support our attack, Liversedge requested air strikes, and the Navy obliged. On July 15, and again on July 17, SBD Dauntless and SB2C Helldiver ("Son of a Bitch 2nd Class" her pilots sometimes called the large airplane) dive-bombers, accompanied by TBF Avengers toting two-thousand-pound bombs in place of torpedoes, droned high over our heads, and then came screaming down from the clouds to pummel the enemy positions. The rumble of the detonations provided us with a grim satisfaction that, perhaps, we might find the Japanese defenses flattened. Then past experience returned and reminded us that no amount of aerial or naval pounding would drive a determined Japanese soldier from his carefully reinforced works.

On July 19, the day before we were to jump off, our planes returned. Nineteen Avengers and eighteen dive-bombers blanketed the Japanese positions with one-thousand- and two-thousand-pound bombs.

Captain Clay Boyd, who had been flown back to Guadalcanal with a severe case of malaria, went AWOL from the base hospital, we later learned, and hitched a ride with a Dauntless pilot. He wanted to observe the bombing of Bairoko from the rear gunner's seat. Ten minutes after the dive-bombers disappeared over the eastern horizon, headed back for the 'Canal, the sky was again filled with the hum of aircraft engines. This time they were eighteen-cylinder Wright "Twin Cyclones" affixed to the wings of eight B-25 Mitchell bombers. The two-engine planes winged over us at ten thousand feet, bomb bay doors yawning open. Once over the Jap lines, the bombardiers toggled their loads, each dumping three thousand pounds of explosives. That done, they wheeled about and changed their role from bomber to gunship. Roaring in on the Japanese, they strafed the enemy with a hailstorm of .50-caliber rounds from at least twelve machine guns in each ship. It was an impressive show. We just hoped it had done some good.

———————

As Tuesday July 20 dawned, we Raiders were preparing for battle, loading weapons, stuffing ammo clips into the empty ammo pouches on our bandoliers, hanging grenades on our web gear, and making sure KABARs and stilettos were razor-sharp. Captain Wheeler made the rounds, giving instructions to his platoon leaders and encouragement to his men.

"How's that jungle rot coming along, Whitey?" he asked me.

"It hurts, but I'll live," I replied. "Unless the Japs have other plans, that is."

"Well you take care today," Wheeler said, patting me on the shoulder. "Once we take Bairoko, maybe we'll get a break and get taken off this island, so we can get you and some of the other guys taken care of better."

Wheeler left, and I turned to Waltrip.

"Who's he kidding?" I asked.

"You're right, son," Bill replied. "This island is totally unfit for human habitation, so you just know they're gonna keep us here."

At 8 a.m. precisely, Wheeler fanned the company out with three platoons abreast and signaled us forward. Initially, the terrain was fairly open and we moved unhindered, but before long the jungle closed in, cutting off one platoon from the next. Our right flank platoon, under Lieutenant Bill Christie, moved parallel to the lagoon and had the easiest time of it, at least initially.

Colonel Liversedge had requested an air strike for 9 a.m., in hopes of clearing a pathway for us to push forward while the Japs had their heads down. He hoped that would put us almost among them before they could use their stout defenses to their benefit. The problem was that Liversedge had made the request too late, and he did not wait for confirmation of the air support. If he had, he'd have known that his message was never received. So by 9 a.m., as we advanced on Bairoko, we kept scanning the skies for friendly aircraft that would never arrive.

Pushing forward along the beach area with almost no cover, Christie's men met the first enemy fire at around 10:15 a.m. They flopped down on the ground, exposed, and returned fire.

The rest of B Company wasn't doing any better. Wheeler kept advancing us, growing more and more worried when he lost sight of the platoons to either side of him, obscured by the increasingly dense underbrush. Then the Japs raked our line with automatic weapons fire, and we heard the all too familiar whir of invisible bullets buzzing through the jungle. Some struck flesh. A man a few feet to my right grunted in pain and dropped, a hand clutching a bloody shoulder. We ducked down, seeking whatever shelter the heavy foliage and twisted tree roots afforded us. Bill Waltrip set up the .30-cal and, with J. T. Allen serving as loader, sprayed the Jap positions before us. To our left, we could hear more gunfire as the balance of Dog Company also began running up against the Jap defenses.

Wheeler was soon among us, moving along his company line.

"We need to push our machine guns forward, Bill," I heard him tell Waltrip. "Try to punch a hole through their line."

At that command, Bill scooped up his gun, a kerchief in one hand to avoid being burned by the hot barrel, and our squad inched forward, followed by other MG squads. It was slow, tedious work. We'd place the gun, fire at the enemy to drive them back, then move the gun forward a few inches more. As we advanced, the rest of the platoon moved with us, laying down as much covering fire for the machine guns as possible. The more we advanced, the stiffer the resistance became. By noon, we had broken through the line of outposts, creeping past shattered Jap machine gun nests manned by dead gunners. Passing them, we ran smack into the main line of resistance, and a wall of lead came at us from Nambus firmly placed in nests chiseled into the hard coral. Our advance was brought to a halt.

We had dribbled casualties during our entire forward movement, but now we were up against an immovable phalanx of machine guns covered by snipers tucked away in treetops. How to get at them and root them out, that was the question. We had no bazookas and flamethrowers, so we were reduced to old-fashioned tactics: hand grenades and fixed bayonets.

Removing grenades from our web belts, we grasped them tightly. At the order, we yanked out the pins, making sure to keep a firm grip on the lever or spoon.

"Now!" came the call, and we hurled the pineapples at the Jap guns. Some men tossed smoke grenades as well. Then, with a yell, we charged with bayonets thrust out ahead of us. It brought back horrible memories of Bloody Ridge as we got among the Jap defenders, slashing and stabbing, until the survivors fled to the rear. But for each machine gun position we took in that daredevil manner, there was another one to attack and then another, and our supply of grenades was soon all but exhausted. We'd made as much headway as we could, but we were now mired down.

On the beach by the lagoon, Christie's platoon was also stuck.

"Cassidy," Christie called, summoning Corporal Vince Cassidy. "Take a squad and try to work your way around the Jap flank."

Cassidy nodded and signaled his squad to follow. They sidled around to the left, but that way was blocked as well. Cassidy reported back to Christie, and the lieutenant sent a runner to find Wheeler and tell him that his approach to Bairoko was hopelessly stymied. In fact, the whole damned

Raider line was stymied. More than one thousand men of the 1st and 4th Raiders attacking on an eight-hundred-yard front were halted in our tracks.

Okumura had used the ten-day delay we had given him to good effect. While we sat on our asses waiting for the 4th Raiders to arrive, the Japanese commander had fortified his line with one thousand well-supplied men holding an arc a thousand yards long and bulging out from the harbor five hundred yards at its deepest point. His position was studded with five-man heavy machine gun bunkers. Covered by logs and coral, with narrow, well-camouflaged gun slits, they proved nearly impossible to spot. These heavy MG nests were supported by lighter machine guns and several 90mm mortars that could lob a twelve-pound explosive four thousand yards—all topped off with snipers tucked away in trees like some sort of deadly orchard.

If combat men ever experienced a Hell on Earth, this was it.

But neither Liversedge nor Griffith was ready to concede defeat.

Liversedge ordered the Army's 3/148 to advance along the Triri/Bairoko Trail and reinforce us. Lieutenant Colonel Schultz moved his regiment ahead slowly, taking six hours to push forward about twenty-five hundred yards. Then, about a thousand yards from linking up with our left flank, they ran into intense Jap fire. Schultz, an inexperienced and overly conservative combat commander, assumed he had run into the main Japanese line, and he hunkered down to form a defensive position. He had not met the main Jap line, but he was now as immobile as if he had. The 3/145 back at Triri was too far in our rear to be of help. A determined and rapid response by the Army was what we needed to break through, but it was not the response we got.

Communication problems, which had plagued us ever since we landed on this stinking island, also hindered Liversedge's coordination of the battle that was rapidly turning against us.

Griffith, whose battalion was fully committed to the fight, fretted over his flank. Thinking maybe Angus Goss's demolition platoon could bolster our front, he sent the irascible Goss and his boys over to D Company to plug a gap that had developed between Dog and our own Baker companies.

The Jap machine guns had us hugging the dirt while snipers picked off men right and left. Three Dog Company Raiders were hit by the same sniper before he was spotted. Then a heavy fusillade of small arms fire riddled the man and he dropped from his perch.

The Japanese seemed to be all around—in front, in back, and even above us. After the war, Frank Guidone, who had recently received a battlefield promotion to second lieutenant, said he thought the volume of fire exceeded what we experienced on Bloody Ridge.[1] We were limited in the amount of return fire we had available. The dense jungle and the leafy canopy overhead ruled out mortars.

Late in the fighting, a joint effort by elements of the 1st and 4th Raiders, led by Lieutenant Joe Cuetara, launched a determined attack to try to relieve the pressure on Wheeler. The assault had some effect, and we were able to fight our way forward a short distance, before we bogged down again under intense Jap fire. I heard Wheeler get on the radio and ask Griffith for support, saying that with a few reinforcements we might be able to break through. But Griffith had no help to send. The entire Raider battalion was just barely hanging on.

The 4th Raiders made a bold attempt to break the stalemate. Companies N, led by Captain Earl Snell, and P, commanded by Captain Anthony Walker, launched a gutsy bayonet charge. Emitting a loud rebel yell, they surged forward. The charge was successful at first, and the Raiders seized a small ridge. However, concentrated Japanese fire cut down many of them, including both brave company commanders, and the attack broke down.

Dog Company, through guts and sheer determination, kept pushing forward amid the hail of Jap fire that cut down many a good Raider. Kemp, promoted to captain after he assumed company command, and his boys penetrated two of the four Japanese lines of defense, seizing a small coral ridge. Three hundred yards away, they could see the shimmering water of Bairoko Harbor. The men took what shelter they could as the Japanese launched a Banzai attack on the ridge. Weight of numbers told, and D Company was nearly forced from the ridge. But then, with a bloodcurdling howl, they surged forward again and the Japs were driven away. D Company dug in. As they held on to what they had gained, Jap 90mm mortars fell like hailstones, killing and wounding men in the close-packed salient.

The slugging match continued, and good men died. Sergeant Jim Walsh, one of the hearty souls who had fished guys out of the rain-swollen Tamakau River, was killed by a Jap bullet. In our company, dead-eye marksman Sergeant Johnny Holladay, whose trusty Springfield, Old Lucifer, had sent many a Jap to meet his ancestors, was crouched down by a tree with Corpsman James Boren. A cry of "corpsman" came up from the fighting just ahead, and Boren responded. As he left Holladay to go forward, he heard a rifle shot, loud and close by. A sinking feeling concerning Holladay suddenly hit the corpsman, and he returned to the tree to find the young sergeant dead, a victim of a Jap sniper lurking in one of the many trees. Johnny would never sing "John Henry" again, and I later read where Vince Cassidy eulogized him by saying, "The last string is broken, the melody died. He is dead at Bairoko, and with him lies 'John Henry.'" [2]

Perhaps the loss that hit us all the hardest was when feisty Angus Goss fell, a bullet through his heart. A chaplain who was traveling with us, Father Paul Redmond, dragged the body to a protective nook by a fallen tree trunk and laid Goss out. Kneeling over Goss's prostrate form, he gave the old Marine last rites. He next removed an American flag he carried tucked away in a haversack, and covered Goss's body. I later saw Angus lying there, a lonely and forlorn figure, the flag covering the upper half of his body, his legs and feet protruding out from under the Stars and Stripes that he had died defending. Once again I had the thought, "What a sad and miserable place to die."

Jap 90mm mortars began pouring down on our lines, blasting men and trees alike. Liversedge again attempted to get the 3/148 to move up and reinforce us, but Lieutenant Colonel Schultz insisted that he could not advance. Liversedge was fit to be tied. Schultz was no more than a thousand yards away but could not, or would not, close the gap.

"Griff," he said wearily. "Make a sweep of our lines and see if there's any way for us to break through the Jap defenses."

Griffith did so, making his way carefully, company by company, as he covered the length of both battalions. Everywhere he stopped, he became more and more disheartened by our losses in killed and wounded. As a unit, we were bleeding profusely and nearing the point of total exhaustion. Finally edging forward to Dog Company's salient, he knelt down by Captain Kemp.

"Frank," Griffith said. "How's it going?"

"We're hanging on by our teeth," Kemp replied. "Any chance of the rest of the battalion pushing ahead?"

Griffith shook his head dejectedly. Just three hundred yards away he saw the harbor, so close and yet it may as well have been on the moon.

"What do you think your chances are of reaching the harbor?" Griffith asked.

Now it was Kemp's turn to shake his head.

"We're losing the daylight, but we can get there," he replied assuredly. "But I don't think many of us would get back unless the other companies move up as well."

It was the answer Griffith had expected. He knew Baker Company was pinned down, and the rest were all confronted with dense jungle thickly studded with pillboxes. With a heavy heart, he slapped Kemp on the shoulder and headed back for HQ. There he delivered the bad news to Liversedge. The Raiders, both battalions, were hopelessly mired down and cowering under relentless Jap mortar fire. We had suffered more than 250 casualties, many of them litter cases who would require being carried out. Ammo was nearly exhausted, as were medical supplies and pure water to quench parched throats. The Japs could re-supply from Vila across the gulf.

"Without air support or the Army coming up to lend a hand, we're stuck," Griffith concluded. "We have no choice. If we want to save what's left of the Raiders, we need to break off."

To Griffith's surprise, Liversedge concurred.

"Give the orders," he said resignedly. "We'll hold our positions for the night, and pull back in the morning."

As Griffith went off to spread the word, Liversedge got on the radio, requesting air support by every available plane for the next day. When the officer on the other end hemmed and hawed, Liversedge's temper flared.

"You are covering our withdrawal," he snapped.

When word circulated that we were pulling back, we were stunned. We knew our assault had been stopped, that we were taking serious losses, and that many of us were fighting despite suffering from dysentery and malaria. But our fighting spirit had not diminished. We all thought that, somehow, a way through the Jap lines would be found and that we would achieve our mission. Bitterly, we dug in. What the hell had it all been for?

As dawn began to streak the Wednesday morning sky, we prepared to disengage. We knew this withdrawal was going to be a tough one. The Jap fire was intense, and it was guaranteed that they'd send a hail of lead after us as we retired rearward.

Captain Wheeler eased some of our concerns when he showed up on our platoon front.

"We are heading back for Enogai," he said with the same sourness in his voice that we felt in our guts. "This is not going to be easy. The bastards let us advance well into their lines and then closed up around us. The flyboys will be providing close air-ground support, and I mean close. They'll be bombing and strafing the Japs in order to clear us a path back, as well as making the Nip bastards keep their heads down. You'll move when we give the order and drop if we say so. You'll get the signal when to move, so get ready."

As soon as it was light enough to see, we heard the planes coming. A flock of B-25 Mitchells swarmed in, engines thrumming so loudly the ground vibrated.

"Here they come, those beautiful bastards," Boyer White muttered beside me.

I watched the Mitchells approach, bomb bay doors open. Then bombs began toppling from the planes, the first of 130 tons of explosives the Air Corps would drop to cover our retreat. The jungle exploded all around. Flames and smoke rose into the sky, mixed with shards of splintered trees and smashed vegetation.

"Let's go," the call went up, and we headed rapidly back the way we had come twenty-four hours earlier.

I think our withdrawal went more smoothly than was anticipated, due in large part to the fact that the Air Corps today more than made up for their failure yesterday to flatten enemy defenses during our advance. They flew 250 sorties on our behalf, bombing and strafing the Japs unmercifully. A few of the enemy who had gotten behind us, mainly snipers, tried to impede our withdrawal, but most of them died in the attempt. The Japs on the main line, now in our rear, did not pursue. My guess is they were too busy cowering in their pillboxes beneath the terrific aerial pounding. That did not mean the way back was easy. The jungle was just as tangled going back as it had been moving up, only now we were encumbered by the many wounded. Almost every man took a turn helping to lug a stretcher. I did my turn, and when I wasn't toting one end of a litter, I was walking alongside one, holding a plasma bottle the rubber tube from which ended up attached to a needle buried in some seriously wounded Raider's arm. As I gazed down at the ashen face on the stretcher, I counted how fortunate I had been. In fighting from Tulagi to Tasimboko to Bloody Ridge and the Matanikau, I had not been touched by an enemy bullet. Now here on New Georgia, I had again been blessed.

Our march back to Enogai was slow, with the column halting every few hundred yards because of delays up ahead. Rubber boats were rowed into Leland Lagoon from Enogai, and some of the worst of our wounded were placed aboard these for more rapid transport back to base, where they could be better tended. It was evening by the time my machine gun squad got back to Enogai, and we collapsed in our company area, tired and dispirited. Out over the harbor we could hear the drone of airplane engines as a couple of PBY Catalina flying boats skimmed in for landings. The men most badly in need of a hospital were taken to the Catalinas by Higgins boats, loaded up, and whisked back to hospitals on Guadalcanal and Tulagi.

The butcher's bill for this screwed up affair was 46 Raiders killed and 198 wounded. The 3/148 lost 3 killed and 8 wounded. This gross disparity of losses could be why we later heard that Griffith chewed Schultz a new asshole and, it was said, threatened to have him hanged from a cherry tree in Washington, D.C., after the war was over.

As for those Raiders who made it back, we were exhausted almost beyond endurance. And in exchange for much suffering and loss, we had gained absolutely nothing.

Just like after the Second Matanikau foul-up, it was time to play the blame game.

Not surprisingly, much of the blame fell on Liversedge, starting with his waiting too long to request the air support that was to precede our attack on July 20. In addition, it was said, he should have opened the attack with a concentrated barrage from our 81mm mortars, which had plenty of ammo. He also could have requested that an artillery unit be attached to him at the same time the 4th Raiders were being sent to join us. A battery of 75mm howitzers saved our asses at Bloody Ridge and might have done the same at Bairoko. And then there were those intact Jap 140mm guns we had captured when we took Enogai, which just sat around unused. A few well-placed rounds from them might have turned things our way as well. Finally, it was said Liversedge should not have assigned the green 3/148 to make the flank attack, but used a Raider battalion instead. Speed was required, and it was the sort of thing we had been trained for. Plus the reserves at Triri were too far to the rear to be of much help.

But there was also blame higher up the command chain. Colonel Merrill Twining dropped it squarely in the lap of Admiral Richmond Kelly Turner, saying the whole mission had been "a vague, ill-conceived, reckless foray."[3] He said the American strategy of a long march by a lot of men through a trackless jungle filled with swamps and mud was the same sort of bad planning Kawaguchi had used on Guadalcanal and which had led him to disaster.

He may have been correct.

But in essence, we felt that our attack was doomed to fail even before we launched it. The Japs had ten days to strengthen their defenses while we sat waiting for the 4th Raiders to arrive. Ten days for one thousand men to fortify their line and make it almost impregnable, especially in so confined an area, where we could not maneuver around their line but had to come at them head-on. So between bad planning, high-ranking screwups, and crappy radios, we Raiders felt we had been ill-used, and we'd lost a lot of good men proving it.

The Joint Chiefs of Staff, looking over the operation some time later, concluded that an attack by troops who are lightly armed against an entrenched enemy supported by heavy automatic weapons, mortars, and heavy artillery will most likely fail. We had proved that beyond question.

So there we sat following our exertions, sick and exhausted, our morale almost at rock bottom. Raider historian Joseph Alexander wrote later that our spark was gone. That was a good summation of our condition. Two weeks later, after examining us poor relics who returned from Bairoko, our regimental doctors, Stuart Knox and J. C. Lockhart, told Liversedge that the Raiders were "unfit for further action" and that if we were again committed to the fighting, it would lead to "unjustifiable slaughter."[4] We spent the last ten days of July sitting in our defensive positions, making just a few patrols in the direction of Bairoko and enduring nuisance raids by Jap aircraft.

The Raiders would be at Enogai until August 28, at which point they boarded a ship bound for Guadalcanal. By this time the 1st Raider Battalion was down to 245 effectives.

I was not among that number.

CHAPTER THIRTEEN

REASSIGNMENT

JULY 1943–AUGUST 1944

By the time the 1st Raider Battalion, or anyway what remained of it, boarded ship on August 28 for its return trip to the 'Canal, I was already back on Tulagi. The jungle rot that had formed around my waist and about my feet, ankles, and lower legs had worsened significantly.

With the fight at Bairoko over, Wheeler approached our machine gun position. He knelt beside me.

"Scuttlebutt says your jungle crud is giving you a lot of problems, Whitey," he said, genuine concern in his voice. "Why don't you fall out and go see the doc?"

"I'll be fine, sir," I replied. "I want to remain with the squad."

Wheeler looked at me like a father would a son and put a hand on my shoulder. He and I had been through a lot together and shared a fondness for one another.

"Damnit, Whitey," he said. "The Marine Corps is not a democracy, so you don't get a vote. You're a good Marine, but you're no use to Wild Bill or me if you can't walk and we have to lug your ass around on a stretcher. Now, git."

"Go along, Son," Waltrip said and smiled. "We can get along without you for a while."

Resignedly, I rose and hobbled off in the direction of what passed for our sick bay. Doc Knox was just finishing lancing a boil on another Marine's left foot. I told him why I was there.

"It was Captain Wheeler's idea," I explained, letting him know I was willing to tough it out.

Knox smiled knowingly and indicated that I was to sit on a nearby tree trunk. I did, and he knelt in front of me.

"Let's have a look see, Whitey," Doc Knox said, as he removed my wet boondockers and saturated socks. He made no comment about trying to keep my feet dry. He knew how pointless such a suggestion was, since he was just as damp as I was from rain, sweat, and humidity. He studied my abused feet, which, I admit, looked nasty, with open sores and cracked, scabby skin that frequently bled. He emitted an occasional "hmmmm" as he checked me out.

"You sound like a man inspecting a used car he might wanna buy," I commented.

"Well, I sure as hell wouldn't want to buy these used cars," he said, indicating my feet. "I have three other men whose feet are as bad as yours or worse. I'm arranging with that Aussie coast watcher Donald Kennedy to have them taken to his hideout up in the mountains for a spell, hoping the change in climate will help. It's drier up there and less humid. I'm sending you along."

That's how I found myself hobbling, assisted by two of Kennedy's Fiji Island soldiers, along a jungle path and up a mountainside. The other three men, in worse shape than me, were being carried on stretchers. Kennedy had about twenty-five of the tough islanders assisting him in his spying activities, and they had been driving the Japs nuts with the information he had been passing along to the Allies. Kennedy's camp was comfortable, and we had better food than down at Enogai. We had the opportunity to relax and were pretty much catered to by Kennedy's men. A corpsman sent along to attend to our needs slathered some sort of salve on my open sores. I never did find out what it was he was using. I only knew that it stank, and since it was on my feet, there was no way I could get away from it. During our stay in the camp, we were well protected, since the Fiji Islanders formed an armed, protective ring around the entire area, a precaution they always performed lest they be surprised by a Jap patrol.

For three days we relaxed and were cared for by the islanders. The natives provided us with light blankets to keep away the nighttime chill, mosquito lotion to fend off the insects and mosquito nets for sleeping. On the fourth day the corpsman decided the jungle rot had not gotten better. We were soon headed back down the mountain and into Enogai.

"Well, Whitey," Knox said as he examined my legs. "I'm shipping you guys back to the Army hospital on Tulagi. There you can get clean, dry clothes, better medicine, and, seeing as it's an Army facility, a damn sight better food than we Marines get. There's a Yippy anchored offshore right now. You'll be put aboard before she leaves at dusk."

That afternoon, hearing that I was being sent back, Bill Waltrip stopped by to see me, as did my old Dog Company buddies.

"I'll see you guys back there," I said. "Stay sharp in case the Japs come calling."

"You stay sharp in case some of those Army nurses come calling," Alex Stewart quipped.

"No chance, Alex," I told him. "I'm not wearing officer's bars."

"Maybe Spike Edwards can steal you some before you leave," Big Stoop Ruble chimed in.

———

An hour before the sun went down, I was helped into a rubber boat and rowed to a YP boat riding at anchor. There some sailors helped me aboard. The stretcher cases were already on the deck. The Navy ensign in command moved among us.

"You fellas just relax," he told us. "It is over two hundred miles to Tulagi, so we won't make it in one hop. We will travel by night, since it is too dangerous in daylight because of Jap planes. We should only have to lay over somewhere for one day, so we'll get you there as quickly as we can."

As he walked away, I watched the young officer and wondered just

who in the hell he had pissed off to be assigned command of this glori-
fied tuna boat.

I'd sailed on a Yippy before, about a year earlier when we were on our
way to smash the Jap supply base at Tasimboko. "Yippy" came from their
designation as YP boats, short for Yard Patrol, and they were basically
close-to-shore patrol craft. YP boats had been in use since before the First
World War. They were originally built for the Coast Guard by various
naval yards, including Philadelphia, and at a few yacht-making businesses,
but the necessities of war had forced the Navy to also use converted tuna
boats, after first reinforcing their hulls with a sheath of steel.

During the course of the war, thirty-one of these boats would be
lost, counting the one we'd sailed to Tasimboko aboard.

As I sat on the deck watching the crew prepare to shove off, I thought
about this vulnerable little craft upon which my life now depended. We'd
be sailing more than two hundred miles on waters frequently patrolled by
Japanese ships and flown over by Japanese aircraft. My ride across this perilous stretch of sea would be on a craft made all of wood and about fifty feet
in length. She was unarmed, and if she had steel sheathing on her hull, I
didn't see it. Then the anchor came up, the engines turned over, and with
a prayer to Almighty God on the lips of myself, and probably several others,
we set off. Where in the hell were the PBY flying boats when I needed one?

It was pitch-black as we rounded the headland of New Georgia's northwest tip and began our run down The Slot. The little boat churned its way
through the water at twelve knots or about twenty-two miles per hour.

I found a comfortable spot on the deck on the port side, where I laid out
my blanket, then curled up, using my pack as a pillow, and tried to get some
sleep. The thrumming of the engine and the slap of water against the hull
was actually quite relaxing. I settled down, knowing that I would soon be
sleeping on a nice, cozy cot in the field hospital instead of in a rain-soaked
mud hole on New Georgia. Plus there'd be better food; this was an Army
hospital after all and not a Marine facility, and the Army always seemed to
go first cabin. All of these thoughts lulled me off to sleep.

I don't know how long I was asleep or what time I awoke, but something brought me back to consciousness. I just wasn't sure what it was. Yes, I was. Someone had shaken me. It was one of the Yippy's sailors. The swabbie who woke me now put a finger to his lips and gave me a "shhhhh." It was like an alarm bell went off in my head and I was fully alert. It was then that I realized the YP boat's engines had stopped and we were practically motionless.

Then a new sound met my ears, the low, deep rumble of larger engines. Other sailors made their way along the YP's deck, signaling everyone to be very quiet and still and to keep low and out of sight. Risking a peek over the gunwall I saw them, black silhouettes on a dark sea in an even darker night. Japanese warships, three or maybe four of them, the nearest one no more than a football field's length off our port side, steaming northward through the black water, coming from the direction of the 'Canal and steaming toward Munda and the Kula Gulf. I was terrified yet unable to take my eyes off the enemy battle fleet. At least two of the ships had the low, sleek profile of destroyers, while the larger one, around which the smaller shapes darted, was most certainly a heavy cruiser.

The hairs on the back of my neck literally stood up as I contemplated this spectacle. I realized now why we had stopped. The night vision skills of Japanese lookouts were well known, and had we been moving, one most certainly would have spotted our wake. The ships were so close the rumble of their engines caused our YP boat to vibrate far more than our own engine had done just below the deck. Frightened that some sharp-eyed lookout might spot my white skin in the dark night, I lowered my face below the gunwale and began to pray. If those bastards spotted our little wooden boat, we'd be blown into matchsticks before their gunners could work up a sweat. I thanked God that our converted tuna boat sat so low in the water. If we would've had any sort of large superstructure, we'd have been spotted easily in such a close encounter.

As the enemy ships continued past us, we were hit by their wakes, and our boat was tossed around as if we'd been riding out a stormy sea. Then the wakes subsided, and slowly, ever so slowly, the rumble of the engines faded and faded until totally gone. The next sound I heard was our own engine turning over, and the familiar vibration of the deck beneath me resumed.

With the danger now over, I began shaking like a leaf from nervousness. That had been too damned close, and I thanked whoever the eagle-eyed swabbie was who'd spotted the Japs in time, and for the quick thinking of the young ensign in command who'd had the presence of mind to shut the boat down and hide in plain sight, shielded only by the blackness of the night.

We steamed on for several hours more, until the first rays of the new morning began to paint the eastern horizon. Off to our starboard side stood a few dots of land, some of the many tiny, nameless islands that are part of the Solomon chain. As I watched, I saw the prow of our boat turn in the direction of one of the dots, and we churned that way through the sea.

Arriving at the island, the skipper found a small cove and cautiously guided his craft into it, aware that the Yippy had about a twelve-foot draft. Inside the cove, he sailed as close to shore as he dared and dropped anchor. This quiet island setting would be our home until the sun began its evening descent.

"Anyone who wants to go ashore and stretch his legs may do so," the skipper announced. "Just don't go too far in case we need to get out of here, and don't do anything to attract the attention of any wandering Nip plane. We have K-rations for you guys to eat, but no hot food or coffee. I don't want any fires lit that might give off smoke. If the Japs find us, we're dead meat. We'll shove off again just before sunset. We should make Tulagi tomorrow."

Within minutes, a dinghy was lowered over the starboard side of the Yippy, and those of us who wanted to walk on shore loaded aboard. Despite my sore and bleeding feet, I yearned to be on dry land, so I stepped onto the dinghy, found a place to sit, and watched as a swabbie pushed us away from the side of the Yippy. Four sailors began rowing us for the beach.

We idled away the day doing whatever pleased us. Some men cracked open coconuts and ate the sweet meat inside. I had sort of lost my taste for coconuts after Tulagi, when the Navy left us stranded and coconuts were all we had to subsist on for weeks. As we whiled away the day, the sky overhead would occasionally come alive with the sounds of airplane engines, and we'd duck for cover. But in every case the planes turned out to be our own, generally Guadalcanal-based dive-bombers and torpedo planes, scouting for enemy targets in The Slot. I'm not sure why our boat's skipper had not tried to make his way toward the 'Canal since we had only friendly aircraft overhead, but maybe he was afraid they'd attack us, thinking we were a Jap boat. I'm not certain our Yippy had a radio. I'd never heard it crackling. Of course, maybe the skipper was just being cautious and keeping radio silence as long as we were within range of the Japs.

As the sun began sinking toward the western horizon, we made preparations to leave. The dinghy that had brought us ashore was reloaded. We pushed off and were rowed back to the Yippy. Once aboard, I resumed my familiar spot on the deck and felt the friendly vibration as the engine restarted. I know not what part of God's earth we had used for our rest—I can't even recall hearing a bird on that little island—but as we got under way, we all gave thanks for that safe haven.

This last leg of our journey proved far less eventful than the first. We could sit up and walk about, talk freely and enjoy the stillness of the night as one can only experience it while sailing on the high seas in the South Pacific, illuminated by a half-moon and a million stars highlighted by the presence of the Southern Cross. The dominance of that constellation is why we Raiders featured it on our shoulder patch.

As our Yippy churned its way toward Tulagi, the corpsman continued to dress my jungle rot with that same damned smelly salve. I must admit, stink as it did, it eased the painful discomfort, but it did little for my actual condition.

As dawn approached, off in the distance we could see land. It was the northern tip of Guadalcanal. Ever so gradually, the island began filling the horizon. Off to port the conical shape of Savo Island seemed to rise up out of the sea. As our boat chugged along between the all too familiar shorelines of the 'Canal and Savo, Florida Island and the smaller landmass of Tulagi came into view. I don't recall any particular feelings of nostalgia as our Yippy drew to the dock on Tulagi, but just over a year before, this same dock had been used by a PBY that was pounded by the same Jap destroyer that kept shelling us day after day following our capture of the island. The only nostalgia I felt for this damned place was for my friend Ken Bowers, who was buried by the cricket field.

After the Yippy tied up, we Marines were taken via ambulance to an Army hospital. Tulagi had changed a lot since I was last there. All signs of the fight had been erased. Many of the original buildings remained, although damaged ones had been removed. Army tents dotted the place, many near the small golf course and in the area of the Residency, which had once served as Edson's HQ. The base hospital was near here also, and that's where the ambulance unloaded us.

Upon my arrival, my rotting Marine dungarees were removed and disposed of, and I was given a bed with clean sheets and a pillow. It was like I had died and gone to Heaven. Clean sheets? A pillow? What next? I wondered.

For a little over three weeks, doctors treated my jungle rot, bathing it in a saline solution, and then leaving it exposed to the drying rays of the sun. I was also served delicious meals. Nothing fancy, mind you, but after weeks of surviving on K-rations and crappy Jap food we had captured on New Georgia, it made me feel like I was dining in some posh New York restaurant.

On August 30, a doctor approached as I was sitting up on my bed at the hospital.

"Good news, Private Groft," he told me. "Your legs are in pretty good shape now, and you are being discharged. Your unit has arrived back on the 'Canal, and transportation is being arranged for you to rejoin them. Pack your gear. You'll be leaving at 1300 hours."

That was wonderful news, and I quickly began making preparations to leave. A new uniform was provided for me, but unfortunately, this being an Army hospital, I was given olive drab Army clothes. It did not matter. I was rejoining the Raiders, and I'd have gone back in my skivvies if I'd had to.

Just before 1 p.m., I boarded a Higgins boat for the twenty-odd-mile ride across Iron Bottom Sound. As I stepped onto the boat and off of Tulagi, not to return for another six decades, it occurred to me that I had not visited the spot where my foxhole had been, where I had spent three weeks back in August of '42. Nor had I visited the grave of Kenny Bowers. In my hours of solitude, when my mind drifts to these faraway places where I grew from a boy to a man, I have regrets about a great number of things and events. Nausea sometimes sets in and I am seized by an overwhelming grief, but thank God reality soon returns.

Stepping back on Guadalcanal, I quickly located the Raiders' camp. I strode confidently through our company streets, followed by the hoots, howls, and derogatory remarks of my comrades because of my Army ODs.

"What did you do, Whitey," one Raider called, "join the enemy?"

"Where'd you get the doggie outfit?" another chimed.

Smiling inwardly at the good-natured drubbing I was taking, I finally located Baker Company. I spotted Captain Wheeler emerging from his tent.

"Captain Wheeler," I said, coming to attention and snapping my hand up in salute. "I'm back."

"Whitey," he replied, returning the salute. "It's good to see you. How're the legs?"

"Healing, sir," I told him, handing him my hospital discharge papers. "I've been officially discharged."

He accepted the papers but did not look at them.

"Great," he answered, then cast a disapproving look at my outfit. "Now get over to the quartermaster, draw a proper uniform, and burn that monkey suit."

"Yes, sir," I said and beamed.

It was good to be home.

I did not have time to make myself too comfortable on Guadalcanal, because by September 4 orders came down saying we were shipping out for New Caledonia again. Our trip back to New Cal was aboard the eight-thousand-ton attack transport USS *Fuller*.

As the *Fuller* knifed its way uneventfully across the deep blue Pacific toward New Cal, we Raiders heard the rumblings of a very disconcerting rumor. It said the Raiders were going to be disbanded.

"That's just more gum flapping, Big Stoop," I told Ray Ruble when he brought me the news. "The Marines wouldn't do that. They need us."

"I don't know, Whitey," Big Stoop said. "We lost a lot of good guys and officers. And Colonel Griffith ain't looking so good, either."

Big Stoop was right, of course. We were just a shadow of that fine battalion that had stormed ashore on Tulagi on August 7, 1942. Many an excellent Raider had fallen on Tulagi, at Bloody Ridge, along the Matanikau, and in the hellish jungle of New Georgia. What remained was merely a remnant. Even Colonel Griffith, as Big Stoop pointed out, was weak and sick, afflicted with some sort of gum ailment that left him drooling blood down his chin. It was not a pretty sight.

As if to confirm our fears, on September 8, Griffith was replaced, his illness having caught up to him. To replace him in command, he appointed George Herring, who had earned a major's gold oak leaf during my absence.

Besides the change in leaders, there also seemed to be a change in attitude. To make up for our losses, we had received a good number of replacements, men not as well trained or as fit as the original unit. Many were lacking in discipline and that fierce unit pride us old-timers all felt.

Simply put, we were used up and we knew it, and it showed in our results. I think most of us, from our officers right down the line, were aware that the New Georgia campaign especially had been subpar for us, that we really had not done the job we had been sent there to perform. Part of the fault, for certain, lay in poor planning and a lack, once again, of support in the way of supplies and naval fire. But many of us had gone into that battle ill and in a weakened state. In the end, the surprise was not that we failed, but that we accomplished as much as we had.

But now, late in 1943, it was not the same war it had been in the summer of 1942. Then America was on the ropes, reeling from the repeated blows dealt us by the Japanese, starting with Pearl Harbor. We needed to strike back at the Japs, to tell the civilians on the home front, as well as the rest of the world, that we might be down for the moment, but we were far from out. We had to hit the Jap where he lived and put him on the defensive for a change. But America did not have the resources in either men or ships for any large-scale invasions, so the brass opted to go with limited attacks, which led to a rapid strike force like the Raiders.

Now America was geared for war. Men marched out of the training camps by the thousands, and ships by the hundreds were steaming for battlefronts on two oceans. An elite force such as the Raiders, geared for limited, hit-and-run, morale-boosting raids, was no longer relevant. Now American muscle was coming to bear in terms of overpowering naval fire and airpower, and landings that included hundreds of tanks and thousands of troops, unlike anything we could have imagined even a year earlier.

Amphibious warfare, in short, had outgrown us and we had become obsolete.

Then there was also the fact that the Marine Corps had never wanted the force to begin with, but had the Raiders foisted on them by political pressure brought to bear by the President through his son, Jimmy Roosevelt. Now the Corps had grown from a handful of brigades to four full divisions and four air wings. We simply were no longer needed.

By the time the *Fuller's* anchor splashed into the harbor at Nouméa, we all had become convinced that this was the end, and that we who remained were going to be dispersed to other established units. Many, in fact, would be taken to form a new 4th Marine Regiment, whose proud predecessor had served in China and gone out of existence in April 1942 when its battered survivors were marched into Jap prison camps on Bataan. The Marines were "authorized" to re-form the regiment because, according to maritime tradition, when a unit like the 4th is lost, its colors are retired and held in reserve until they can be redeemed in honor.

For some reason, however, not every Raider was being rolled into the new 4th Marines. Many men, largely those with two or more battles under their belts, would be shipped back to the States to become part of new regiments that were, even then, forming in camps from San Diego to Quantico.

The demise of the Raiders was a bitter pill to swallow.

Over the span of years since the Raiders ceased to exist I have tried to figure out the logic used in deciding who would become part of the 4th Marines and who would be reassigned to other units, but I have never been able to figure it out. Logic would seem to dictate that seniority and experience would be deciding factors, that those Raiders who set sail from the States for New Caledonia in the spring of 1942, and who took part in every action in which the Raiders were engaged, would be the most likely to be assigned to the newly designated regiment. But one thing that's consistent among the United States military top brass, is that common sense seldom comes into play. So when the assignment lists came out, posted on the bulletin boards outside the HQ tent, we flocked around to see what would be our fate. For whatever reason, I saw my name listed among the men who would not be going to the 4th Marines. For me, it was both a happy and a sad moment. Sad because I was leaving the Raiders for good, a unit I had grown to love and in which I had a fierce pride. Happy, because my orders read that I would be catching the next ship heading for the United States.

I was going home. And I was not going alone. Dick "Mac" Mac-Neilly, Spike Edwards, and "Big Stoop" Ruble would be shipping over with me. Things began moving rapidly now. Orders came for those of us who were shipping out to pack our gear because we were being taken to a new camp. I hurriedly looked up my buddies who were staying. I hugged Alex Stewart, who had shared the terror of Bloody Ridge with me, and shook hands warmly with Captain Wheeler.

"You be careful, Whitey," he said. "We'll catch up with each other after the war."

"It was a pleasure serving under you, sir," I told him sincerely.

I had a warm handshake and a bear hug for Bill Waltrip, whom I had grown quite fond of. We exchanged addresses.

"Look me up after this is all over, son," he told me. "We'll tie one on together."

"Damn right we will," I told him. "And the first round is on you."

He laughed and we parted ways. Bill would ship out later and end up with the 1st Marines and land on Iwo Jima.

Boarding trucks, we waved a final farewell to our friends whom we had fought beside in so many hard battles. Bouncing along the rough New Cal dirt roads, we at last came to our new home, Camp Goettge, named after Colonel Frank Goettge, Vandegrift's intelligence officer who led that doomed patrol back in August of '42. Here we received a new clothing issue and turned in our web gear as we were preparing to leave for the good old USA.

I was filled with excitement at returning to the States, yet remorseful about the many friends I was leaving behind, and of those who would remain on these islands forever. This last was very strange for me. I was just eighteen years old when I enlisted in the Marines. I had never had a friend die, much less seen a buddy killed in battle, sometimes horribly. Now, in the fall of 1943, I was almost twenty, and we young men who sailed off to war a little more than a year ago were now older than our actual calendar years. Our experience seemed to make us quieter and more guarded in our conversation with each other. Could it be that we were concerned about becoming too close to one another and being at risk of repeating the loss we'd experienced with our comrades now departed? The war was far from over, and there was no telling when it would stop. Gone was the thought of a quick end to the Jap threat. We believed our return to the States would be of short duration, so the prospect of our returning soon to a world of sudden and violent death in the South Pacific was very real. There was even talk we might be shipped over to Europe.

As I waited with the others for our transportation back home, I happened across a Charlie Company man I recalled seeing before, but had never really gotten to know. So I introduced myself.

"Charlie Pacini," he replied with a smile, and we shook hands.

Charles V. Pacini hailed from Phillipsburg, New Jersey, and had a college degree, which impressed me, a mere high school graduate from Lebanon, Pennsylvania.

We talked for the longest time, and as we shared our experiences, each of us discovered a kindred spirit in the other fellow. We would become friends for the next half century, and I would serve as a grooms-man in his wedding.

But that was all still years in the future.

Now it was back to America as we boarded a ship bound for a nonstop cruise to San Diego. The farther east we steamed the more remote was the chance of any sort of enemy interference, and with the end of that threat, the long voyage became a tedious one, broken only by games of poker or craps and speculation about our futures. One thing was certain: Our days as Edson's Raiders were over, and we would have to march to a new drummer for the first time in our military careers. This would not be easy, for we had served in the finest and most elite battalion the Corps had ever produced, and bonded forever to men and officers without equal.

I do not recall my initial emotion upon seeing the coastline of the United States come into view, but I am sure it was one of relief and gladness. But it was tinged with sorrow as well, for I knew I'd be head-ing back across the Pacific before the war was over.

As our ship arrived in San Diego, I noticed that the Navy Yard seemed larger and a helluva lot busier than it had been when I was headed the other direction eighteen months ago. The ship tied up at dockside and a gangplank was shoved to its side. We began debarking, carrying our worldly possessions in our seabags. Directed to a line of waiting trucks, we tossed our bags onto the back, climbed up into the truck bed after them, and sat on the benches that lined the sides. Once we were all aboard, the trucks set out with a jolt and rolled through the base and out the main gate. I do not recall how long we drove, but we rumbled along for several hours in those damned uncomfortable, springless trucks, swaying and bouncing over every bump in the road. Now we were out in the desert somewhere.

"Where on God's earth are they taking us?" Pacini, seated to my left, asked.

"I'd say Hell," I replied. "But I think we already passed it a few miles back."

The trucks jolted to a halt at what was obviously a temporary camp in a remote part of the desert.

"Everybody out," came the call. "Move ass. Out!"

We hopped down from the trucks, and as we looked at the rickety camp we were being placed in, our spirits fell.

"Do you believe this place?" Big Stoop said. "The general in charge of setting up Marine camps must've looked for a helluva long time to find a spot this crappy."

"No Marine general would stick us in a place like this," Pacini replied. "Had to be an Army guy."

We now were shown to clapboard barracks buildings with cots, each with a thin, lumpy mattress, lining the inside walls. Big Stoop and I figured that the government had spent a total of $12 on materials to erect this entire camp. I'd seen Jap POWs living better. Everything about this camp was bad; the accommodations were bad, the food was bad, and the garrison assigned to man the camp seemed like they were pissed off at the world, and I can't say I blamed them. If this had been my assigned duty station, I'd have been pissed off as hell. I couldn't even be sure the camp had a name. All I knew was that unless you were some big shot officer or a Medal of Honor winner, they treated you like shit here.

We remained in this lousy rat hole camp until the end of November, when orders for each man came through. Most of us, including Pacini, Mac, Big Stoop, and me, were given thirty-day passes to go home, travel time not included, after which we were to report to Camp Lejeune, North Carolina. That meant we would be home for Christmas.

———————

Since Mac was from New York and Big Stoop and Pacini were both from New Jersey, we traveled east together. After the tropical hell-holes I had seen the last sixteen months, I greatly enjoyed watching the bountiful United States glide past my train window. The cross-country trip was fabulous, and at each stop where we could get off to stretch our legs, people treated us with great respect. They shook our hands, bought us coffee, and extended all sorts of niceties. During layovers where we had to change trains forcing us to line up at the window for tickets, people would move aside and allow us to go to the front of the line. Men patted us on our backs and give us thanks for the service we had performed. Women gave us affectionate pecks on the cheek. It was very touching and went a long way toward making all of our bad times seem worthwhile. As the landscape continued to roll by, I lost my friends one by one, as they had to step off to catch different trains going to other destinations. By the time the train huffed and puffed into Harrisburg, and then on to Lancaster, I was traveling alone.

Stepping from the Pullman at the McGovern Street station in Lancaster, I made my way through the depot, down the marble staircase, and out of the terminal. I caught a taxi, and arrived at my parents' home a short time later. They knew I was coming and were naturally overjoyed to see me, and we spent a lot of time catching up on news of family and friends. My brother Luther, the only one of the fourteen children younger than me, had just graduated from high school and was living at home. He, too, was glad to see me, and we spoke about what had happened in our lives since we were last together. But seeing the extreme misery and death of war firsthand, and having killed other human beings in combat, had changed me in ways I was not even aware of until then. The result for me was that my little brother and I, once so close, now had almost nothing in common anymore.

Of my two brothers who, like me, were of prime military age when the war began, Charles was in the Navy Seabees and was stationed in Oakland, California, while Richard, who had served four years in the Army before the war, was exempted from the service because he had a job with the railroad, which was considered important to the war effort. My two older brothers Paul and John had long been married with large families, and quite frankly, we were strangers, as I had never grown up with them. Like most of my seven sisters, they had moved out of the house while I was quite young.

I took a bus to Lebanon to see my friends, and found that all but two had gone into the military after me. The two who remained had failed to qualify for service and were classified as 4-F. We spent a good bit of time together. However, neither of my two buddies had a car, and I didn't either. In fact, I didn't even have a driver's license. That limited our activities to what we could get to by bus. Still, we got around to some of our favorite haunts, like the Little Crystal restaurant on Ninth Street, and for a short time, it was like the old days, before the war forced me, a teenage boy, to grow up into a man.

While I was at home, the movie *Guadalcanal Diary* was playing at the Colonial Theater in Lancaster. My younger brother, Luther, two years younger than me, had failed the physical to get into the service, but he got a real thrill out of going to see the movie with me. What made it interesting from my perspective, besides having fought on the 'Canal and defended Henderson Field against the Japs on Bloody Ridge, was that I had known Richard Tregaskis, the war correspondent and author of the book the film was based on. However, I was sorely disappointed in what I saw portrayed on the screen. It did not even begin to tell the story of what it was like for us on that island—the hunger, the fear, and courage. It did, however, prove to be an effective recruiting tool, I later learned.

Seeing my mother and father again and being with them for Christmas was really wonderful, but my time at home was drawing to a close. Reflecting back on those last moments with my mother as I prepared to leave, I can still see the agony in her beautiful old Pennsylvania Dutch face, and although she made no sound as I prepared to return to war, the tears ran freely.

———

But I was not heading back to war just yet. My first stop was Camp Lejeune. Begun in the spring of 1941 on an eleven-thousand-acre tract in Onslow County, North Carolina, the camp was named for John A. Lejeune, thirteenth commandant of the Marine Corps.

I traveled by train, first to Washington, D.C., and then on to Camp

Lejeune. My orders were to report to the 2nd Guard Battalion as an MP. Sergeant stripes went with the job.

Arriving at Lejeune was like Old Home Week, because waiting for me were Charlie Pacini, Big Stoop Ruble, Mac MacNeilly, and Spike Edwards, among a number of other Raiders. Charlie and I grew very close, despite the vast differences in our personalities and temperment. Charlie had a much calmer demeanor than many of us and did not drink, smoke, or use foul language, which made him a rarity in the Marine Corps. The rest of us did all of the above, and often with too much frequency. I'd lost track of the number of scraps I had gotten into, especially while I was overseas, and of how many days I'd sat in the brig living on piss and punk.

I enjoyed hanging around with Charlie, and we spent a great deal of off-duty time together, doing things like traveling to Jacksonville to see a movie and have dinner. I would kick back and enjoy a few beers, while Charlie tossed down a cold Coca-Cola.

While some of us were at Camp Lejeune, the rest of the Raiders were bouncing back and forth between camps in New Caledonia and New Zealand.

On September 29 part of the battalion, which had now been divided into two echelons, sailed from New Cal, arriving in Auckland on October 3. At that same time, Major Herring was replaced as battalion commander by Major Charles Banks, who, as things developed, would be the proud Raiders' final CO. Three weeks later, on October 20, the first echelon boarded the USS *Rixey* (APH3), which was designated as a casualty evacuation transport, for a ride back to New Cal, at which point the second echelon made the rest-and-rehab cruise to Auckland. By mid-November, the entire battalion had been reunited at Camp Bailey on New Caledonia. On January 21, 1944, they set sail for Guadalcanal, where they landed three days later.

Then, on February 1, 1944, the news reached us. The Raiders had officially been disbanded. The 1st, 4th, and 3rd Raider Battalions were now designated the 1st, 2nd, and 3rd Battalions of the 4th Marines. The 2nd Raider Battalion became the weapons company. Our proud unit that we had volunteered for, had trained with and fought beside, and under whose banner many of our friends had died, no longer existed. It was a sad day for us, and for all Raiders everywhere.

———————

L ife was quiet at Lejeune, and boring as hell. Elsewhere the war was still going on, and men we knew were out there fighting and dying. Meanwhile, we were stuck at Lejeune, assigned to a guard detail and put in charge of Marines who had been arrested for some infraction or other. What pissed us off even more was that these brig rats we had to wet-nurse were quite comfortable staying off the firing line. After about four months of this crap, we were about fed up.

"I don't know about you guys, but I've had about all of this shitty detail that I can handle," Charlie Pacini told us one evening.

That got my attention. I felt the same damned way, and I knew my other buddies did as well.

"What do you plan to do?" I asked. "Request a transfer?"

"That's exactly what I plan to do," Pacini said. "Who's with me?"

"Count me in," I told him. I had been entertaining the same thoughts. "Maybe we can request shipping over to the 4th Marines and rejoin the outfit."

Ruble, Spike Edwards, and Mac agreed.

We really wanted to get into the 4th Marines, not just because most of the Raiders were assigned there, but because of the unit's proud history. The original 4th was part of what the Corps refers to as the Old Breed, China Marines who had served in that country for nearly fifteen years. As diplomatic relations worsened between China and Japan in November 1941, the 4th was ordered out of Shanghai and posted on Corregidor in the Philippines. When the Philippines were invaded in December 1941, the Marines were put under Army control, and General Douglas MacArthur ordered them, along with a mix of sailors and Filipinos, to fortify the island. When the Japs landed on Corregidor on May 5, 1942, the Marines of the 4th Regiment fought bravely against hordes of enemy infantry, mounting two gutsy but doomed counterattacks. With the surrender a day later, and with about seven hundred Marines killed or wounded, the 4th's commander, Colonel Samuel L. Howard, burned the regimental colors before leading his regiment into three years of captivity.

(It was said that when the men of the original 4th Marines were released from POW camps at war's end and learned that their proud flag had been revived and had fought on to final victory at Okinawa, they wept for joy. I am happy that it was the Raiders who helped make that possible.)

Now the 4th Marines had been reconstituted, and we wanted to be a part of it. But that was not to be. When our requested transfers came through, we five comrades were assigned to the newly formed 29th Marines. The regiment, comanded by Colonel Victor F. Bleasdale, was forming here at Lejeune and was about to ship out for the West Coast. We would be going along. But not without first being assigned one last babysitting job.

———————

The 29th Marines were bivouacked outside of the Marine post grounds, at a place simply called Tent City because it was comprised mostly of pyramidal squad tents that could comfortably house eight men. The atmosphere at this temporary camp was by far lacking in the rigid spit and polish one would encounter at a more formal post. The only actual buildings at Tent City were the headquarters and the mess hall. A dirt road ran along one side of the camp, and out in front was a ramshackle array of shacks selling all types of booze, from beer and rotgut whiskey, to champagne and moonshine that would eat the paint off a tank.

These sorts of fly-by-night entrepreneurs seemed to gather around American military bases everywhere, all of them designed to separate us servicemen from our pay. And we were all too willing to allow them to do just that.

We dubbed this particular strip of shacks the Second Front because, the legend went that surviving one night there was the equivalent of a day in combat. On a big night like Friday or Saturday, the place was a war zone, and many a Marine or sailor who entered those portals came away wounded. We loved it even when, being MPs, we had to wade into one drunken brawl after another.

What little proper furniture may have existed in the Second Front, if there ever had been furniture, had long ago given way to orange crates and makeshift, plywood beds. Some of the more "luxurious" shacks had wooden floors, but most settled for simply dirt. To this day, I remain astounded that the Marines Corps and local law enforcement allowed this place to remain. Perhaps the logic was that if we were going to raise hell and get loaded, we may as well do it close to home and not wreck any nearby towns.

Coming from a Guard unit, when Charlie, Mac, Spike, Big Stoop, and I reported to the 29th Marines Regiment HQ, we met 1st Lieutenant Moto, an American-born Nisei officer who commanded the 29th's MPs. As he looked over our transfer paperwork, Lieutenant Moto was thrilled.

"Excellent," he said with a broad smile as he read our papers. "Not only are you guys combat veterans, but you were with Colonel Edson on the 'Canal, so I know you're a tough bunch of bastards." He looked up at us. "Were you men on Edson's Ridge?" We nodded, and he smiled even more "That's good. That's very good. I need hard-assed combat vets."

It was more than a little odd to us to hear a man of Japanese ancestry praising us, when we had killed so many men who looked like he did. Sometimes war is strange.

Moto's face grew serious.

"This regiment is shipping out for San Diego soon," he said. "Naturally, you men will be going along, but you will not be riding with the rest of the regiment. We are placing in your charge six men who currently reside in our brig. These guys are deserters, men who'd rather run than fight. The Corps wishes to change their perspective, so we are sending them west and placing them on the first ship heading for a combat zone. We are putting them in your care, and your job will be to get them to San Diego, then on to Camp Linda Vista, and deliver them to the brig." He smiled. "How you care for them is up to you, as long as they are able to walk up the gangway under their own power. You'll get further instructions when you board the train. Is that clear?"

It was clear. We didn't like it. But it was clear.

At the end of April 1944, we boarded the train that would carry us west. Our six charges came to us chained together, looking somewhat disheveled from their time in the hoosegow. A couple of them acted pretty tough, while the rest seemed like average joes, as we herded them on board.

Unlike the other Marines on this trip, who rode in Pullmans, our accommodations were in a boxcar specially fitted for us and our guests. Inside the boxcar the prisoners slept on mattresses laid out on the floor. There were a few chairs to sit on, wooden chairs bolted to the floor so they could not be thrown as weapons. One part of the boxcar was partitioned off. Beyond its doorway were four bunks made of two-by-four boards and plywood, with a thin motel mattress and some blankets on each. These were for us MPs during our off hours.

For the most part, the trip was long and boring. The prisoners did not speak much, and we did not engage them in conversation. Nor did we see much in the way of our fellow Marines. We assumed there were troops on the other cars, but never really saw them. During stopovers, we shackled our charges together and took them into whatever town we had stopped in, to get a meal at a local restaurant, paid for by the American taxpayer. I recall during one such break, an elderly woman cautiously sidled up to Spike Edwards.

"Are they German prisoners?" she asked him.

"Yes ma'am," Spike replied, trying to sound official. "Nazis."

Looking sufficiently frightened, the woman hurried away. Spike smiled at us and winked. We grinned back. We did not mind fibbing to the woman. American morale was still recovering from the bleak early war reverses, and there was no point in telling her we were guarding Americans who refused to fight. Plus, we were in the Deep South, where the Great Depression had been especially brutal and folks worried about where their next meal was coming from, and here we were, taking deserters out for a meal paid for by their tax dollars. The fact that she thought we were feeding the enemy was bad enough.

The trip across the country was made without incident, or at least no major incident. As the train chugged across the Great Plains, one of our charges, an especially tough-sounding fellow who, had he channeled his anger into doing his duty, might have made a good Marine, boasted about how he was going to desert again, no matter if we did deliver him to the West Coast.

"I'll find a way," he bragged. "I ain't gonna fight and maybe get killed. I'm not a chump."

We told the guy to shut his yap, but that only fired him up even more.

"You guys can be suckers if you want," he said, goading us, "but there'll be an opportunity for me to get away, and when it comes, I'm gone."

Finally, Big Stoop had had enough of this clown. He slid open the boxcar door and glanced outside.

"OK, Bub," he said. "You're so damned eager to skedaddle, go ahead. We're in wide open country. There are no trees or bushes or fences to get in your way, just open fields, so jump. But you're gonna have to do it from a moving train."

The man gaped at Big Stoop, fishlike.

"Go on, wiseass," Big Stoop continued. "You want an opportunity. This is it. Shit or get off the pot."

The man swallowed hard, as if gathering his courage, and made a run for the door. Just as he got there, however, Big Stoop, gripping his nightstick like a baseball bat, delivered a Babe Ruth–style swing that caught the would-be escapee across the chest and threw him backward into the boxcar. He landed on the floor curled up in a ball, the wind knocked out of him.

"Stupid son of a bitch actually would've jumped," Big Stoop said, awe in his voice.

"I'll give him an A for effort," I intoned.

"Yeah," Pacini offered. "But an F for brains. He'd have killed himself at this speed."

"That's right," Big Stoop said, his face brightening. He leaned over the prisoner, who was still on the floor. "I just saved your life, Sport."

There was no more talk of escaping.

After the train pulled in at San Diego, we piled our charges into a truck for the ride to Linda Vista, one of the sites in the Camp Elliott complex, where we dropped them off at the brig. I never learned what became of them after that, nor did I care. Being around them was depressing and I was glad to be rid of them. I just hoped they didn't get stuck into our regiment.

Now we were free to rejoin our unit, and enjoy some free time while we waited to ship out. During one of our liberties, and while off-duty as MPs, I and Pacini linked up with a big, boisterous Irish Marine named Patrick Henry O'Shanahan, a former Raider I'd known since Guadalcanal who was also assigned to the 29th Marines. At one of the nightspots we visited that night, O'Shanahan, who, like the rest of us, had a snootful, demanded that the bandleader play "The Marines' Hymn." When the man refused, O'Shanahan strode up to the bandstand, grabbed the hapless man by the neck, and tossed him out onto the dance floor. The swabbies and doggies in the club took exception, and this touched off a fist-swinging melee. I took part for a while, then realized my position as an off-duty MP and ducked under a table, taking Pacini under with me. We scurried into the men's room as Shore Patrol arrived to break things up. Charlie and I slipped out in the confusion. Perhaps there was some truth to the scuttlebutt that Eleanor Roosevelt wanted to have returning Raiders confined because we were "half-nuts" and a threat to society.

On August 1 the 29th Marines steamed out of San Diego harbor, bound for that all too familiar destination: Unknown.

CHAPTER FOURTEEN

"I HEAR THE RUMBLE OF HEAVY GUNS"

GUADALCANAL TO OKINAWA
AUGUST 1944–AUGUST 1945

In point of fact, our destination was far from unknown, at least to us veterans. We were bound for Guadalcanal. For me, it would be my fourth time setting foot on that shore. This was exciting news to Charlie, Spike, MacNeilly, Ruble, and me. Not just because we were headed back into action, but the scuttlebutt circulating around the ship was that the 29th was to become part of the 6th Marine Division that was being formed on the 'Canal. The 6th Division, we knew, comprised the 22nd Marines and the 4th Marines, which meant we'd be fighting alongside our old Raider unit.

Among the three regiments forming the 6th Marine Division, only the 29th was not combat tested, with the exception of course of veterans like my friends and me. The other two regiments, the 4th and the 22nd, had seen action in recent months at Eniwetok and Guam, where Raider Lee Minier, a Bloody Ridge survivor and member of the Singing Eight Balls, died storming a Jap machine gun nest.

As I watched the skyline of San Diego fade and all about me was the Pacific Ocean, my thoughts flashed back to the last time I had come this way, an eighteen-year-old kid, all piss and vinegar and itching for my first combat. Now that seemed a lifetime ago and that young boy was almost a stranger.

I had taken a seat on the fantail of the ship, alone with my thoughts of August 7, 1942, and Tulagi. I was gripped by a deep nostalgia and powerful emotions as that day came rushing back to me.

In my memory, Tulagi was being pounded by our Dauntless dive-bombers and our Navy escorts, three light cruisers and five World War I destroyers. As we stood along the rails waiting to depart the ship, I watched the pre-invasion bombardment in total awe. The tortured island appeared to be exploding before my eyes, disgorging all life and matter to the heavens above. Heavy black smoke and flames enveloped Tulagi, and as I descended the cargo net into our landing craft less than fifty yards offshore, the thought crossed my mind that we would not have to do much killing this day. How wrong I turned out to be. The fight was hot and swift, but in three days the prize was ours.

My thoughts turned to Kenny Bowers, and in my mind I had a vision of Ken and me standing by the ship's rail as we cut our wrists and mingled our life's blood together. We were young, inexperienced, and raring to get into the fight. Ken was now gone, buried in a grave by the cricket field on Tulagi, and I had survived no less than four battles before spending most of the past year back in the States. But the war had moved on in my absence. Tarawa, Cape Gloucester, Kwajalein, Eniwetok, Saipan, and Guam had been fought over and won, and Marines were still dying at the Point and Bloody Nose Ridge on Peleliu. Still to come, although we did not know it then, were Iwo Jima and Okinawa, both of which would prove to be among the bloodiest fights in Marine Corps history.

Now I was to become part of the 6th Division, commanded by Major General Lemuel C. Shepherd. Until this point, the Corps had been comprised of just five divisions. I would now be part of the largest division in the Corps—three infantry regiments, along with artillery, motor tranports, and a medical corps with combat military police, of which I was part. This type of work was all new to me, and by the time we dropped anchor off Guadalcanal, I was beginning to have second thoughts about having volunteered for this duty. So was Charlie Pacini. My other friends seemed content to remain with the MPs, so it was just Charlie and I who trekked over to the headquarters tent of the 1st Battalion, 4th Marines, which was formerly the 1st Raider Battalion, to see its CO, Major Jack Kemp. He greeted us warmly.

"It's really great to see you boys," he said, pumping our hands.

"Thank you, sir," I said. "It feels wonderful being back here among the Raiders."

Then we told him why we were there, that we wanted to transfer to his unit.

"It goes without saying that I'd love to have you fellas back, and I have a couple of men who'd like out of this battalion," he said. "But it's up to Lieutenant Moto if he wants to part with you two. I'll speak with him."

We thanked Major Kemp and left.

Kemp made the request, followed up by our own request, made in writing, but until a decision was made, we were to remain MPs, so we decided to make the best of it. Half the time we spent being traffic cops. Guadalcanal was a world different in 1944 than it had been in 1942. Instead of a shoestring operation, it was now a main staging area for the war, with men, planes, and vehicles crowding everywhere. With only one main road on the 'Canal, on which all this traffic had to travel, we spent much of our time directing traffic. Part of this hustle and bustle, as 1944 drew to a close, was in anticipation of the upcoming invasion of Iwo Jima. That invasion happened on February 19, 1945, and we all knew men who were involved in the desperate fighting there. Our first Dog Company commander, Justice "Jumpin' Joe" Chambers, would win the Congressional Medal of Honor on Iwo, just two days before a Jap machine gun sent rounds crashing into his chest. Chambers was lucky. He would survive. Eight other former Raiders would not.

As news from Iwo reached us on the 'Canal, anyone of us who could look at a map became aware that America's next strike, if not directly at the home islands of Japan itself, would most likely be at the Ryukyu Islands, probably Okinawa, which sat less than three hundred miles from Japan.

Even as we speculated on this objective, training intensified. In fact, it got really rough for the guys in the combat rifle companies that made up the 1st, 2nd, and 3rd battalions of the 29th. Our commanding officer, Colonel Bleasdale, was a true blood and guts type of Marine officer, and the slogan circulating in our regiment was "the 29th and a star," meaning Bleasdale wanted to wear a star on his shoulders even if it meant grinding all of us into the dust to achieve it.

Meanwhile, we MPs had an easier time of it. Dick MacNeilly and I became a twosome. The two of us, along with a third MP whose name I have since forgotten, were usually assigned to the same task, and spent much of our leisure time together as well. Mac was a scrounger. If he or any of his buddies needed something, Mac had a way of getting it. That's how he managed to gather the materials we needed to build our own boat. The young Marine who hung out with us was from New Jersey and had boat-building experience, a point we discovered one day during a casual discussion. We'd been lounging on the beach during our off-duty time, watching Higgins boats scuttering to and fro from ships anchored on Iron Bottom Sound to the beach, most loaded with supplies. Then an officers' whaleboat cruised by with some Navy brass on board.

"I used to have a boat," Mac mused. "It was small and had a puny little outboard motor, but I used to take it out on the Finger Lakes and do some fishing." He paused. "I'd love to have one now and go out and cruise on the Sound a little."

"Why don't you build a boat?" our friend asked.

"I said I owned a boat," Mac replied. "I didn't say I built it."

"If you have the materials, I can build one," the man said. "It's what I did back in Jersey."

Mac gazed at him with newfound respect.

"What do you need?" he asked.

"Depends on what size boat you want," our friend said. "A small boat for just a few guys is a snap."

From there, we were off and running. Mac and I put our heads together to say what size boat would be right for us, and our friend began telling us what we needed. With his experience and Mac's ability to beg, borrow, or steal the needed parts, combined with my strong back, we went to work. Here my hat is off to the generous nature of the Seabees who happily supplied a few combat veteran Marines with wood and tools. For the motor, Mac managed to acquire—how I did not know nor did I ask—an engine and the transmission from an Army jeep. With those materials, we sawed, hammered, glued, bolted, and caulked together a nice little twenty-foot runabout that we christened *Stormy*. For the next few weeks we putted around Iron Bottom Sound off Tassafaronga, shirtless in the sun, as if we were members of some highfalutin yacht club. We were the envy of everyone.

We sailed *Stormy* every day we could wangle some free time, right up until the day in early March 1945 when we learned we were heading back to war. *Stormy* would have to remain on the 'Canal, but we were now tasked with finding her a good home. A group of Seabees made us an offer of $500 and we sold our beloved boat. As luck would have it, just before we departed, but before the Seabees could take possession, a fierce tropical storm blew in. Huge waves, driving rain, and high winds smashed *Stormy* beyond repair. I guess her demise was appropriate given her name. Over the years, I often thought about the guys we had sold her to and what they thought of us, because we had no time to inform them of the wreck before we departed. I'm sure some choice words were said when they found her battered remains on the beach, but we will never know.

Steaming out of Iron Bottom Sound, we left Guadalcanal behind. I would not come this way again until the twilight of my life, when, in 2002, at age seventy-eight, I would return to find a different world from the one I left in 1945. On that day I was just twenty-one and, although I did not know it yet, bound for Okinawa.

Our cruise to Okinawa was pleasantly interrupted by a brief layover in the Ulithi Atoll, about thirteen hundred miles south of Tokyo. The U.S. Navy's deepwater anchorage and main staging area since January 1945, Ulithi had been transformed by the Seabees from a remote island where a few hundred natives lived a quiet existence into a bustling naval base to repair and refit the Navy's ships but also, more importantly to many of us common sailors and Marines, provide a place of rest and relaxation.

About forty islets, none of which are big enough to warrant being called islands and none of which are more than a few feet above sea level, make up the Ulithi Atoll. The islets surround the loveliest lagoon you'd ever want to see. In fact, it is one of the largest lagoons in the world, being twenty-two miles long and twenty-four wide. The eighty-seven-square-mile lagoon ranges in depth from eighty to one hundred feet and could hold more than seven hundred ships, more than almost any other American base, including Pearl Harbor.

The islet that most concerned us was Mogmog, the northernmost in the atoll and one of the largest, being about a half mile in length. Some three hundred people lived on Mogmog before the United States decided it was vital for the war effort. After some negotiations with the ruler, King Ueg, the people were all moved to another island, Fedarari, for the duration.

As our troopship convoy glided through the channel in the barrier reef that helped form the lagoon, Pacini, Big Stoop, and I hung on the rail, staring in wonder. Much of the Pacific Fleet was standing at anchor in the lagoon, including no less than six fleet carriers, among them the *Hornet*, the *Intrepid*, the *Lexington*, and the *Ticonderoga*. Battleships sat close by, as cruisers, both heavies and lights, and a myriad of destroyers bobbed at anchor around the capital ships. Between all of these vessels, small whaleboats and Higgins boats scurried on their way between the shore and the fleet, like water bugs between lily pads.

The sun shone down brilliantly, making the blue water so transparent we could almost discern the wreck of the USS *Mississinewa* as we sailed by berth number 131. The brand-new fleet oiler, in service for just six months, had proved that, while the lagoon was a perfect haven for our ships, it was not immune to attack. On November 20, the ship blew up with a tremendous roar and sank, burning fiercely, her spine broken. She had been hit by a Kaiten, a manned Japanese suicide torpedo, that had slipped into the anchorage. She went down in fifteen minutes, taking along sixty-three of her crew and the Jap suicide pilot. The *Mississinewa* was the first ship lost to the Kaiten, which roughly translates as "the turn toward heaven," which is true, I guess, if you're the guy driving it.

Our transport came to a stop at its designated berth, and the anchors plunged into the water.

"Attention, Marines," the PA boomed. "Welcome to Ulithi, the Navy's Pacific rest area. Boats will begin arriving at 1300 to take you ashore. Once there, you will be given a chit that will get you two bottles of beer. Your time will be your own. You can rest, read newspapers or magazines, swim, or play baseball if you want. There is also a movie theater. So enjoy yourselves. The island secures at 1800, so you must leave by then."

We hurriedly got ready and, when the boats arrived, piled in for the ride. On shore, we were welcomed to Mogmog and given our chits, which we took to the refreshment stand. There, two sailors took them from us and handed us two bottles of beer. It was warm, to be sure, but beer was beer. Plus, it was not difficult for us to get more. We easily located guys—often they were youngsters fresh from the States and therefore gullible targets for old salts like us—who would sell us their chits. If a guy was desperate for an extra beer, some of the Navy's old tars would sell theirs for a small fortune, and we bought them. We were going to war. What good was cash to us?

Mogmog could support fifteen thousand enlisted men and officers per day, most of whom engaged in the "Four Bs": bathing, baseball, boxing, and beer drinking. Some guys went to the sixteen-hundred-seat theater to see the movie, "canned morale" we called it, while others sought the solace of the five-hundred-seat chapel. My friends and I just relaxed, sititing on a coconut log, quaffing down our warm beers and talking.

Everywhere around us, men lounged in the sun. Well, not everywhere. We enlisted men were banned from the portion of the island dubbed "Officers' Country." This area featured thatched-roof cabanas, and the officers could drink all the beer they wanted. Between 3 and 6 p.m., they were also entitled to shots of whiskey and bourbon.

Officers above field grade—colonels, generals, and admirals—went one notch higher. They had free run of King Ueg's palace, which boasted modern conveniences, we were told, such as actual furniture that wasn't made from nailed together scrap wood from packing crates.

Officers' Country had one more thing that we enlisted men were not permitted: women. Navy nurses also relaxed on Mogmog, and they were allowed to fraternize freely with officers of any grade, from the lowliest shavetail lieutenant to the four-star generals. But never were we grubby enlisted men allowed to chat up the ladies.

"Wish I could steal me a major's uniform here," Spike Edwards mused, while we watched from afar as half a dozen nurses enjoyed the sun and the beach with a few guys wearing brass.

"I wish you could steal one for me, too," I told him.

"That's it," Pacini said. "Next war, I'm getting a commission."

At 6 p.m. we were back in the boats and returning to the ship, and the next day, our convoy slipped back out of the lagoon heading north. I never found out why we stopped over on Ulithi. Maybe the brass wanted us to have a good time before going back to war, or maybe it had to do with the timing of our arrival off Okinawa. Whatever the reason, I never forgot my day in paradise. We Marines enjoyed our time on the island and were grateful. Those of us veterans who had fought on other islands were all too aware of what was going to take place in a few days. We also knew that some of the men who shared the day on Mogmog with us had downed their last beers.

So it was aloha to Mogmog as we slipped back into our shipboard routine of calisthentics and preparing our weapons and ourselves for war.

————————

As our convoy, designated Task Force 56, drew closer to our target with every turn of the propellers, men became very quiet. There was a sense, largely unspoken, that this could be the last fight of the war, and in the minds of some of the men—especially among us Guadalcanal vets—that this could be the last time we would have to answer the call. I, for one, was somehow convinced that, having survived all that I had so far, I was not destined to meet my death in combat.

For the first time I was going into battle as a sergeant, and my experience had earned me the job of helping to prepare young Marines to go to war. I drilled into their heads some of the vital information they needed about survival, like not to bunch up, to listen to their NCOs, to keep sharp at all times, to avoid souvenir hunting because of the danger of booby traps, to shoot or bayonet dead Japs because live ones were known to lie down among their own dead comrades and smear themselves with the blood of the slain, in order to kill an unwary American.

From all indications, the upcoming fight would be our biggest one yet. Experience had shown us that the Japanese soldiers always fought hard and seldom gave up, and as we approached the home islands of Japan, we expected that they would double and even triple their efforts. Okinawa, we veterans felt, and based on what news was coming to us from Iwo Jima, would be much harder than anything we had been called upon to accomplish before.

As we drew closer to our objective, our officers began briefing us on what to expect and how to respond to events in the forthcoming invasion, which we all prayed would be our last battle. My role in the upcoming fight was still a question mark. Charlie and I were still sweating out our request out of the MPs and into the 4th Marines.

The convoy moved on in company with a protective screen of destroyers and cruisers. During one of the quiet times during this final leg of our voyage, with Okinawa lying in wait for us just ahead, I relaxed on deck enjoying the warming rays of the evening sun and taking in the naval might that surrounded us, I was moved to write a short poem. I had always enjoyed reading poetry, and as I sat on the well deck of the ship, that section just aft of the bow, I found myself reciting these words without pen or paper:

Far off into the distance where the horizon meets the sky,
I hear the rumble of heavy guns as we go passing by.
It is not the guns of the Japanese, but of a mighty fleet at sea.
A fleet that bears the insignia of the United States Navy.

It is very strange, for although more lines occurred to me, I was never satisfied with any beyond those four, so I decided to forgo my aspirations to be a poet and concentrate on being the best Marine I could be.

I found myself engaged with an odd attitude in regard to the coming fight. I had a group of young men whose minds I needed to prepare for a fight that could end their lives. I had had these same talks with myself many times over the past three years, and had never found it difficult to steel my resolve and place my fate in God's hands, while simultaneously praying for personal courage to serve my country and the Corps. Luckily, for this fight, my job was made easier because of the nature of the unit. We were a combat military police force and would not be joining the assault on the enemy line. It was certainly safer than being in a front line rifle unit, but therein lay my personal problem: I had no heart for the work of an MP. I was a combat Marine who had trained and fought with what I firmly beleived to be the greatest group of men the Marine Corps had ever fielded: Edson's Raiders. In my mind, there was no comparing the Raiders with any other infantry unit, be it a squad, a company, or a battalion.

We had received specialized training from top-notch experts schooled in the art of silent death, of hand-to-hand combat with the bayonet and stiletto knife. Our training had included some moves of martial arts like judo and jujitsu, and we could kill quickly and quietly with our bare hands. No regular Marine infantry to that time had been subjected to such training. We had the utmost confidence in our abilities and had a great respect for our officers, particularly Colonel, now Brigadier General, Edson, whom we would have followed to hell and back. As far as we were concerned, he had no peer in the Pacific Theater in regard to small group actions and tactics involving company- and battalion-size units. I believe this, even in my ninetieth year, and with so many moons having passed over the horizon, and with them many memories, some sad and some happy, and some like that old moon continuing to roll around.

Now here I was on my way to Okinawa in an outfit I cared little for and faced with the biggest fight of my life, and just maybe my last. Okinawa is a big island, sixty-four miles long and eighteen miles across at its widest point. It was home to about 435,000 civilians, including 60,000 in Naha, its capital city. I had never engaged in street fighting, but that seemed about to change. But the city aside, we would discover that Okinawa overflowed with craggy ridges of coral as tough as hardened steel to penetrate, laced with caves and ravines, all stoutly held by an enemy determined to kill as many Americans as possible before they, themselves, would be killed. It was a bleak prospect. Our bleakest yet, in fact.

This was a whole different nut to crack than, say, Guadalcanal. While Okinawa wasn't as big as Guadalcanal, we would have to fight for every inch of the place. We had fought desperately to hold Henderson Field, allowing the Japs, by repeated attempts to wrest it from us, to simply wear themselves out and finally give up. Here it would be different. The Japs had had three years to prepare this island's defenses. Okinawa would be like Iwo Jima, Saipan, and Guadalcanal all rolled into one bloody bundle. It was estimated that we would be facing one hundred thousand troops, in addition to well-placed artillery, and plenty of it.

The ships and men around me, sailors, soldiers, and Marines, all belonged to Task Force 56, a subunit of Task Force 51, under command of Admiral Richmond K. Turner, the same man who, many Raiders felt, had left us hanging, ill-supplied and ill-supported, at New Georgia in the summer of 1943. This invasion force, we were told at our briefings, would be a joint Army/Marine assault force consisting of the Army's 7th and 96th divisions (jointly called the XXIV Corps), side by side with the III Amphibious Corps, made up of General Shepherd's 6th Marine Division and the 1st Marine Division under Major General Pedro de Valle, the same Pedro de Valle I had seen on Bloody Ridge, measuring out firing grids for his 11th Marine Artillery, which saved our asses during the Jap assaults. Our four divisions comprised 10th Army, 102,000 Army personnel and 88,000 Marines, under Major General Simon Bolivar Buckner Jr., whose father had surrendered Fort Donelson to his old friend, General Ulysses S. Grant, in 1862.

The plan, as outlined to us, was to come in from the west, the East China Sea, landing on beaches in the Hagushi sector. We were to move directly east, sieze the Yontan and Kadena airfields just inland of the beaches, and keep going until the island was cut in two. At that point, the Army units were to wheel south and the Marines north, completing our conquest of the island. It looked and sounded easy on paper and sand tables, but anyone experienced in fighting the Japanese knew otherwise.

S unday, April 1, 1945, dawned beautifully, with a bright, warm sun and crisp blue sky. A true springlike day. It was Easter Sunday and, we feared, the day many of us would die under enemy fire. April 1 was L Day, L for Landing, L for Love, both were suggested. Perhaps only a few also realized it was also April Fools' Day.

Waking early, we ate our invasion breakfast of steak and eggs, washed down with hot coffee, preferably with cream and sugar, otherwise known as "joe with sidearms" or "blonde and sweet."

Outside there was one hell of a racket as the Navy and the flyboys pounded the invasion beaches in advance of our landing. After breakfast, we were ordered to climb into our gear and move topside to our debarkation stations. The scene outside is beyond my poor powers to describe. Ships of every size, numbering far above what I could count, stood offshore and poured every caliber of shell imaginable at the smoking, burning island. I heard later that there were more than fourteen hundred ships and half a million men involved in the Okinawa operation. Overhead, I watched our planes swoop in low, dropping bombs and napalm on suspected enemy positions. It all looked impressive as hell, but I'd seen it before. I hoped this time it would do some actual good.

But the Japanese were also active, for anti-aircraft fire soon erupted all around. Small dots in the sky grew in size, and as I watched, a few peeled off from the others and skimmed in low. Too low, it seemed to me. Then I realized their intent, as one plane, the big, red meatball insignia standing out starkly on its side and wings, splashed into the water less than fifty yards from a ship. These were Kamikazes. I'd heard of them—who in the Pacific had not—but had never seen them in action. Now, standing there watching the awesome spectacle of airmen intentionally trying to blow themselves to bits by crashing their aircraft into one of our ships, all I could think of was "get me the hell off this floating target."

I soon had my wish, and within thirty minutes we were packed into the amtracs and churning toward shore, four divisions abreast in a wave of invaders eight miles in width. I fully expected to land under heavy fire or, if very lucky, light enemy fire. The last thing I expected was to land with no enemy fire at all. But that's what happened. Our landing was a veritable cakewalk, and we began our inland thrust almost right away. We encountered a little enemy resistance at Yontan Airfield, but quickly quashed it and seized the airstrip. That was quite an accomplishment, considering we'd taken in just a few hours what planners thought would take three days to seize. I believe I heard that, overall, only nine Marines were killed that first day.

The idea of letting us land so easily, we would learn after the war, came from the Jap high command. They figured to hold our fleet in the offshore waters of Okinawa so that their suicide planes and boats could decimate our Navy, stranding us ground pounders on shore, ripe for annihilation.

That strategy came close to working at Guadalcanal, but this was not 1942. Then, they could chase away our Navy, gun-shy as it was after Pearl Harbor, and had they been able to muster more resources, they might have succeeded in driving us into the sea. Now we were no longer so easy to annihilate, despite the fact that our fleet lay within range of nearly every Japanese air base capable of launching planes. The Kamikazes would take a heavy toll of men and ships during the eighty-three days of battle on Okinawa, but the Navy held station offshore the entire time.

Besides an easy landing, Okinawa proved different in other ways that were outside of my experience. The main example was civilians. As we Marines wheeled left and began our drive northward, we found the roads choked with civilians fleeing south, trying to avoid getting caught up between us and retreating Japs. As MPs, my buddies and I were tasked with herding these refugees into established safe areas, away from the flow of military traffic and the threat of Japanese mortar or artillery fire. The civilians were a pathetic lot, and my battle-hardened heart went out to them. They were old men, women, and small children, some crying in fear, others quietly bearing their lot. They had not asked to be caught between two warring armies, but now they were being driven from their thatched roof homes, carrying all their worldy possessions in carts drawn by water buffalo or by hand, or lugged on their backs in huge bundles.

We MPs also had to set up roadblocks and direct truck and jeep traffic.

I was most unhappy with this kind of work, and so was Pacini. We were combat veterans, Edson's Raiders, who still had that fire in our gut to be part of the action. So we began to harass our superiors about our requested transfers to the 4th Marines or any combat unit within the 6th Division. It finally worked.

On April 13 a news flash was passed on to us. President Roosevelt was dead, we were told. He had died a day earlier in Georgia. It would be later that we learned that FDR had succumbed to a cerebral hemorrhage.

This news hit us like a ton of bricks. I had been just short of nine years old when Roosevelt had first been elected, in 1932, and he had been the only president many of us had really known. His sudden death so close to seeing the war come to a victorious conclusion brought a tear to many an eye on Okinawa, including my own. Though I was a Republican, I admired FDR. He was our leader and had always been there to guide us. We wondered what this Harry Truman fellow was going to be like.

That same day, April 13, the Marines reached Hedo Misaki, the northernmost point on Okinawa. The seaport of Nago at the base of Motobu peninsula was ours, and supplies began flowing ashore. We had taken in twelve days what had been anticipated to take at least three weeks to conquer. The only stiff defense the Marines faced was at Motobu peninsula. A few days later, Pacini and I were called to Lieutenant Moto's tent.

"You win, fellas," he said, handing us each a sheet of paper. "Here are your transfer orders. You want combat, you got combat."

We accepted the papers, saluted, and left, both of us eager for the move. We had heard that both the 4th and the 22nd needed replacements. We hoped to be sent to the 4th Marines, but our papers assigned us both to the 22nd, specifically King Company, 3rd Battalion. Charlie and I were not disappointed. We were overjoyed to be back in the fight, and for the first time in six months we felt we could hold up our heads. I shook hands with Big Stoop, Spike Edwards, and Mac, all of whom opted to remain with the MPs.

"Take care, Whitey," Mac said to me. "It's tough seeing you go, but I know it's what you want. But we had some great times together."

"We'll go out and get roaring drunk when this is all over," I told him.

Fighting in the southern half of Okinawa was a far different ball game than what we had faced in the north. At first we Marines bitched because we had rapidly taken the entire northern part of the island while to the south, the Army was slogging it out for just a few yards of ground. They'd barely made a dent in Japanese defenses. We bemoaned the Army's lack of fighting ability and aggressiveness. We had no way on knowing, until we got into it ourselves and were forced to eat our words, that the Japs had concentrated nearly all of their troops and heavy weapons in the southern third of the island. There, amid a tangle of coral ridges, ravines, and fortified hills, they'd built a defensive network that was nearly impervious to our heaviest naval and artillery fire. This was the Shuri Line, anchored around historic Shuri Castle, which had been built more than five hundred years earlier as the palace for the Ryukyu Kingdom. Once elegant, with a graceful Tori gateway, it lay in ruins as our guns and planes tried to root out the stubborn defenders who lived in and fought from the many underground catacombs. One single half-mile sector of the Shuri Line contained sixteen well-hidden mortar pits, eighty-three light machine guns, forty-one heavy machine guns, seven anti-tank guns, six field guns, two mortars, and two howitzers.[1]

But the immediate concern for me and my new comrades was a vile little hill called Sugar Loaf. Just two hundred feet in height, the bald, battered hill was a nightmare maze of machine gun emplacements, fortified caves, mortar pits, snipers, and hidden artillery. The 2nd Battalion of our regiment had struck it on May 10, and again on May 12 and 14, and in three days suffered horrific casualties, losing four hundred men killed or wounded. They'd taken the crest of the hill twice, but both times were tossed off by artillery fire and counterattacks. G Company, which had had 215 men, was down to 75 effectives.

Sugar Loaf, or Hill 51.2 to the Japanese, was not just one hill, but part of a larger triangle-shaped position that included an area called the Horseshoe and Halfmoon Hill, both of which provided Sugar Loaf with interlocking fields of deadly machine gun and mortar support. Japanese mortars firing from reverse slopes of Sugar Loaf and nearby hills, and heavy 150mm artillery support from emplacements at Shuri Castle, a mile to the east, wreaked havoc on our Marines. Many of our guys who died fell on Hell's Half Acre, an area in front of Sugar Loaf, devoid of cover and so scarred with shell pockmarks that it resembled the surface of the moon. In fact, Sugar Loaf and all the ground around took on a lunar appearance.

Tank support wasn't much help. As armor approached the hill, Japanese suicide squads would storm them, using smoke grenades to get close and then finishing the tank off with twenty-two-pound satchel charges tossed underneath or a one-and-a-half-pound TNT charge affixed to the steel hull. Sometimes their infantry would swarm over a tank and try to pry open the hatches. After the battle, someone counted thirty-three knocked-out tanks around and on Sugar Loaf.

In the midst of this fight, we were told that Nazi Germany had surrendered, and that the war in Europe was over. Charlie Pacini and I just looked at each other and shrugged. All around us friends were being killed, so the end of the European war meant almost nothing to us.

Our entire regiment was heavily engaged in this hellish fight, swapping fire with an enemy that, for the most part, we could not see. They fought from caves and holes in the coral, and the only way to get at them was grenades and flamethrowers.

Finally, after ten days of the worst fighting I had seen, someone came up with the right plan. Tanks and Marines were sent around the right side of the hill to engage the Japs on Sugar Loaf. Once the enemy had given them their full attention, more tanks and Marines were sent around the left, and sixty men charged up the face, gaining the crest. King Company was not involved in this intense and violent action, but from our position at the base of the hill, we heard the nonstop rattle of tank and small arms fire and the distinctive *whoosh* of the flamethrowers. For an hour the fight raged, then the shooting died away. Sugar Loaf was ours, but we had suffered about three thousand casualties, more than fell in seventy-six hours of battle on Tarawa. Our regiment, the 22nd, was down to 62 percent of combat strength.

Fighting on this island defies description. In some places the enemy actually fought from Okinawan tombs. The islanders, in their tradition, buried relatives in limestone and concrete tombs, and these now made ideal defensive positions for the Japs. After losing a good many men assaulting these fortified positions, we found that to take one of these effectively required an entire platoon. First we called in artillery and mortar fire. The Japs in the tombs survived almost intact, but the fire killed or drove off any Japs on the outside. Next, covering fire was provided by tanks and 105mm guns mounted on self-propelled howitzers. As this supporting fire was being poured in, infantry moved up. Riflemen fired on the Japs while bazooka men, BAR men, and Marines with flamethrowers flanked the Jap position and finished it off. We grimly referred to this as the "blowtorch and corkscrew" method, and it proved effective.

It was around this time that I received my only wartime injury. We were advancing slowly on the Shuri Line behind a blanket of naval gunfire when something hot burned across my back, slicing my shirt and skin. I moaned and carried on. The wound burned like hell, and I had this vision of a large hole in my back. Charlie Pacini was by my side, and I asked him to take a look. He did and started to laugh.

"What the hell are you laughing at?" I snarled through clenched teeth.

Charlie plucked the metal shard from my back and showed it to me. It was flat and about the size of a quarter, but still hot to the touch.

A corpsman arrived and patched me up.

"You're lucky," he said. "It didn't go in very far. Congratulations. You've been tagged by the U.S. Navy."

I was back in action the same day. Because the wound was a result of friendly fire, it did not qualify me for the Purple Heart. This would have been all right except that I knew another Marine who was injured when a Jap shell struck one of our supply trucks. The deuce-and-a-half went up with a roar and the man was bowled over, not from the blast or the concussion, but from the truck's tailgate, which was tossed into the air like a leaf, then came down and struck the man. My wound was a result of friendly fire, his of being hit by a flying tailgate from a damned truck, yet after the battle I had to stand in formation and watch him get a Purple Heart, while I still had the scar from the shrapnel on my back. That pissed me off.

To this day I try to envision the guy showing his medals to his grandson, who asks him, "Grandpa, how'd you get this?" To which he would respond, "Well, I got hit by the tailgate of a truck."

By May 23 we were advancing on the capital city of Naha or, rather, where Naha used to stand. As we crossed the rain-swollen Asato River, we found nothing but square mile after square mile of rubble. No houses or buildings remained. Streets were so clogged with rubble that tanks could not maneuver. The stench of death in the city was sickening and battle-hardened Marines puked. Largely, this stink came from bodies of civilians buried under these mountains of debris. It was reported that the smell even nauseated pilots hundreds of feet over the city. I had no reason to doubt that claim.

As sniper fire began coming our way, we dispersed and took shelter, and began picking our way forward with extreme caution. This was the part of the battle that, I think, many of us most feared. We had been trained for fighting in thick jungles, not in city streets. We feared shooting other Marines in the jumble of streets and shattered buildings, or being shot ourselves by friendly fire. Because of our losses at Sugar Loaf, I was a squad leader, and as I led my eight men through Naha, I realized I was out of my depth here. This was unlike any experience I had gone through. Guadalcanal and New Georgia had no cities, just a few ramshackle huts in native villages.

As we entered an intersection, I signaled my men to caution. Some Marines had passed through here before us, and a couple lay dead on the roadway, indicating to me that a Jap machine gun might still be nearby and have the place sighted in. I turned to the men.

"We're gonna go across here one by one," I told them. "Run like hell. Don't stop for anything." I pointed to one of my men and said, "Go."

The first guy took off and ran like a deer across the intersection. Sure enough, a Nambu opened up, and I saw dust and bits of masonry fly as bullets chewed up the gound behind my man. He made it across safe and sound. I tried to spot the machine gunner, thinking that if we knew where he was, we could lay down suppressing fire to cover our crossing, but he was too well hidden.

I turned to a young private who was right behind me.

"Carefully, work your way forward," I told him. "Try to spot that damned gun."

The young man nodded, slinked out away from the wall we were sheltered behind, and crawled forward. I watched him from my vantage point as he moved from one pile of debris to the next, doing his damnedest to spot the Jap. As he took a peek from behind a pile, the Jap, who was probably watching him the whole time, opened fire, catching my man square in the forehead. My heart sank as I saw him lying there. I didn't even know his name. However, because of his effort, I had a pretty good idea where the machine gun was. I indicated a heap of masonry directly diagonal across the square, by the base of a ruined building that had once contained some sort of store.

"When I give the word," I said, pointing to one of my guys, "you take off across the intersection. The rest of you will pour a suppressing fire on that store opposite us. Ready? Now."

The next man sprang up and ran as the rest of us laid down a hail of gunfire on the spot I suspected of housing the machine gun. It worked. My guy made it across, so we repeated the plan six more times, until all of my men were safely over. Then it was my turn. Taking a deep breath, I yelled, "Now!" and bolted across the square, my squad covering me as I ran. As I raced across the open expanse, I heard the rattle of the Nambu. Objects began buzzing by very close to my face, one so close I felt the wind of its passing. I reached the other side safe and sound, but sweat poured off me and I sat down to calm my nerves. Of all the action I had ever been in, including Bloody Ridge, I instinctively knew that those bullets that had just passed me by came closer to ending my life than anything in any other fight I'd experienced. I had escaped death almost literally by a hair's breadth.

More Marines were coming up now on the side of the street we had crossed over from. I signaled them to halt, then pointed to the square.

"Machine gun," I called. "Shop on the corner."

An NCO waved that he understood and brought forward one of his men. I watched the guy attach a rifle grenade to his Garand, then fire. The man was good. The grenade burst dead on target, and the machine gun was silent. Whether the gunner was dead or had just vacated, I don't know. I retrieved the dog tag from the man I'd lost, and we moved on.

We secured Naha the next day and went into a brief bivouac while waiting for orders to move farther south. It was during this brief respite from combat that I lost my close buddy Charlie Pacini. We'd been sitting around jawing. A few other Marines from another company were nearby, and one young man was fumbling with his rifle. Suddenly the weapon discharged, and I heard Charlie yelp in pain and fall to the ground. The bullet had struck him in the neck, passing clean through. I was at Charlie's side in an instant, ripping open my first aid kit for bandages to stem the bleeding and yelling, "Corpsman! Corpsman!"

"Looks like you have to finish off the Japs without my help, Whitey," he said and smiled through teeth clenched in pain.

"You're just trying to get a pass home, you goldbrick," I joked with him. "You're barely scratched."

But the wound was bad, and I knew Charlie's war was over.

A corpsman responded to my call, gave Charlie a syrette of morphine, and bandaged the wound. As he worked, I stood and walked over to the ashen-faced Marine who was still holding his rifle. He was scared, but I didn't give a shit. I was thoroughly pissed off.

Stepping right up into his face, I snarled, "If my friend dies, you die. So you'd better pray."

I scared the crap out of the guy, but I meant every word. I returned to the corpsman.

"Can you get your friend back to the aid station?" he asked me.

"Sure," I replied, then hefted Charlie up on my back. He grunted in pain despite the morphine.

"You're about as gentle as a professional wrestler, Whitey," he said.

"Bitch, bitch, bitch," I told him, and we started back.

I carried Charlie to the aid station, where we said good-bye. We had become friends upon leaving the Solomons for the States more than a year ago, served together in the 2nd Guard Company in Camp Lejeune in 1943, volunteered together in spring 1944 to go back overseas with the 29th Marines, landed on Okinawa, and been shipped over to the 22nd Marines. I would not see him again until his wedding in summer 1947 in North Tonawanda, New York.

Now I was on my own on Okinawa as the fight became more intense and brutal. I can't recall a more violent action during my time in the service, where we lived life second by second, except for maybe Bloody Ridge. The battle for Sugar Loaf, the attacks on the Shuri Line, the final assaults against the Japs' last line of defense on the island's southern tip were brutal, grinding affairs. And death was no respecter of rank. On June 18, we heard that General Buckner, our overall commander on the island, had been killed by shrapnel while watching his troops advance. A number of aids and other officers were with him at the time, but he was the only person struck by the exploding shell. He was replaced by Major General Joseph "Vinegar Joe" Stilwell, who had so ably commanded forces in China, Burma, and India early in the war. I saw General Stilwell arrive a few days after Buckner's death—riding in a jeep, his walking stick in hand and that famous battered old campaign hat planted firmly on his head. Seeing him was one of the high points of my military career.

Looking back on all the death and suffering, the pain and misery and horror of the battle for Okinawa, I wondered if there wasn't a better way. I guess the answer to that is part of the reason why I was a lowly enlisted man and not a general.

The battle for Okinawa ended on June 12 after eighty-three days of bitter, sustained combat. We killed more than 110,000 of the enemy and captured another 10,000. About 7,500 Marines and soldiers and approximately 4,300 sailors and Navy air personnel died in action, and another 39,000 of all services were wounded. An additional 26,000 servicemen were lost to combat fatigue. The Navy lost 36 ships sunk during the battle and 368 damaged, including 43 so badly that they were not repaired but scrapped.

Perhaps saddest of all was the number of civilians who perished. It is estimated that more than 100,000 noncombatants lost their lives, or nearly a third of the island's pre-invasion population. Many were inadvertently killed in cross fires between us and the Japs. Others, especially infants, died of starvation. The worst was the number of civilians who killed themselves. Just as had happened at Saipan a year earlier, the Japs told them we would torture and kill them, and many believed it. Whole families died together, often by jumping from cliffs. Parents killed their children before killing themselves. It was unbelievable. Nothing in our training had prepared us for anything this gruesome or tragic.

With the Battle of Okinawa over, we Marines of the 6th Division were soon loading back onto troop transports and steaming off to the east. Our destination was Guam, where we would immediately be given new men to replace the many who had fallen. Then it was back into training. Everyone knew what the training was aimed at: the upcoming invasion of the Japanese home islands. Knowing we had just gone through a fight where we suffered over eighty thousand casualties, plus the twenty-six thousand we had endured on Iwo Jima, each one of us knew that the upcoming landing would be desperately contested by the enemy and could very well mean our deaths. I knew my chances of getting killed or wounded were extremely high, because we were told that our losses were expected to be severe.

Settling in on Guam, we prepared for "The Big One." As we trained for what was guaranteed to be a nightmare of an operation, it was with an odd feeling of nostalgia that my mind replayed the past three years, beginning with Tulagi and Ken Bowers's death, and moving on to the endless Japanese Banzai charges at Bloody Ridge and the horrible death of Stan Kops and the loss of Ken Bailey on the Matanikau, and lastly to New Georgia and to Angus Goss's body lying forlornly under our flag and the never-to-be forgotten shells bursting overhead, as rain fell in torrents on a pitch-black landscape that left water running in swift-moving streams over our bodies. My mind marveled about that specific night when, in the midst of the shell fire and intense rain, I lay down and slept like a baby until awakened by the Aussie coast watcher after most of the guys were all saddled up. Amazingly, I could not recall a night when I had slept so soundly.

So much for the memories. Now it was back to the grind of preparing to invade Japan. The scuttlebutt was that the entire Marine Corps would be involved. We speculated that the 1st and 6th divisions would be the spearhead because we had performed so well on Okinawa, and although both divisions had been loaded with new men untested in battle, they had performed very well and were all now veterans.

An intensely lonely feeling descended over me when I realized that this would be my first fight without a single Raider at my side. Gone were Charlie Pacini, Bill Waltrip, "Mac" MacNeilly, Alex Stewart, Big Stoop Ruble, Spike Edwards, and the rest. I wondered how many times a man could face death as I had done since 1942 and expect to escape unscathed. I had been in close-up combat and killed men face-to-face. I'd had more close calls than a man is entitled to, especially those sniper rounds that pierced my backpack on Guadalcanal and that extremely close shave in Naha. Yet I had never been touched by a single bullet. I thought about the Jap soldier I had bayoneted on Bloody Ridge, and saw his horrified eyes in my mind. He now lay with his comrades in an unmarked mass grave on the 'Canal.

How many more times could I do this?

I shook the negative thoughts from my head and went back to the business at hand.

I don't recall how I found out that Bill Waltrip was on Guam with the 9th Marines. No matter. I went looking for him. When we met, we embraced heartily and exchanged "Thank Gods" over each other's safety. We headed for the base "slop chute" for a couple of beers. I filled Bill in on my experiences on Okinawa, and he told me of the horrors on the black, volcanic sands of Iwo Jima. We expressed hope that we'd soon be heading for home, but in the back of our minds was Japan and the upcoming fight. Finally, we had to say good-bye and promised to keep in touch when we got back home. It is a promise I am glad we were both able to keep.

On the way back, I had more luck. Walking along the dirt road toward where the 22nd Marines were billeted, I heard a jeep approach me from behind. I stuck out a hand to thumb a ride. The jeep stopped and a voice called out to me.

"Hop on board, Whitey," the voice said.

I looked into the face of Clay Boyd. My own face revealed my glee.

"Captain Boyd," I said and saluted. Then I noticed the gold oak leaf on his collar. "I mean, Major Boyd."

He grinned and returned the salute.

I had not seen Boyd since New Georgia, when he and some natives greeted us on the beach the night we landed. After Enogai, he had been evacuated with a severe bout of malaria. It was certainly good to see him, and we chatted about the Raiders the whole way back to my camp. He returned me to the 22nd Marines, right to my company area. We shook hands and he drove off. I would not see him again until the 1950s, at a Raider reunion in Quantico, Virginia.

Our training in Guam was in full swing, and the days rolled by. July came to an end, and we were now into the first week of August. I was having a cup of coffee in the mess hall when a report came over the radio that we had dropped something called an atomic bomb on the Japanese city of Hiroshima.

"What the hell is an atomic bomb?" I thought as I listened to the report.

The announcer continued, saying President Truman was calling on the Japanese to surrender, promising that there'd be similar bombings if they did not give up.

All training on Guam was now temporarily suspended as the men were in such a state of excitement. Would the Japanese surrender? Considering how much turmoil there must be in Japan right now, it was hard for us to conceive of the thought that they would not. We veterans understood better than the new guys about the Jap warrior code and their fanaticism, but even I thought they must toss in the towel. Yet several days passed, and no word of any surrender came over the radio. Then, on August 9, came the news that, true to his promise, Truman had ordered our bombers to drop a second bomb. This time it fell on Nagasaki.

This one brought results. Word came down: The Japs had given up. The war was finally over. It is difficult after all these years to describe our elation, but one thing I am sure of: We all thanked the Lord that we were spared. Knowing I had, by the Grace of God, survived, my thoughts again turned to my departed buddies, those lost from our first landing on Tulagi through the invasion of Okinawa.

Now events moved rapidly. My former Raider comrades in the 4th Marines soon boarded a ship bound for Japan. The old 4th, which had been captured on Corregidor, had earlier in the war been shipped to Japan to work as slave laborers. The new 4th now marched on the prison camp where the men of the old 4th were being held and proudly presented them with their colors. My heart ached. I so wanted to be part of that wonderful event.

In early October, the 22nd Marines boarded ship and set a westward course. Were we going to Japan as well? we wondered. We soon had our answer.

Our port of call was to be mainland China.

CHAPTER FIFTEEN

"FOR WE'RE THE LAST OF THE RAIDERS"

CHINA AND HOME

OCTOBER 1945–JANUARY 1946

The Second World War was over, and while most Marines, sailors, and GIs were thinking of home and family, I and my comrades of the 22nd and 29th Marine regiments were en route to Tsingtao. This seaport city in northeast China's Shantung Province would be our base for the next five months. We were being dispatched because our division commander, General Shepherd, had been assigned to accept the formal surrender of the Japanese 8th Army.

As our convoy steamed north from Guam, I settled in for the long voyage. The official history of the 22nd Marines says the division traveled aboard twelve transports and five cargo ships. I'm not sure which category the ship I was on fit into. It was a British vessel and little more than a scow. Not much good could be said about it. The food, mostly mutton, was horrible, and the sleeping quarters were filthy.

General Shepherd traveled on board the attack transport USS *Dade*. Shortly after we left the warmth of Guam, he released information about our mission. The memo said we were to assist in the occupation of the Tientsin-Tsingtao area until the arrival of Chinese government troops, the Kuomintang. We would then assist them in occupying the

Tsingtao-Chefoo region of Shantung Province, helping to maintain order and do what we could to alleviate hunger and disease. We were also to help in the recovery and evacuation of Allied prisoners and the disarming and confinement of the surrendering Japanese. Such a massive mission required access to air and sea transportation for the arrival of supplies and the evacuation of men—ours and, eventually, repatriated Japanese. We were specifically tasked with guarding Tsingtao itself, the nearby Tsangkou Airfield, and the seaport at Chefoo.

At dawn on October 11, someone yelled that land was in sight. We Marines sat down to another unpalatable breakfast—thank God the last one on this hulk—packed our gear, and went topside for a welcome view of China as our ship entered Kiaochow Bay.

I shall nerver forget my first sight of the Chinese mainland as we approached Tsingtao, which I have heard referred to as the Pearl of the Orient. I certainly never viewed it that way. The approaching coastline looked gray and dull. While landmasses, be they continents or islands, and including our West Coast, all lack color when seen from far out on the ocean, they come alive with shapes and colors as you close the distance. Not so with China. The drab landscape we saw ten miles out was what we saw as we prepared to dock.

Suddenly, here I was in China. I recalled as a boy, dreaming of such faraway places. Where might China be? I wondered. Someone had told me it was below my feet, and that I'd reach it if I dug straight down. Now I was grown up. I was ten thousand miles across the Pacific, and I arrived via the Solomons to Okinawa and, finally, to China.

The war was over, I thought. I had made it.

Thoughts rushed through my brain like a runaway train as we left the ship and formed into companies in preparation to march to our quarters in Tsingtao. As we tramped through the crowded streets, tens of thousands of cheering men, women, and children lined our way, making it almost impossible to hear our band and equally impossible to keep a marching cadence, so we moved at route step.

We were the first Marines—in fact, the first of any American troops—these people had seen since God knew when. The entire 22nd Regiment was strung out for a mile through the streets. Girls, old men, and children touched us as we passsed by; others saluted or gave us the thumbs-up sign. For the first and only time in my life, I realized what it was like to be a conquering hero. This idolatry on the part of the people of Tsingtao was not a one-night stand either, but continued throughout our stay. They simply loved us.

Our march ended at our assigned billet, the buildings of Tsingtao University, located on the edge of the city, the same structures the Japanese had occupied when they were masters of this part of China. Our quarters were single rooms large enough to accommodate a squad or more, much like we would have had at home. The school itself was a three-sided structure, wrapped around a large compound. Here we would conduct our drills. It was also here that our medical staff had us drop our pants while they conducted "short-arm inspection," checking our genitals for signs of venereal disease. VD checks were not at all unusual in the service. This one, however, was conducted in the open, within sight of Chinese laborers who cheered and laughed every time one of us dropped his trousers. This was a bit much, even for us hardened Marines, and we allowed our displeasure to be known. The procedure was never conducted outside again.

Once inland from the dreary dock area, Tsingtao proved to be a beautiful city, sitting, as it does, on the western coast of the Yellow Sea, opposite the peninsula nation of Korea. There had been a settlement there for more than six thousand years, but it was the Germans in the nineteenth century who had made the biggest impact. During China's colonial period, in the latter part of that century, while Western nations were carving out sections of China as their own territorial fiefs, the Germans occupied and fortified this region, remaining until the outbreak of World War I in 1914. They focused especially on the fishing village of Tsingtao, widening the streets, erecting private housing and government buildings, electrifying the city, building sewers, and providing safe drinking water. Being German, they even built the

Germania Brewery in 1903 and brewed beer. Examples of German architecture were everywhere. When Russia turned red after the first World War, white Russian refugees fleeing Vladivostok and other Russian towns and cities, took up residence in places like Shanghai, Tientsin, and Tsingtao. Later, the city became a sort of playground for the rich and famous, hence its "Pearl of the Orient" nickname.

After settling in to our new home, we took up various duties, including patrolling the streets and keeping tabs on the Japanese garrison, which numbered some ten thousand men. This was an unsettling time for us. First, the number of prisoners almost exceeded the number of Marines we had on hand, and we knew that a good many of the Japs did not relish the idea of surrendering. Plus, Nationalist Chinese troops were pouring into the city on a daily basis, and they had no love for the Japs. If that weren't enough, China was a nation in revolt, Communist forces were not far away, and they had no love for either the Japs or the Kuomintang. The handwriting was on the wall, and we were sitting on a diplomatic powder keg.

In fact, just a few days after we arrived, General Shepherd received a note from the Communist Chinese commander of the region, offering his help to destroy the Japanese still there and then enter Tsingtao in order to assist us in establishing order and stability. Shepherd replied that our intent was not to destroy the Japanese, but to accept their surrender, and that the Communist forces' presence in the city was neither needed nor desired.

The day the Japanese Army surrendered, October 25, 1945, will live in my mind forever. This was the culmination of events that began, for me, on August 7, 1942.

With the exception of the 4th Marines, who were still in Japan, the entire 6th Division took part. A day earlier, General Shepherd had issued a special memorandum to the troops.

"You are about to participate in the formal surrender of the Japanese military force in the Tsingtao area," the 22nd Marines official history recorded him saying. "It is an historical event which each of you shall long remember. It is the goal for which we have fought during these past four years, and I am sure the personal satisfaction each of you obtains from witnessing the local Japanese Army commander lay down his sword in complete defeat will, in a small measure, compensate for the dangers and hardships to which you have been exposed during your service in this war."

The surrender was a solemn, hour-long ceremony held at the Tsing-tao racetrack. I was one of about twelve thousand Marines of the 22nd and 29th regiments who stood stiffly at attention around the oval race-course. Off to one side, our tanks and field artillery were neatly lined up, all cleaned but still looking menacing in case any Japs felt disin-clined to surrender.

We Marines were not alone in watching this ceremony. The race-course and the open fields around it were jam-packed. Near where we were formed up stood eight thousand Jap soldiers, fully armed and look-ing not at all happy. More unsettling was that surrounding all of us, Marines and Japs alike, were at least eighty thousand Chinese. I can't begin to tell how volatile this situation was, and how high the danger was of some spark setting it all off. The worst of it was that we Marines, though we carried our weapons, had not one round of ammunition among us. It was decided that the chance for an incident was too great, considering all of us combat veterans who had fought in so many battles during the past three years. All it would take would be for one man to lose his cool and God only knew what consequences would result.

Also present to watch the surrender were civilian internees, in-cluding Americans, only just released from the nearby Wei H'sein in-ternment camp.

In the middle of this massive ocean of humanity was a platform upon which sat a table where the surrender documents had been spread out. Lined up on one side of the table were General Shepherd; Lieu-tenant General Chen-Pao-tsang, representing Chiang Kai-shek's Na-tionalist forces; Major General Keller E. Rockey, commander of the III Amphibious Corps, of which we Marines were a part; and Vice

Admiral Daniel E. Barbey, commander of the 7th Fleet Amphibious Forces. On the other side of the table stood a sullen Major General Eiji Nagano, commander of the Japanese 5th Independent Mixed Brigade, and members of his staff.

From atop the racetrack's grandstand, the flags of China and the United States fluttered in the morning breeze. Similar flags also flew around the surrender platform, along with the flags of Great Britain, Russia, and France. I never understood this latter. The only French I had encountered in the Pacific were on New Caledonia, and we considered them Vichy-loving traitors and did not trust them.

As we watched, Nagano sat at the table and signed ten copies of the surrender documents. They were next signed by General Shepherd and Lieutenant General Chen-Pao-tsang. With the surrender now inked, I watched as General Nagano rose from his chair. As he did so, there began a muffled roar from the Chinese around us, which rose in tempo like an approaching thunderstorm. With a flourish, Nagano held out his sword with both hands, bowed slightly, and laid it on the table in front of General Shepherd. The climax had arrived, and the roar of the Chinese crowd erupted like a thunderclap. They were beating on anything they had and loudly yelling. I thought that surely the sound would reach the heavens. The boisterous clatter raised the hair on the backs of our necks as we understood the mounting danger of this situation. We were fully aware of the hatred that existed between the two forces, fueled by the Japanese attrocities against civilians, including mass killings, rape, and the burning of towns and cities.

Upon hearing of the formal surrender in Japan, Nagano had withdrawn his men in order to avoid any incidents when we Marines arrived in Tsingtao. Now, with the Japanese and Chinese forces in such close proximity, and with the intense emotion both sides felt as the surrender ceremony progressed, every Marine there realized we were between a rock and a hard place should the Chinese lose control and swarm onto the field. Fortunately, the exchange went well and the Chinese displayed more bravado than bite.

After Nagano surrendered his sword, his staff officers followed suit. All of this was done slowly, as if it caused them great pain, which I'm certain it did. Not physical pain, of course, but deep pain to their pride and devotion to their lost cause. After the officers surrendered their swords and belts, the soldiers laid down their arms as well, under the supervision of their officers and as directed by Marine MP officers. Once all of that was accomplished—without incident, thank God—our Military Police escorted the Japanese from the field, and we snapped to attention and saluted as the division played the American national anthem, the Chinese national anthem, and "The Marines' Hymn."

Being present to watch this surrender ceremony was one of the most satisfying experiences of my life. I had come a long way, endured almost unbearable hardships and faced death any number of times, to witness this moment in time. I had friends buried on distant islands who had died in order to make this day possible, and I felt a deep humility in the knowledge that I was there, representing them.

One man not present at the surrender but who should have been was General Stillwell, who, as I mentioned earlier, replaced General Buckner as overall commander on Okinawa after the latter's death. But Stillwell, who had arrived in China back in 1911 as a young lieutenant, was conspicuous by his absence. Always somewhat controversial, the general knew the Chinese people like no one else did. He spoke the language fluently and loved the Chinese. He saw more front line action than any other general in the war, and commanded Chinese troops under Chiang Kai-shek, whom he called "The Peanut." To deprive him of seeing the war in China come to an end was, to me, a slap in the face by the powers that be in Washington.

Vinegar Joe would die of stomach cancer almost a year later.

The surrender ceremony finally ended, we were marched back to our quarters. Men were assigned to escort the Japanese POWs to the ship that would carry them home to Japan, while the rest of us resumed our duties, such as going on patrols and standing guard. We drilled in the courtyard at the university and continued servicing our weapons, which to a Marine is a sacred act.

Part of our duties involved assisting American civilians who had been stranded in Shantung Provice when the war erupted and interned by the Japs, losing all of their possessions. A great deal of captured American property had been discovered, so we posted guards around the area and tried to reunite the civilians with their lost items. That was not possible in many cases since Japanese soldiers had looted the place.

One pleasant thing about duty in China was that we were given a great deal of liberty to see the sights of Tsingtao. Like most of the other Marines, I did a lot of my traveling by rickshaws, operated by prideful coolies who displayed affection for their vehicles much as we do for our cars here in America. Leaving our quarters to begin our liberty, we'd find as many as twenty or thirty rickshaws lining the lane outside the gate, each driver hawking his service as the best available.

The military had also established recreational facilities for us, including Enlisted Men's Clubs and a Red Cross, this latter established in what had once been the old and prestigious Tsingtao International Club. These places contained Ping-Pong tables, a snack bar, a library, and, a welcome sight for sore eyes, American girls serving as hostesses.

We also had our own radio station, XABU, which went on the air on November 10, the 170th anniversary of the founding of the Marine Corps.

I soon established a network of my favorite bars and restaurants, such as the Green Lane Villa, located in the city's outlying area, and far enough from most of the potential fares that the rickshaws did not like going there. On my first trip there, I made the mistake of paying the coolie his fare up front. When I was ready to leave, I found that he had already headed back looking for another fare. I also discovered it was a really long walk back to quarters.

One place that was popular with a good many men was a whorehouse in Tsingtao that we, with typical Marine gutter humor, dubbed the House of a Thousand Assholes. An ornate, three-story wooden building, it was staffed by surprisingly nice young ladies who, unfortunately, had no other way to earn a living in war-torn China than to provide sexual favors for servicemen far from home, for a mere $2 a visit.

Most of us respected these women and were kind to them, even bringing them extra food. Our concern for them was how we got involved in the only real "battle" we Marines "fought" while in China, not against the Japanese or the Communists, but against Nationalist Chinese soldiers who invaded the house one night. Naturally, we did not begrudge the soldiers of the Kuomintang blowing off steam—hell, we did it all the time. Our problem came when the Chinese refused to pay the women. Granted, the soldiers were no doubt underpaid and probably had not seen $2 in two years, if ever. But they not only refused to pay, but grabbed the women, even those who were not hookers but simply cleaned the place, and started slapping them around. They even hit a few with rifle butts.

It was a typical "Marines to the Rescue" scenario, as we laid into the Chinese, fists swinging. What followed resembled a barroom brawl straight out of Hollywood, with Chinese soldiers being tossed over banisters and flying from doorways and through windows. We mopped up the place with them until the MPs broke it up. The women never got their $2 each, but at least they got justice, and we had a lot of fun while blowing off steam of our own. All of us Marines got hauled off to the brig, but we were soon released. No Marine, so far as I know, ever faced any charges for the donnybrook, and many of us even helped chip in for the repairs.

Aside from the Battle of the House of a Thousand Assholes, there was one other time I got into some trouble while we were in Tsingtao.

Oftentimes we Marines were required to pair up on our leaves. All my closest friends since I'd been in the Corps were no longer with me, so I didn't like to buddy-up if I could get away with it, but there was once when I was very glad to have complied. It occurred on our way back to the compound following a jaunt into the city, when I noticed a group of Marines on the porch of a tavern having a loud discussion with the Chinese proprietor. The man was trying to convince the Marines that he was closed in order to give a private party. The Marines he was trying to explain this to, I noticed, were young guys, newly arrived and all under the effects of Al K. Hall. I felt sorry for the poor Chinese businessman, dealing with a group of drunken gyrenes, so I stepped in and pulled rank.

"All right, fellas," I told them. "Enough's enough. Why don't you just move along."

"Ahh, come on, Sergeant," one man whined. "We just wanna have a couple of drinks, and this Chink won't serve us."

"I think you've had plenty to drink," I told them. "But if you need more, go find another place. This man is telling you he's closed."

The face of the Marine who spoke up, and appeared to be the group's leader, reddened with anger. I decided to put on a tough front. I stepped close to him and pointed to the Pacific Campaign ribbon on my blouse and to one of the three small bronze battle stars attached to it.

"This is for Guadalcanal," I told him, sounding as menacing as I could. "Edson's Raiders. Bloody Ridge. You really don't want to screw with me."

He looked at the ribbon, then back to me. Then he glanced at the other Marine with me, also a combat veteran.

"Come on, fellas," he said to his friends, and they staggered away. I smiled to my buddy.

The owner of the tavern was pleased to have had my help and invited the two of us to come inside and join the party.

As we entered, I could see that the crowd was mostly Russian men and women, with a few Chinese sprinkled in, all having a grand time. We joined in. It was during my conversation with one of the Russians that the real trouble arose. The man said something—I can't recall what it was so many years later, and it was so insignificant—but at the time, it made me laugh. A Russian man strumming a balalaika stopped suddenly and shouted that I had insulted their national anthem with my laughter. The man spoke very good English, and he demanded an apology and challenged me to a duel. What he did not know was that, concealed under my jacket I carried a fully loaded .45 automatic, and I had shot expert with it during basic training at Quantico.

Of course, I had no intention of dueling with the fellow, possibly killing him, and thus making U.S./Russian relations frostier than they already were. Instead, I placed a case of vodka on the table.

"If we're going to duel," I said. "Let's make it a duel of bottoms up."

The man smiled his agreement. We began removing small bottles, about four ounces each, from the case and setting them on the table. The rules of the game were simple. Each of us in turn picked up a bottle, removed the cap, and chugged down all the alcohol inside in one swift motion. Once the vodka was drained, the dead soldier was thrown against the wall with a flourish, and another bottle opened. The Russian was good, and after each bottle he'd yell something in his native language. After four bottles, the Russian was still able to stand upright, but I was totally trashed. The crowd roared with delight as my buddy lugged me outside and dumped me into a rickshaw and we headed back to camp. I guess we made it back to the barracks all right, but I really don't remember a damned thing. Next day, my throbbing head felt so big I didn't think my overseas cap, or "piss cutter," would fit. I vowed to never again challenge a Russian to a duel with vodka. The gun would have been more merciful.

———————————

The days wore on and our duties became repetitious, and before I knew it, we had reached November 23, my twenty-second birthday. I thought back to when I turned nineteen on New Caledonia. Birthdays had come and gone without fanfare during my time in the service, but I don't remember ever fighting on any of them.

Winter was now drawing closer, and the weather grew colder. On these frosty nights, I enjoyed hitting the sack early. Life here in China was great compared to my time in combat. There, I slept in muddy foxholes, many times in pouring rain. I went for weeks on end without ever being dry. Here in Tsingtao, I was inside a warm building, on a reasonably comfortable cot. Life in the Marines didn't get much better.

One night I nodded off shortly after the bugle sounded Taps. I don't recall how long I was asleep when I was jarred awake by the bugle again sounding. Only this was not Taps, but Assembly. During the day, Assembly was not an unusual call, but late at night, with nothing outside the barracks windows except darkness, the suddenness of the call carried with it the frightening feel of dread.

"Up! Up!" the company sergeant yelled, entering the barracks. "Gather your combat gear! Light marching packs. Grab your weapons and draw ammo."

Not knowing what the hell was happening, I dressed quickly, shoved my necessities into my LMO pack, and picked up my M1 carbine. Outside in the compound, six-by-sixes were rolling up. They squealed to a halt, and tailgates dropped. After drawing a bandolier of .30-cal ammo, I climbed into the back of one of the trucks. Once all of the men were aboard, tailgates slammed shut and the trucks rolled out of the main gate.

"What's going on, Sarge?" a man seated beside me stammered.

I looked at him. He was more nervous than a long-tailed cat in a rocking chair showroom.

"I have no idea, son," I told him. Then I thought, "son." He was about the same age as me, except he had no combat experience, which made me "the old man."

Our trucks did not have far to go, only to the city's airfield. There we hopped down from the truck beds. Squad leaders were called forward. I told my guys to stand fast and hurried over to the platoon meeting.

"The Communist Chinese Army is approaching the city," we were told. "We will form a perimeter to defend the airfield. Deploy your squads and dig in. If they approach, do not, I repeat, do not fire, unless so ordered. Caution your men, especially the replacements. We don't want any trigger-happy fresh fish starting World War III. You may build fires for warmth. This is not a secret move. The Commies know we're here."

After deploying my guys and overseeing their positioning, I let them huddle around the fire, contemplating our situation. If the Commies approached, I figured we'd have plenty of time to get back to our foxholes.

The men held muffled conversations among themselves for a time. Then one young guy, possibly verbalizing what was on all their minds, asked me, "Do you think they mean to attack us?"

I shook my head in what I hoped was a convincing manner.

"I doubt it," I replied. "They might be eager to kick Chiang Kai-shek's ass, but I don't think they'll be too eager to fight us."

I prayed that what I had said was true, but in reality, I had no idea what the Communist Chinese might do. I learned back in 1942 to never underestimate the Oriental mind. All I was certain of was that I sure as hell did not want to die here. Not now. During the war, I had never allowed myself to think much about the possibility of dying in battle, even during my darkest hours on Bloody Ridge, with a sea of Japs seemingly coming straight at me. But now the Pacific War had ended. I could see the light at the end of the tunnel I had been traveling for three years, so suddenly self-preservation had become a major concern.

The men chatted awhile longer, ridding themselves of some pent-up nervousness. Then, one by one, we all left the warmth of the fire to bed down and await whatever tomorrow might bring.

Slowly, the dawn began to paint the eastern sky. Overhead, the stars gradually disappeared as the night gave way to the sun's rays flooding across the earth. As the cold earth warmed, vapors arose to form a mist that lay thickly across the airfield like a billowy blanket. Marines moving along our perimeter appeared to be walking on a cloud. Other men, invisible due to the ground mist, seemed to appear as if by magic as they rose up from their foxholes.

We heard the roar of Detroit engines as a fleet of trucks rumbled into view, pushing aside the mist as they approached. These were a welcome sight because they were bringing our breakfast—powdered eggs and Spam—and, best of all, hot coffee and more wool blankets. Both of these were greeted with open arms after the cold night just passed.

The regimental and company mess cooks also began to set up the necessary equipment to serve us a hot dinner later in the day.

The smell of food, even Marine chow, brought hordes of uninvited guests: local Chinese who lived near the airfield in rickety shacks or, in some cases, mere holes dug into the ground, covered by wood or tin if they were fortunate.

I felt sorry for these people as they crowded around us, begging for food. I had never dealt with this type of thing before, and it made me keenly aware that, no matter how bad we had it, we still lived like royalty compared to these poor bastards. We gladly gave them what food and assistance we could, if not out of compassion, then at least as a means of preventing them from interfering with our task at hand.

The day was uneventful, and as nightfall began to descend, we posted sentries, three men to a post. The blankets that the trucks had brought up that morning were issued and were a welcome addition as the nighttime chill began to surround us.

"What's the latest?" I asked the company gunny sergeant when he came around to check our lines.

"Just scuttlebutt, Whitey," he replied. "The feeling is that we'll soon be pulled off this line and return to our billets. The Commies don't want to get into a shooting war with us, which of course would thrill old Chiang. Nope. The Reds know we won't be here much longer, and they're content to wait where they are until we leave."

I relayed the scuttlebutt to my guys around the fire that night, reminding them it was just rumor. Later, still deeply concerned, we again left the friendly fire to bed down. The warmth of our blankets gave us some small comfort.

Few guys got much sleep that night, and next morning men were stirring early. The mess cooks, judging by the early morning echoing rattle of pots and pans, were already busy, and from the aroma wafting our way, we knew we were in for a wonderful breakfast. In my humble opinion, the cooks should all have gotten medals, Bronze Stars at least, for they were unsung heroes of the war.

Our new friends, the displaced Chinese civilians, caught the scent of breakfast as well, and began moving our way. Strangely, they never bothered the mess cooks, but waited patiently for us to return from the chow line with our rations.

As we ate, the picket sentries returned from their outposts to report that all was quiet.

Our company officers finally announced that we were to be withdrawn in a day and would be returning to Tsingtao. This was welcome news if for no other reason than that we would be once again able to shower, shave, and change into fresh clothes.

It was the end of November by now, and the days were growing colder and colder. I had been at war since 1942. Now it was late 1945, and frankly, I was growing weary of it. I had lost all my friends; too many had gone to the beyond, while others, by the Grace of God, had returned safely to the States. I was ready to join them.

My enlistment was to be up in a month, and I was looking forward to boarding a ship to San Francisco, and then home.

Home!

That word sent chills down my spine, and left me in a state of nostalgia, although I am not sure why. For three years I had lived in a world dominated by horrible violence, death, and hardship, going days and sometimes weeks without a decent meal. My mind once again flashed to the jovial face of my best friend and blood brother Ken Bowers, who left me in our first action on Tulagi. We had pledged to look out for each other. Now, in Tsingtao three years later, I had only to look at the scar on my right wrist to remind me of the moment when we had pledged brotherhood. It was a pledge cut short by a machine gun bullet.

We continued our patrolling duties around the airfield throughout the day, and it was with extreme gladness that we welcomed the news that we would be pulled off guard duty the following morning. Next day, just as promised, we loaded up on trucks and returned to the comfort of our university hall.

T he year 1946 brought me the best sort of news. On New Year's Day, I was told to pack my seabag, turn in my web gear and weapon, and be ready to leave China the next day. My emotions began rising and falling like an ocean wave. Just a day or so before, I had been in a dark mood thinking of home, and now I was so giddy with excitement that I felt more like a boy on his sixteenth birthday than a man of twenty-two.

Eagerly, I began preparing to leave. Shoving all my worldly possessions into my seabag, I reflected on how little I really owned. Was this the sum total of a man's worth? Not by a long shot! I was alive. I had lived through the hell of war by God's good grace, and I would soon see the Golden Gate. Yet as significant as was my departure for the States, I felt nowhere near the level of emotion I had experienced when the Raiders were disbanded just under two years earlier. That had been a family the likes of which would never be seen in the U. S. military again.

Lying down on my cot late on January 1, 1946, I was turning in for my last night under China skies. But sleep did not come easily. The departure of me and a good many men of the 22nd Marines was the beginning of the end for the 6th Marine Division, which would officially disband on March 26. Formed on Guadalcanal, it was the only division in Marine history to be established overseas. So there would be no homecoming for the men of the 6th, no ticker tape parade, no returning of the colors. The 6th Marine Division would just die here, far from home. But its death was only physical, for it would live on in the hearts of all of us who had served in its ranks. We were known as the Slashing Sword Division, but I recall it as the Tiger Cub Division, because of its balance of young men and old-timers.

On Wednesday morning, January 2, 1946, a fleet of trucks rolled into the university compound to take us to the dock where we would board the ship for the fourteen-day voyage home.

My passage across the Pacific would be aboard the SS *Lurline*, formerly property of the Latson Line and a far cry from the garbage barge that had brought me to China. The twin-stack liner had been launched in 1932. Weighing in at 18,163 gross tons, the ship was 632 feet long and 79 feet wide at the beam, and was able to plow through the water at twenty-two knots, or about twenty-five miles per hour. In peacetime she carried a crew of 359 and 715 passengers, 475 in first class and 240 in tourist. When she pulled out of China on January 2, 1946, she would be weighed down with close to six thousand Marines, all going my way.

The line of six-by-sixes came to a stop on the dock, and we began unloading, clutching our seabags, all of us in neatly pressed uniforms, complete with neckties and our piss cutter caps planted firmly on our heads. Getting into line to climb the gangway to board the ship, I was shocked by the number of men involved. From where had they all come? It reminded me how the individual soldier, like me, traveled in a small circle, concerned only with his squad, platoon, or company. Beyond that small scope, such as my regiment stationed at Tsingtao, lay hundreds of miles of occupied territory. North and south along the Yellow Sea, from Shanghai to Peking, and inland almost to the Mongolian border, Marines who had landed here just as the 22nd did back in October, now converged on Tsingtao to be the first to exit China.

China was a nation in turmoil. Ambassador Patrick J. Hurley had come here to meet with Generalissimo Chiang Kai-shek and Chairman Mao Tse-tung, leader of the Communists, in hopes of the two sides reaching some form of amicable agreement, but the talks had failed. President Truman would next send retired general and future secretary of state George C. Marshall to give it a try, and those talks would fail as well. We heard that trouble was brewing up north with the Communists around Peking. A group of Marines, the story said, had supposedly been ambushed, though we heard no word of any casualties. None of us doubted that the Nationalists would lose all of China. It was just a matter of when.

War between the two sides was inevitable, and America wanted our Marines out before the nation exploded.

My group was the first to leave, and as I approached the gangway, I looked at all the thousands of men around me, and for some odd reason, possibly my love of food, I thought how difficult it would be to get all of these men into the mess hall to be fed. Even on a normal troop ship, one spends most of the day in line.

My problem was soon solved when a sergeant I had befriended, and who loved to eat just as much as I did, suggested we volunteer for mess duty.

The idea of washing pots and pans did not appeal to me at first.

"I'm not sure I want to spend the entire trip home bubble dancing," I told him.

"So you pot wallop for a couple of weeks," he said. "We're guaranteed our meals. We eat first and we get quarters right by the galley."

That convinced me, which is how I ended up on KP duty for the trip home. This suited me, because while it meant spending a great deal of time in the scullery cleaning pots and pans, it also provided a place where I could be alone, and I had much to think about. And it wasn't just thoughts of home that begged for my attention, but my pending separation from the Corps as well. At this point I had not the remotest idea what I would do in the future. It was a scary and unsettling time for me. How would I fit back into a peacetime world?

The skyline of China had long disappeared, and all around us stretched the vast emptiness of the northern Pacific Ocean. We were on a course due east, above the Tropic of Cancer, and far enough north so as not to catch a glimpse of Midway or the Hawaiian Islands as we passed them by. Sitting pensively on the ship's fantail, I found myself thoroughly intrigued by the wave action in the North Pacific that was so different than in the south. Here, the waves came at you in more rapid succession and the distance between each peak was much shorter, while in the South Pacific, there were huge swells that opened up into wide canyons, so that the bow of the ship dipped down into that trough, making you feel as if you were riding a roller coaster. For a terrifying moment your stomach turned into a hard knot, and then a force from beneath drove the bow up, but only long enough to set you in position for the next dive.

The ship's stern was my favorite haunt, and I spent almost all of my off-duty time sitting there, deep in thought as I puffed on my pipe, a habit I had recently taken up in China, watching the ocean and the world of war recede behind me. It was quiet there, with very little foot traffic, and I could be alone with myself to watch the wake trail away. It felt as if I was rushing forward ever closer to a rendezvous with whatever fate had in store for me next.

Two weeks after we hoisted anchor at Tsingtao, the west coast of the United States began coming into view. This would be my first look at San Francisco. When I shipped overseas in 1942, and again in 1944, it had been out of San Diego.

Home again, home again, home from the sea, I thought.

It is difficult even today to describe the emotions I felt as the skyline turned into a mass of gray objects I could recognize and feel. As the *Lurline* steamed into the harbor, gliding under the Golden Gate Bridge, I looked up at this massive symbol of America. It was a moment of my life that I will always remember, and as we passed under the bridge I gave thanks to God. After six years of conflict, the world was at peace, and I felt a sense of being delivered. Like many other Marines jam-packed shoulder to shoulder on the deck, I shouted and cheered our return as the ship's crew hurried about, making sure all the proper lines were in place from bow to stern so the *Lurline* could be secured once we reached the dock.

As we cruised into the harbor, I saw a boat approach and pull alongside. It carried the harbor pilot, who would guide our ship safely to its berth. The pilot now took over, assisted by the ship's captain, and steered the vessel expertly to its assigned berth and eased her up to the dock. The ropes were tossed down to the pier and secured, and the gangway was rolled into place. Trucks lined up at dockside to carry us to the naval station on Treasure Island, where we sat down to a good meal. After that, each man was processed, given his orders, and handed his pay. My orders were to board a train bound for Great Lakes, Illinois, the Navy's training base, not unlike the Marines' Parris Island.

I made this trip in relative luxury, riding in a Pullman sleeper car with upper and lower bunks and being fed in a dining car, just like the civilian passengers. Instead of being treated like government property, as we had been when we headed for war, I now felt like a guest of our government, and I thoroughly enjoyed the sensation. During the trip, countless numbers of fellow riders, civilians all, shook my hand or patted my shoulder, thanking me for my service. When we Marines entered the dining car, people rose and offered us their tables. But the most wonderful experience of all was just sitting back and taking in the sights of this grand and beautiful country, mile after mile, state after state, from the snowcapped mountains of Colorado to the flat, grassy plains of the Midwest. I was in a high state of emotion, tears welling in my eyes, my heart racing, as I thought, "This is my country and woe to the person who tries to take it from us."

Two days out of California the train drew close to Chicago's Union Station. Here I was to leave the Corps.

Leave the Corps.

To me, that statement was the equivalent of saying I was leaving home or mother. I was eighteen when I enlisted. I was now twenty-two, and for the last four years I had either been in battle or preparing for battle. I knew nothing else. Uncertainty filled my mind, but I resolved to be the best civilian I could, just as I had been the best Marine possible.

I found myself traveling with three other men, all heading east, they en route to Philadelphia, and me to Lebanon. I got along pretty well with them, especially one Marine named Feenie, and we talked a great deal, mostly about the Corps and home. They had all been drafted in 1943 and received their separation through the military's point system, which did not apply to me since I had signed a four-year enlistment that just happened to coincide with the end of the war.

Because of some transportation snafu, we had a three-day layover in Chicago, so the four of us went out drinking. I recall meeting a woman in a bar. We got to talking, I bought her some drinks, and we ended up spending a couple of days together. On the third day, I left her to go meet my buddies at the hotel where they were staying. Our seabags were packed, and one of the Marines and I were seated in the hotel bar downing a cold beer. Feenie and the other Marine were walking the streets of the city, doing some sightseeing. In short, we were killing time until we were due to head for Union Station. Suddenly Feenie, looking disheveled and upset, raced into the bar.

"Whitey!" he shouted. "We're being attacked! Come help us!"

We leaped off our stools and bolted out the door. Feenie and the other of my Philadelphia traveling companions were being assaulted by three men. I later learned that one of the civilians had offered to give my friends a brief tour before we left the Windy City, when in fact, it was an ambush and robbery. Even as I raced to the scene, two of the men were beating on the other Marine, who was starting to sag. I and the man from the bar rushed into the fray. Once the odds were even, the outcome of the brawl was never in doubt. I grabbed one of the attackers and delivered several hard punches to the gut and jaw that drove him to the sidewalk. The other Marine from the bar took his man out as well. Feenie went half-nuts and punched and kicked his man repeatedly.

Someone began yelling for the cops, so I grabbed Feenie while my bar companion helped our injured friend to his feet and we all took off, leaving the sidewalk littered with the trio of would-be robbers. We raced into the hotel, grabbed our seabags, and headed for Union Station. The last thing we wanted to do was get tangled up with Chicago's finest, even if we did fight in self-defense. Besides, we had a train to catch and didn't have time for giving police statements. At the station, keeping a low profile in case any police officers came looking for some wayward Marines who might have beaten the crap out of three civilians, we waited until our train was called. When it was, we made our way to the platform and boarded. Sinking into our seats, we gave a collective sigh of relief, then had a good laugh, as the train lurched forward and we left Chicago behind.

The whole of our trip I was impressed with how considerate people were of us, four men in uniform, heading home from the war. They bought us drinks in the club car, shook our hands and asked us where we had been and where we were going.

Next day we rolled into Pittsburgh, where there would be a fifteen-minute stopover, just long enough to get off the train, stretch our legs, and grab a soda and sandwich before the conductor yelled, "All aboard," and we filed back into the Pullman.

As the train chugged out of Pittsburgh and continued its eastward journey, I sensed a difference in attitude among me and my three new-found friends. All of us now became aware that within a few hours we'd be parting company, and the chances of any future contact would be remote. We were about to come face-to-face with a future that was uncertain and, to be truthful, somewhat intimidating. Before I enlisted, I had begun training for a career in silk-screen printing, but that was no longer in my thoughts. I'm sure I was not alone. Thousands of men were coming home at this moment, just like me, with the same question marks concerning their futures.

As the four of us sat talking, the train rolled into a station.

"Harrisburg," the conductor called as he walked through the Pullman. "All off for Harrisburg."

The others would continue on to Philadelphia, but for me, this was the end of our time together. I needed to catch the Reading Short Line to Lebanon. Shaking their hands, I departed, then stepped off the train and watched it roll away.

A couple of hours later, I was home from the war.

Shortly after arriving back in Lebanon, I temporarily moved in with one of my hometown buddies until I could get settled. But first I had a decision to make. My enlistment was up. Did I want to try my hand at civilian life or remain in the by now familiar world of the U.S. Marine Corps. Initially, I chose the former and went back to silk screening for a short time, but in the end, I reenlisted, but not before that fateful day in 1946 when a friend lined me up with a date. We had traveled to West Chester State College with another pal in order to attend a dance. There I met a pretty young coed named Vivian. We soon became engaged.

In 1947, I reenlisted for a four-year hitch and was sent to Quantico. I was able to keep my sergeant stripes and landed a good job in the camp armory. My main problem was my CO, a major who had seen no combat in the war. This "stateside commando" took a dislike to me because I had "fruit salad" on my blouse that included the Asiatic Pacific Campaign Medal with three small battle stars and a Presidential Unit Citation from my time with the Raiders. The major couldn't muster much more than a Good Conduct Medal and a few other noncombatant decorations. It pissed him off, and when he thought I wasn't giving him the proper respect an enlisted man should show for an officer of his stature, he threatened to court-martial me. He was correct. I did not respect him, and I wasn't worried in the least about what he said he would do. Another officer who worked in the armory with me told me that if the court-martial ever came about, he would testify on my behalf.

The major never court-martialed me, but he did transfer me to Parris Island, where I spent time as a drill instructor. I enjoyed Parris Island duty much more than I'd thought I would, but by 1950, I was stationed in Cuba, at Guantánamo. There I was put in charge of water transportation, making sure Marines heading out on leave or coming back made their connection. They traveled by water from the base itself, north on Bahía de Guantánamo, to the town of Caimanera. There they caught trains going to other destinations, or unloaded as they returned.

That's how it happened that in May of 1951, I was sitting on a bench at the train station, awaiting the arrival of a load of guys, mulling over what I would do come July when my enlistment ended. Was I going to reenlist again? I doubted it. Vivian and I had arranged to get married in June, and another four years in the Marines was not in our plans. That's when a middle-aged woman walked up to me and sat on the other end of the bench. I knew who she was. She was the madam of a whorehouse in Caimanera.

"I understand you are soon not going to be a Marine anymore," she said. "That you don't reenlist."

"That's right," I told her.

"I wonder," she mused. "I would like you for a partner to help me run my business. A lot of good money."

I politely turned her down, then laughed to myself after she walked away. The last thing in the world I pictured myself being was a partner in a whorehouse.

In June, as planned, I was home and Vivian and I were married. A month later, I removed my Marine uniform for the last time and took a job with RCA in Lancaster, where I worked for the next thirty-four years as an experimental tube builder for televisions and radios. After I retired in 1985, I spent a great deal of time golfing, fishing, and traveling the country with my wife and growing family.

Although I left the Marines, I never left the Raiders. In 1949 Sam Griffith and Lew Walt, in direct disobedience of Edson's orders, proposed that the 1st Raider Battalion officially became known as Edson's Raiders. That same year, the Edson's Raiders Association was born, and we veterans began holding annual reunions at Quantico. Six years later, in 1955, we were stunned by the news that General Edson had been found in the garage at his home in Washington, D.C., dead by his own hand of carbon monoxide poisoning. I never heard a reason for his suicide. Perhaps the horror of the war caught up to him as it did to other men as well. War scars any man who serves in combat, and we all cope in different ways, if we cope at all. Suicide is an all-too-frequent consquence of postwar trauma.

Of the pride I feel after ten years as a United States Marine, I am most proud of the two-plus years I spent as a member of Edson's Raiders. From our first combat at Tulagi in August 1942 to our last action at

Bairoko in July 1943, 213 of our comrades died in action. In that time, we took on Japan's best troops, both in the Imperial Army and the Special Naval Landing Forces at Tulagi, Tasimboko, Bloody Ridge, Matanikau, Enogai, and Bairoko, killing more than eleven hundred of the enemy. In the process, four of our members won the Medal of Honor and we were awarded a Presidential Unit Citation.

Today, at age ninety, I realize I am one of the few Raiders left to carry on our proud legacy. So I am reminded of a poem written years after the war by Captain Art Haake, a platoon leader with Edson's Raiders. Now, even more than when it was originally penned, I feel it is a fitting epitaph for our fine unit:

Here's some news to make you hot
They're doing away with the best they've got.
And throwing us in with the common lot
For we're the last of the Raiders.
So put away your boots and knives
As souvenirs of Raiders lives
And do your fighting with your wives
For we're the last of the Raiders
Our chow was poor, we had no snacks
Just ammunition in our packs
We've never seen the WAVES or WACS
For we're the last of the Raiders
So throw away your Raider schemes
And throw away your Raider dreams
We're going to join the 4th Marines
For we're the last of the Raiders. [1]

BLOODY RIDGE: AUGUST 2002

The ridge was not as I remembered it. Largely coated by knee-high grass, the dusty terrain was all but barren of the bushes and small, scraggly trees that once studded this ground. The steep slopes leading down to the jungle floor, once so sharply defined, looked softer and more rounded, worn down by six decades of wind and rain. In short, the ridge had aged over the last sixty years, just as I had. When I first stood on this crest, I was a boy just two months short of my nineteenth birthday. Now I was a seventy-eight-year-old man.

Lost in the memories of a lifetime ago, I walked slowly along the ridge, the tall grass separating before me with a gentle whooshing sound. I was alone, surrounded by the spirits of my fallen brethren, who bid me "welcome back."

———

I had returned to Guadalcanal for the sixtieth anniversary of the American landing. I had planned to be here ten years earlier for the fiftieth anniversary, but back surgery forced me to miss the event. I'd read in the *Lancaster New Era* about this trip being organized by a Virginia-based company that specialized in military history tours, and resolved that I would not miss this opportunity a second time. I asked my son Brian to go along. I thought that as a West Point graduate, he might appreciate the trip at least as much as I did. However, he was unable to go, so my younger son, Eric, agreed to accompany me.

We'd left Dulles International Airport with some members of our party, then rendezvoused with the rest in Los Angeles. Then we were off to Fiji. As I became familiar with my traveling companions, especially the World War II veterans, I discovered that not only was I the only Edson's Raider in the group, but the only veteran who had actually fought on Guadalcanal.

Landing in Fiji, there was an overnight layover, followed by a 5 a.m. breakfast before boarding a Solomon Islands Airways plane for Guadalcanal.

The nearer we drew to our destination, the more anxious I became. Between 1942 and 1945, I had been on the 'Canal four times. I was familiar with the island, and in that familiarity, there had been a sort of comfort. But I had left there for the last time in March 1945, bound for Okinawa. That was fifty-seven years ago. How would I feel when I once again saw the 'Canal? Would I still feel that nostalgic familiarity?

Then a group of islands came into view below our plane, and as the aircraft banked, I looked out the window. A large landmass was passing under the wing, with a smaller island nestled just a few hundred yards off its shoreline. I didn't need our guide to tell me the smaller island was Tulagi. I'd have recognized the deadly little lump of God's earth anywhere. It was here that I had experienced my baptism of fire.

Then we soared over Sealark Channel and I spotted the conical shape of Savo, standing its silent watch at the mouth of what we dubbed Iron Bottom Sound. I remembered sitting in my foxhole on Tulagi watching the naval battle taking place just off the coast of Savo, unaware that the Japanese were giving our fleet a shellacking.

Then the plane banked again, making its final approach to Henderson Field. I choked up as Guadalcanal passed underneath us, and was more than a little taken aback by the number of houses and roads I saw sprawled across land that six decades earlier had just been jungle.

Then the runway was below us and our wheels touched the ground. Every other time I had been here, I had arrived from the sea, so coming in by air was a novel feeling. The aircraft finally rolled to a stop and I rose eagerly. After I'd descended the short stairs pushed up to the plane, my foot touched the soil of Guadalcanal. I had walked maybe ten or fifteen feet, when I was suddenly overcome by a deep sense of emotion that ran through my body. Acting on an impulse, I knelt down and kissed the ground. I admit it was somewhat theatrical, but I found I'd never let go of Guadalcanal. It was an inseparable part of me. The locals seemed to enjoy my action because they clapped and waved.

Turning to Eric, I said, "I'm home. I'm really home."

I had expected the airfield to look different, and indeed, it did, having been greatly enlarged and modernized. The familiar pagoda was gone. In fact, the only familiar remnant I noticed was the original iron signal tower, which had been restored so visitors could climb to the platform on top. But I found I was not ready for the many other changes I would find on this island.

Vans were waiting for us at the airport to take us to our hotel, the Kitano Solomon Mendana, and we climbed aboard. As we traveled west, I was dismayed to see that our beloved coconut grove was gone and replaced by what passes on the 'Canal for urban sprawl, spilling over from the city of Honiara, which sat astride the Matanikau. In fact, I was astounded by the amount of development that had taken place since I had last been here. To begin with, the unpaved government road that skirted the coast, and along which we Marines had marched to battle numerous times, was now a paved four-lane road called the Kukum Highway. The highway morphed into Mendana Avenue once we crossed the modern bridge that spanned the Matanikau River and entered Honiara. Right there, on the east side of that bridge, was where our A Company had suffered heavy losses and killed scores of Japanese during the "Second Matanikau" battle. Where those men bled and died now stood several of what looked like commercial buildings and a cluster of homes, these latter nearly blotting out the sandbar position held by the Raiders. Perhaps it was appropriate that the Honiara Central Hospital also stood near where so much blood was spilled.

Progress, in fact, had obliterated the entire Matanikau battlefield area. Where once there had been just jungle and a small native village, there now stood the sprawling city of Honiara. Houses—some modern, some traditional Solomon Island types—seemed to be everywhere.

As our van crossed the bridge spanning the Matanikau, I noticed another road branching off to our left. This was Chung Wah Road, which followed along the east bank of the river. Sixty years earlier, it had been little more than a path we hacked through the rain forest as we attempted to cross the river upstream at the One Log Bridge, which was also long gone. I remembered well how we moved cautiously along that path under Jap sniper fire, and somewhere up Chung Wah Road, possibly violated by modern construction, was the spot where Ken Bailey had died. I hoped there was some type of historic marker to note the loss of this fine officer, but I doubted it. In fact, nearly all the battle sites we Marines and our Army comrades had fought over in this area, such as Hill 84, where Chesty Puller's men were cut to pieces during "First Matanikau" on September 27, 1942, were gone forever.

Our hotel was extremely nice, but staying there did vividly bring back memories of some of Guadalcanal's inconveniences. Each evening as we took dinner in the hotel's open-air restaurant, the waitresses would remind us to please keep our feet on the bottom rungs of the chairs and not on the floor. Doing so kept our feet from being overrun by the hordes of island rats, some of them the size of small cats, that migrated daily from the inland region to the beach. I'd forgotten about the rats.

"Thank God we all have cocktails in hand," Eric observed.

It was also interesting to note that our hotel room came with assorted spray bottles to repel Guadalcanal's myriad of bugs. I hadn't thought about them in years, either.

Our nearly two weeks on the island were filled with traveling from site to site. First there was Red Beach, where the 1st Marine Division had landed on August 7, 1942. We stopped briefly by the American Memorial, where there was to be a dedication the next day that we would be attending. We also visited a monument dedicated to Martin Clemens and other coast watchers, and the bronze statue of Jacob Vouza that stands in front of the Honiara police station.

On the evening of the first day, we attended a pre-dedication reception at the American embassy in Honiara, where we met Susan S. Jacobs, the United States ambassador to the Solomon Islands region.

Overall, I got along well with the other folks on our tour, except for this one veteran who was what we who trained at Parris Island called a "Hollywood Marine" because he trained in San Diego. The guy was a braggart, always shooting his mouth off about how he was a "'Canal veteran." One night at the Guadalcanal Yacht Club, located next to our hotel, we got into it. I told him one was considered a Guadalcanal veteran even if he was just passing through and never fired a round while on the island, while others of us actually fought on this ground. I called him a blowhard. Luckily, Eric got between us and took me away from the guy. We didn't speak the rest of the tour.

The next day, August 7, we were all bussed to the American War Memorial, located on Skyline Road, for the dedication ceremony that had been an annual event since 1992. Before leaving the hotel, I was informed that there would be a small group of Japanese veterans attending the ceremony as well. I was also asked to lay the wreath at the monument, assisted by a Japanese vet.

"You really should be the one laying this wreath," I was told.

As I have stated earlier in these pages, I had never fully forgiven the Japanese for the horrific brutality they exhibited against my fellow Americans who fell into their hands. Stan Kops's screams still ring in my ears.

I turned to Eric.

"I have reservations," I told him. "There will be Japanese at the service. I don't know how I'm going to react to that. What should I do?"

"Dad," Eric replied. "They've asked you to do this as a representative of our country, so you'll be fine. But if you can't face the Japanese and turn and walk away, that's OK. Nobody's expecting you to do anything you can't do."

On high ground four hundred yards west of the Matanikau River, on Skyline Road, the monument is a large, horseshoe-shaped plaza featuring one four-by-four-foot-square, twenty-four-foot-tall red marble pylon on which is inscribed "This memorial has been erected by the United States of America in humble tribute to its sons and its allies who paid the ultimate sacrifice for the liberation of the Solomon Islands 1942–1943." The American flag and the flag of the Solomon Islands fly from poles to either side of the tall pylon.

Several smaller red marble markers denote the battles fought for the Solomons, including Bloody Ridge, Tassafaronga, New Georgia, Cape Esperance, and Mount Austen. Also listed are the names of ships whose hulks lie rusting at the bottom of Iron Bottom Sound, which can plainly be seen in the distance. At the center of the plaza, set into the stone walkway, is a star. Dedicated ten years earlier, on the fiftieth anniversary of the battle, the monument was a joint effort of the American Battle Monuments Commission and the Guadalcanal–Solomon Islands Memorial Commission.

The ceremony was held with a great deal of pomp. Ambassador Jacobs was present, along with a neatly uniformed band and a contingent of U.S. Marines in their dress blues. Gathered around the memorial to watch the ceremony were hundreds of natives and the Japanese veterans. Chairs were provided for us aging vets, and we sat, solemnly listening to various speakers tell of the valor and sacrifice shown here by men of both the United States and Japan. As the ceremony wound down, a Japanese veteran and I were called forward. A Marine colonel handed us a large wreath and saluted. The Marine band stopped playing as the Japanese vet and I, each holding the wreath, slowly walked forward, toward the tall pylon. It was so quiet that you could have heard a pin drop. This was an emotion-charged moment for me, and my heart was almost literally in my throat.

Reaching the tall marker, the Japanese vet and I reverently laid the wreath down before it, then stepped back and saluted. We turned to face each other, and I looked at the man for the first time. I mean, truly looked at him. What I saw was a little old man, just like me. His skin was wrinkled, he was slightly stooped, and his hair was thin and graying, just as mine had turned snow white. In essence, this man was a sort of mirror image of me, and I realized it had been an intensely emotional moment for him as well. He had, I am sure, lost comrades in the fighting on this island, just as I had. For all I know, he and I may have shot at each other on Edson's Ridge or across the brown waters of the Matanikau just east of where we now stood.

Tears welled up in our eyes, and the Japanese man and I embraced.

Watching us, Eric thought, "Oh my God. Maybe there can be world peace." Then, caught up in the moment just as I was, my son walked off behind one of the marble obelisks, sat on the ground, and wept.

Later in the day, we boarded an actual Higgins boat for a trip across the Sound to Gavutu and Tanambogo, which the Paramarines had fought so hard to secure. Then we crossed over to Tulagi. As our Higgins boat pounded across the waves en route to those islands, it felt like old times, at least to me. I had made this trip several times in my youth, without ever the slightest twinge of seasickness. I am happy to say that, even though I was now considerably older, my stamina remained intact. Not so for some of my traveling companions, who turned all shades of white.

Arriving at Tulagi, we did not land at Blue Beach as I had done on August 7, 1942, but at the more settled southeastern tip, near Hill 281, where the heaviest fighting took place. Like its larger neighbors across the channel, Tulagi had also experienced a spurt of modernization, although I could still spot some familiar landmarks. At places like this, our tour leader would give an overview of the fighting, then simply turn things over to me.

"Why don't you take it from here, Marlin," he said. "You were here. I wasn't."

I explained my part in the battle as best I could recollect. I spoke of Ken Bowers, of our blood oath, and indicated the approximate spot where he was killed. This was without a doubt the most emotional part of my Tulagi visit. After his death, Bowers had been buried in a temporary cemetery near the cricket field, but I did not get to visit there during this trip.

The visit to Tulagi was especially memorable for me because the people of the island greeted me so warmly. They had heard that I was a Marine Raider, and people flocked around me, shaking my hands and introducing themselves. I was bombarded by more names than I can ever hope to remember. The only person who sticks in my mind was a woman named Catherine Pule, whose father had worked with coast watcher Martin Clemens during the war. Catherine took my hand and escorted me around during my all-too-brief stay, not just here, but on Guadalcanal as well. We hit it off very well, and I became a close friend of her and her family. Needless to say, I was deeply honored when, during our stay on the island, her son's wife gave birth to a child, a son, whom they named Marlin Pule. Catherine still writes to me.

Over the course of the next week, we made numerous treks to the sites of various battles, many of which I was not a part of, including Alligator Creek, where the Ichiki detachment was annihilated on August 21, 1942, the spot where, on the night of October 24–25, John Basilone used a machine gun to hold a section of the Marine line almost single-handedly, winning for himself the Congressional Medal of Honor. We also visited the Japanese Memorial on Mount Austen, as well as Galloping Horse Ridge (both areas fought over after the Raiders had departed the island) and what battle sites still remained along the Matanikau.

Dotting the island were rusting reminders of the war, such as American amtracs, wreckage from airplanes, and similar relics. They looked old and worn, just like the rest of us who fought here.

I was disappointed that we did not visit Tasimboko, site of the 1st Raiders' only true behind-the-lines raid of the war. Classified as a raid rather than a battle, I guess it did not rate a spot on our agenda.

One deeply personal moment for me on this trip came the day before we were to head for home. We were at the Yacht Club enjoying cocktails when Catherine Pule and another woman approached us.

"Marlin, may we speak with you?" Catherine asked.

"Of course," I said, and they took seats at our table.

"You know I teach at the Chung Wah Primary School," Catherine said. "American veterans come to the Solomons quite frequently. They tour the islands' historical places and then leave. They never visit our school or talk to our kids about what happened here. Would you honor us by paying a visit to our students?"

I didn't even have to think about it.

"I certainly will," I said.

Bright and early the next morning, a jeep arrived for me. I climbed in and we were off. I had wanted Eric to go along, but he said that I was being honored and it was something I needed to do on my own. When we arrived at the school in Honiara's China Town section, Catherine ushered me onto the stage. Spread out in front of me were more than a hundred smiling faces. Some were descendants of Jacob Vouza and a few, thanks to Catherine, knew I had fought on the island and were holding banners proclaiming they were "Whitey's kids."

I was very uncertain about how I was going to talk to these kids because a number of them were of Japanese ancestry. The Japanese have become a very prominent part of the community in Honiara, and in fact, Japan is a major economic supporter of the Solomon Island nation.

So I told them about my life in America, and how I came to their island during the time of war. I did not refer to the Japanese by name, preferring to just say "our enemies." I was very careful in that regard. The kids listened attentively as I spoke of my home and how it was not that much different from their own. I told them about American kids and their schools, and how they were very similar to them and their own schools, despite their living in opposite corners of the world.

After my talk, we moved to another room, where I sat down at a desk and kids had their picture taken with me. Many wanted my autograph. They hugged me, and one little girl just clung to me the whole time. It was such a gratifying experience and really brightened my spirits, for I had been somewhat saddened by the abject poverty I had seen in some parts of Honiara.

"I'll love you all my life," I told the kids as I climbed back in the jeep, my visit over. And I meant it. By the time I got back home, I found I had received seventy-four letters from the kids.

As emotional as this trip had been for me overall, the singular event I had most anticipated, in fact the driving motive for my returning at all, was revisiting Edson's Ridge. It was the one stop about which I felt both a high sense of excitement and a great deal of fear. How would I react once I got there? Could I take it? Would the ghosts of my departed comrades haunt me or bid me welcome?

I had seen the ridge when I stepped off the plane on our arrival, still rising above the flat plain some thousand yards south of the airfield. I had paused and looked at it standing there, silent and foreboding. Yet at the same time it appeared somewhat peaceful, with its grass covering standing out against the crisp blue sky and no longer wreathed by the angry smoke of battle.

On the day of my visit there, I found myself in a four-wheel-drive vehicle, bouncing up the crude road to the top of that familiar ridge. This was pretty much the same road I had led the Paramarines along when Edson moved the battalion into position. I remembered how proud I'd felt at the head of that column of paratroopers, leading them forward into battle.

The little convoy of vehicles stopped, and I stepped out, planting my feet on Bloody Ridge for the first time since September 14, 1942. On that day, I was a battle-shocked veteran, exhausted by two days of almost constant fighting. Sixty years later, I was back, an old Marine who had survived a terrible war and returned to face his demons.

As I had for much of this trip, I wore my Marine jungle helmet with the globe and anchor device on the front, hoping, perhaps, that the spirits of my friends who had lost their lives on this tortured hill might recognize the little white-haired old man who was intruding on their turf.

We were standing in a clump in the area of Hill 120 where we Raiders had made our stand against the nearly overpowering ranks of Japanese who stormed the crest. After a brief outline of the battle, our guide, as he had done on Tulagi, said, "Marlin. Why don't you tell the story from here."

So I did, and the group listened with keen attention.

Among our knot of people were two members of a Canadian public television crew, Bill Casey and Colin King, who were on the island to shoot a documentary. Since they were staying at our hotel, I was aware of their presence, and they were interested in the veterans, especially me. They'd asked if I'd allow them to film me on the ridge, and I agreed.

Now, after I addressed the tour group standing around me, Casey and King took me aside and wired a microphone to me. Their instructions were simple. I was to stroll along the ridge, reliving my memories and talking about how it felt to be back.

For me, this was the most gut-wrenchingly emotional part of the entire visit to the ridge, for I was walking alone; just me and the spirits of the past. I remember saying that I was treading on sacred ground, and how I felt humbled to have survived and been able to return to honor my departed friends.

Tears welled up in my eyes as I walked Hill 120, trying to recall where my fighting position had been. In my mind's eye, I once again heard Alex Stewart ask me how many Japs there were and if they'd be back after we repelled them the first time. I heard Lieutenant Ed Wheeler kneel by my side and wish me luck. I recalled Mo Cooley batting away imaginary Japanese beetles as the strain became too much for him, and I "saw" Edson again standing erect on the hill just behind me during the height of the battle, warning that he'd shoot any man who broke for the rear. Once again I felt the horror of hearing Stan Kops scream for help and beg for mercy, neither of which he received. I recalled how the adrenaline rush of seeing wave after wave of Japanese charge my position pushed aside my fears and helped me perform my duties as a Marine. I recalled the terrific bombardment as our 11th Marine artillery blasted apart the Jap lines as they raced toward us. I saw men on both sides fall, and I recalled the unfortunate enemy soldier I had run through with my bayonet, somewhere near where I was standing at that very moment.

As I strolled alone across the ridge, I found reminders of the struggle, mostly in the form of rusted tangles of the barbed wire we'd strung for defense and the steel spikes we'd hammered into the ground to secure the wire.

Once, lost in my thoughts, I wandered out of sight of the camera, and they had to cut and call me back, and then reshoot that portion. They filmed me from a distance, and then did a close-up sequence.

The one dismaying moment during this visit occurred when I walked to the battle marker that stood stark and alone amid the tall grass at Hill 120. This pyramid-shaped marble marker about seven feet tall was badly weathered and chipped. But what was most disheartening was that it had been vandalized. A rectangular brown stain about four feet from ground level showed where a bronze plaque had once been. Pry marks around the periphery indicated where it had been forcibly removed. I knew how the plaque had read:

"During the six-month battle for Guadalcanal from 7 August 1942 to 9 February 1943, the 'Battle of Edson's Ridge' stands out as one of the most fiercely contested engagements between U.S. Marines and Japanese forces. During 12–13 September, the Japanese launched a determined counterattack from the jungle south and east of this hill against Raider and Parachute troops commanded by Colonel Merritt A. Edson as the first phase in a coordinated offensive to recapture Henderson Field. After two nights of savage fighting, the Japanese under the command of Major General Kiyotake Kawaguchi, were defeated with severe casualties and never seriously threatened the airfield again. This monument stands in the area where Colonel Edson's men rallied and repulsed the last enemy attacks."

I resolved that when I returned home, I would have a new plaque made, shipped here to Guadalcanal, and affixed to the monument, which is exactly what I did.

Aside from that insult to the memory of brave men, my visit to the ridge was soul-satisfying. I felt at ease with the spirits that surrounded me, and it gave me an inner peace and a unique opportunity to reconnect with my own youth.

Then it was time to go.

Stepping back into the jeep, I took one final glance around. I knew I would never be returning to Bloody Ridge, so I bid it a final farewell. I also said adieu to the spirits of my friends, as well as to an eighteen-year-old Whitey Groft who, like the rest of Edson's Raiders, would remain a part of this lonely ridge until the end of time.

A few days later, we boarded a plane and flew back to Fiji.

NOTES

CHAPTER 2: TRAINING AND DEPLOYMENT

1. Joseph H. Alexander, *Edson's Raiders: The First Marine Raider Battalion in World War II* (Annapolis, Md.: Naval Institute Press, 2000), pg. 19, citing Richard Tregaskis, *Saga XIX,* "The Best Soldier I Ever Knew" (February 1960), pg. 18.

CHAPTER 3: THE BLOOD OATH

1. George W. Smith, *The Do-or-Die Men* (New York: Pocket Books), pg. 104, 2003.
2. Alexander, *Edson's Raiders*, pg. 96.
3. Smith, *Do-or-Die Men*, pg. 119.
4. Ibid., pg. 131.

CHAPTER 4: THE PERFECT RAID

1. Smith, *Do-or-Die Men*, fn. pg. 187.
2. Ibid., pg. 200.
3. Richard Tregaskis, *Guadalcanal Diary* (New York: Random House, 1943), pg. 204.
4. Ibid., pg. 207.
5. Alexander, *Edson's Raiders*, pg. 128.
6. Smith, *Do-or-Die Men*, pg. 209.
7. Alexander, *Edson's Raiders*, pg. 130.

CHAPTER 5: "THIS IS WHERE THEY'LL HIT"

1. Alexander, *Edson's Raiders*, pg. 149.

CHAPTER 6: "THEY'LL BE BACK"

1. Alexander, *Edson's Raiders*, pg. 151.
2. Ibid., pgs. 152–153.
3. Ibid., pg. 153.
4. Smith, *Do-or-Die Men*, pg. 236.
5. Ibid, pg. 263.
6. Alexander, *Edson's Raiders*, pgs. 164–165

CHAPTER 7: "I'LL SHOOT ANY MAN WHO HEADS FOR THE REAR"

1. Smith, *Do-or-Die Men*, pg. 158.
2. Richard Frank, *Guadalcanal: The Definitive Account of the Landmark Battle* (New York: Random House, 1990), pg. 240.
3. Alexander, *Edson's Raiders*, pg. 143.
4. Smith, *Do-or-Die Men*, pg. 296.

CHAPTER 8: "THIS PLACE IS LOUSY WITH NIPS"

1. Smith, *Do-or-Die Men*, pg. 199.
2. Alexander, *Edson's Raiders*, pg. 200.
3. *Ibid.*, pg. 201.
4. *Ibid.*, pg. 203.

CHAPTER 9: BACK TO THE MATANIKAU

1. Smith, *Do-or-Die Men*, pg. 324.
2. Alexander, *Edson's Raiders*, pg. 216.
3. Smith, *Do-or-Die Men*, pg. 332.
4. *Ibid.*, pg. 332.
5. *Ibid.*, pg. 336.
6. *Ibid.*, pg. 338.
7. *Ibid.*, pg. 342.

CHAPTER 10: REST AND REFIT

1. Alexander, *Edson's Raiders*, pg. 245.
2. *Ibid.*, pg. 240.

CHAPTER 11: THE DRAGONS PENINSULA

1. Alexander, *Edson's Raiders,* pg. 260.

CHAPTER 12: "YOU ARE COVERING OUR WITHDRAWAL"

1. Alexander, *Edson's Raiders,* pg. 283.
2. *Ibid.,* pg. 287.
3. *Ibid.,* pg. 289.
4. *Ibid.,* pg. 290.

CHAPTER 14: "I HEAR THE RUMBLE OF HEAVY GUNS"

1. George Feifer, *Tennozan: The Battle of Okinawa and the Atomic Bomb* (New York: Ticknor and Fields, 2002), pg. 233.

CHAPTER 15: "FOR WE'RE THE LAST OF THE RAIDERS"

1. Alexander, *Edson's Raiders,* pgs. 309–310.

INDEX